D1596181

MUSKINGUM UNIVERSITY LIBRARY
NEW CONCORD, OHIO 43762

THE FATHERS
OF THE CHURCH

A NEW TRANSLATION

VOLUME 127

THE FATHERS
OF THE CHURCH

A NEW TRANSLATION

EDITORIAL BOARD

David G. Hunter
University of Kentucky
Editorial Director

Andrew Cain
University of Colorado

Joseph T. Lienhard, S.J.
Fordham University

Brian Daley, S.J.
University of Notre Dame

Rebecca Lyman
Church Divinity School of the Pacific

Susan Ashbrook Harvey
Brown University

Wendy Mayer
Australian Catholic University

William E. Klingshirn
The Catholic University of America

Robert D. Sider
Dickinson College

Trevor Lipscombe
Director
The Catholic University of America Press

FORMER EDITORIAL DIRECTORS
Ludwig Schopp, Roy J. Deferrari, Bernard M. Peebles,
Hermigild Dressler, O.F.M., Thomas P. Halton

Carole Monica C. Burnett
Staff Editor

ST. CYRIL OF ALEXANDRIA

FESTAL LETTERS 13–30

Translated by

PHILIP R. AMIDON, S.J.
Creighton University

Edited with notes by

JOHN J. O'KEEFE
Creighton University

THE CATHOLIC UNIVERSITY OF AMERICA PRESS
Washington, D.C.

Copyright © 2013
THE CATHOLIC UNIVERSITY OF AMERICA PRESS
All rights reserved
Printed in the United States of America

The paper used in this publication meets the minimum
requirements of the American National Standards for Information
Science—Permanence of Paper for Printed Library Materials,
ANSI Z39.48-1984.
∞

LIBRARY OF CONGRESS CATALOGING-IN-PUBLICATION DATA
Cyril, Saint, Patriarch of Alexandria, ca. 370–444.
[Correspondence. English. Selections]
Festal letters 1–12 / St. Cyril of Alexandria ; translated by
Philip R. Amidon ; introduction and notes by John J. O'Keefe.
p. cm. — (The Fathers of the church : a new translation ; v. 118)
Includes bibliographical references and indexes.
ISBN 978-0-8132-0118-4 (cloth : alk. paper)   1. Cyril, Saint,
Patriarch of Alexandria, ca. 370–444—Correspondence.
2. Christian saints—Egypt—Alexandria—Correspondence.
3. Christian life—Early works to 1800.   4. Theology, Doctrinal—
Early works to 1800.   I. Title.   II. Series.
BR65.C952E5 2008
270.2092—dc22
2008029287
Festal letters 13–30; ISBN 978-0-8132-2184-7

CONTENTS

ABBREVIATIONS AND NOTES
TO READER

Abbreviations

FOTC   The Fathers of the Church. Washington, DC:
The Catholic University of America Press.

LXX   Septuagint.

MPG   Patrologia Cursus Completus: Series Graeca.
Ed. J.-P. Migne. Paris, 1857–1886.

SC   Sources chrétiennes. Paris.

Notes to Reader

Letters 13–17 are translated from SC 434.

Letters 18–30 are translated from MPG 77: 809–981.
The text is of indifferent quality, but is translatable as long
as occasional repairs are made along the way. Where we
have translated according to one of the alternate readings
listed by the editor at the bottom of the page, we have put
"reading X" or "reading X for Y," or "reading X instead of
Y." Where we have corrected the text when that seemed
necessary, we have put "correcting X to Y."

The numbering of the Psalms in this volume is that of
modern versions of the Bible. Where the Septuagint has
been followed, a footnote indicates this fact.

SELECT BIBLIOGRAPHY

Primary Sources

Amidon, Philip R., SJ, and John J. O'Keefe, ed. and trans. *St. Cyril of Alexandria: Festal Letters 1–12*. Fathers of the Church 118. Washington, DC: The Catholic University of America Press, 2009.

Azéma, Yvan, ed. *Théodoret de Cyr, Correspondance*. 3 vols. SC 40, 98, 111. Paris: Cerf, 1955–1965.

Burguière, Paul, and Pierre Évieux, eds. *Cyrille d'Alexandrie: Contre Julien*, Tome 1, Livres I–II. SC 322. Paris: Cerf, 1985.

Durand, G. M., ed. *Cyrille d'Alexandrie: Deux Dialogues Christologiques*. SC 97. Paris: Cerf, 1964.

———, ed. *Cyrille d'Alexandrie: Dialogues sur la Trinité*, Tomes 1–3. SC 231, 237, 246. Paris: Cerf, 1976–1978.

Évieux, Pierre. *Cyrille d'Alexandrie: Lettres Festales I–XVII*. Sources chrétiennes, 372, 392, 434. Paris: Cerf, 1991–1998.

McEnerney, John I. *St. Cyril of Alexandria: Letters 1–110*. The Fathers of the Church, vols. 76, 77. Washington, DC: The Catholic University of America Press, 1987.

Migne, J.-P., ed. *Patrologia cursus completus*. Series Graeca, vols. 68–77.

Pusey, P. E., ed. *Sancti Patris Nostri Cyrilli Archiepiscopi Alexandrini*. 7 vols. Oxford, 1868. Reprint. Brussels, 1965.

Socrates. *Ecclesiastical History*. PG 67.

Sophronius. *Laudes in SS. Cyrum et Joannem*. PG 87: 3411–13.

Wickham, Lionel R., ed. *Cyril of Alexandria: Select Letters*. Oxford, 1983.

Secondary Sources

Boulnois, Marie-Odile. *Le paradoxe trinitaire chez Cyrille d'Alexandrie: Herméneutique, analyse philosophique et argumentation théologique*. Paris: Institute d'études Augustiniennes, 1994.

Boyarin, Daniel. *Intertextuality and the Study of Midrash*. Bloomington, IN: Indiana University Press, 1994.

———. *Dying for God: Martyrdom and the Making of Christianity and Judaism*. Stanford: Stanford University Press, 1999.

Cameron, Averil. *Christianity and the Rhetoric of Empire: The Development of Christian Discourse*. Berkeley: University of California Press, 1991.

Casiday, A. M. *Evagrius Ponticus*. London and New York: Routledge, 2006.

Chadwick, Henry. "Eucharist and Christology in the Nestorian Controversy." *JTS N.S.* 2 (1951): 145–64.

Clark, Elizabeth. *The Origenist Controversy: The Cultural Construction of an Early Christian Debate*. Princeton, NJ: Princeton University Press, 1992.

Dawson, David. *Allegorical Readers and Cultural Revision in Ancient Alexandria*. Berkeley: University of California Press, 1992.

Dysinger, Luke. *Psalmody and Prayer in the Writings of Evagrius Ponticus*. Oxford: Oxford University Press, 2005.

Evagrius of Pontus. *The Praktikos & Chapters On Prayer*. Translated by John Eudes Bamberger. Kalamazoo: Cistercian Studies, 1981.

Frankfurter, David. *Religion in Roman Egypt: Assimilation and Resistance*. Princeton, NJ: Princeton University Press, 1998.

Gorday, Peter. *Principles of Patristic Exegesis: Romans 9–11 in Origen, John Chrysostom, and Augustine*. New York: Edwin Mellen, 1983.

Guillaumont, Antoine. *Aux Origines du Monachisme Chrétien. Spiritualité Orientale*, no. 30. Abbaye de Belle Fontaine, 1979.

Haas, Christopher. *Alexandria in Late Antiquity: Topography and Social Conflict*. Baltimore and London: The Johns Hopkins University Press, 1997.

Hardy, E. R. "The Further Education of Cyril of Alexandria (412–444): Questions and Problems." *Studia Patristica* 17, vol. 1 (1982): 116–22.

Harmless, William. *St. Augustine and the Catechumenate*. Collegeville, MN: Liturgical Press, 1995.

———. *Desert Christians: An Introduction to the Literature of Early Monasticism*. New York: Oxford University Press, 2004.

Hirshman, Marc. *A Rivalry of Genius: Jewish and Christian Biblical Interpretation in Late Antiquity*. Albany, NY: State University of New York Press, 1996.

Hurtado, Larry W. *One God, One Lord: Early Christian Devotion and Ancient Jewish Monotheism*. Edinburgh: T&T Clark, 1998.

Jones, A. H. M. *The Later Roman Empire*. Vol. 2. Baltimore: Johns Hopkins University Press, 1986.

Jouassard, G. "L'activité littéraire de saint Cyrille d'Alexandrie jusqu'à 428: Essai de chronologie et de synthèse," in *Mélange E. Podechard*. Lyon, 1945.

Kelly, J. N. D. *Golden Mouth: The Story of John Chrysostom, Ascetic, Preacher, Bishop*. Ithaca, NY: Cornell University Press, 1995.

Kennedy, G. *Greek Rhetoric under Christian Emperors*. Princeton: Princeton University Press, 1983.

Kerrigan, Alexander. *St. Cyril of Alexandria: Interpreter of the Old Testament*. Rome, 1952.

Koen, Lars. *The Saving Passio: Incarnational and Soteriological Thought in Cyril of Alexandria's Commentary on the Gospel according to St. John*. Uppsala: Acta Universitatis Upsaliensis, 1991.

Liébaert, J. *La doctrine christologique de Cyrille d'Alexandrie avant la période nestorienne*. Lille, 1951.

————. "Saint Cyrille d'Alexandrie et la culture antique." *Mélanges de Science Religieuse* 12 (1955): 1–21.

Malina, Bruce. *Christian Origins and Cultural Anthropology.* Atlanta: John Knox, 1986.

Malley, W. J. *Hellenism and Christianity: The Conflict between Hellenic and Christian Wisdom in the* Contra Galilaeos *of Julian the Apostate and the* Contra Julianum *of St. Cyril of Alexandria.* Rome, 1978.

Mango, Cyril. *Byzantium: The Empire of New Rome.* New York: Scribner, 1980.

Manoir, Hubert du. *Dogme et Spiritualité chez Saint Cyrille d'Alexandrie.* Paris, 1944.

McGuckin, John A. *St. Cyril of Alexandria: The Christological Controversy: Its History, Theology, and Texts.* Leiden: E. J. Brill, 1994.

————. *Cyril of Alexandria: On the Unity of Christ.* Crestwood, NY: St. Vladimir's Seminary Press, 1995.

McKinion, Steven. *Words, Imagery, and the Mystery of Christ: A Reconstruction of Cyril of Alexandria's Christology.* Leiden and Boston: Brill, 2000.

Meunier, Bernard. *Le Christ de Cyrille d'Alexandrie: L'humanité, le salut et la question monophysite.* Paris: Beauchesne, 1997.

Neusner, Jacob. *Judaism and Christianity in the Age of Constantine: History, Messiah, Israel, and the Initial Confrontation.* Chicago: University of Chicago Press, 1987.

O'Keefe, John J. "Impassible Suffering? Divine Passion and Fifth-Century Christology." *Theological Studies* 58 (1997): 39–60.

————. "'A Letter that Killeth': Toward a Reassessment of Antiochene Exegesis, or Diodore, Theodore, and Theodoret on the Psalms." *Journal of Early Christian Studies* 8, no. 1 (2000): 83–104.

O'Keefe, John J., and R. R. Reno. *Sanctified Vision: An Introduction to Early Christian Interpretation of the Bible.* Baltimore: Johns Hopkins University Press, 2005.

Prestige, G. L. *Fathers and Heretics.* London: SPCK, 1940.

Quasten, Johannes. *Patrology,* vol. 3. Westminster, MD: Christian Classics, 1986.

Russell, Norman. *Cyril of Alexandria.* The Early Church Fathers. New York: Routledge, 2000.

————. *The Doctrine of Deification in the Greek Patristic Tradition.* Oxford: Oxford University Press, 2004.

Schäublin, Christoph. *Untersuchungen zu Methode und Herkunft der Antiochenischen Exegese.* Cologne and Bonn: Peter Hanstein, 1974.

Simon, Marcel. *Verus Israel.* Translated by H. McKeating. Oxford, 1986.

Simonetti, Manlio. *Biblical Interpretation in the Early Church: An Historical Introduction to Patristic Exegesis.* Translated by John A. Hughes. Edinburgh: T&T Clark, 1994.

Smith, Jonathan Z. "What A Difference A Difference Makes." In *To See Ourselves as Others See Us.* Edited by Jacob Neusner and Ernest S. Frerichs. Chico, CA: Scholars Press, 1985.

Stark, Rodney. *The Rise of Christianity: A Sociologist Reconsiders History.* Princeton, NJ: Princeton University Press, 1996.

Visotzky, Burton. *Fathers of the World: Essays in Rabbinic and Patristic Literatures.* Tübingen: J. C. B. Mohr, 1995.

Vaggione, Richard Paul. *Eunomius of Cyzicus and the Nicene Revolution.* Oxford: Oxford University Press, 2000.

Wilken, Robert. *John Chrysostom and the Jews: Rhetoric and Reality in the Late 4th Century.* Berkeley: University of California Press, 1983.

———. *Judaism and the Early Christian Mind: A Study of Cyril of Alexandria's Exegesis and Theology.* Reprint of 1971 edition. Eugene, OR: Wipf & Stock, 2004.

Young, Frances. "The Rhetorical Schools and their Influence on Patristic Exegesis." In *The Making of Orthodoxy: Essays in Honour of Henry Chadwick,* edited by Rowan Williams. Cambridge: Cambridge University Press, 1989.

———. *Biblical Exegesis and the Formation of Christian Culture.* Cambridge: Cambridge University Press, 1997.

———. *The Art of Performance: Towards a Theology of Holy Scripture.* London: Darton, Longman and Todd, 1990.

FESTAL LETTERS 13–30

FESTAL LETTER THIRTEEN

A.D. 425

T IS GOOD, or rather opportune, now for us to come forward with our greeting couched in holy words, and to announce in advance our holy and all-praiseworthy feast, saying, "Grace to you and peace from God the Father and our Lord Jesus Christ, who gave himself for our sins to deliver us from the present evil age, according to the will of our God and Father; to whom be the glory forever and ever. Amen."[1]

For sin mocked those prostrate from of old, and the innate motion of the flesh warred [against them] tyrannically, since pleasure, wild and uncontrollable, poured unceasingly into the souls of all like a river current, always pushing them down to where they had to choose an earthly way of thinking. And death perhaps smiled at everyone's weakness, and, infected with the contempt befitting the devil and dear to him, cried out with him, "I will seize the whole world in my hand like a nest, and I will take it like eggs abandoned; and there is none that shall escape me or gainsay me."[2] But since our situation had sunk and been shaken to such a degree of wretchedness, the merciful God, all but distressed by everyone's misfortune, said through Isaiah's voice, "Therefore my people have been taken captive, and there has been a multitude of corpses, because they do not know the Lord; and hell has enlarged its soul, and opened its mouth, so as not to cease."[3]

---

1. Gal 1.3–5.

2. Is 10.14. For a similar image of the devil, see *Letter* 1.6, *Cyril of Alexandria: Festal Letters 1–12*, trans. Philip R. Amidon, SJ, ed. with intro. by John J. O'Keefe, Fathers of the Church 118 (Washington, DC: The Catholic University of America Press, 2009), 50.

3. Is 5.13–14.

But even if "death has swallowed up when it prevailed, still God has wiped away every tear from every face; the reproach of the people he has removed from all the earth."[4] For when we were delivered to transgression and disobedience, and failed to live lawfully from love of the flesh, we had Satan and the wicked gang of demons laughing loudly and reproaching us in their love of fault-finding. For he is, he truly is, an enemy and avenger, as is written.[5] And indeed we wretches spent our life upon earth embarrassed at these things and at the accusations of our conscience, deprived of freedom of speech with God for this reason, and ill with every sort of wickedness. But when the Creator of all took pity on those prostrate, who had involved themselves in evil without stint, he consoled them, speaking through the holy prophets: "Fear not because you have been put to shame, nor be confounded because you were reproached."[6] "I, even I, am he who blots out your transgressions, and I will not remember them."[7] He sent to us from heaven the only-begotten God the Word, "born of a woman,"[8] and of Abraham's seed,[9] in order that, being made like his brothers in everything,[10] he might put to death sin in the flesh, and, having filled nature with spiritual strength through himself and in himself, might refashion it to what it was of old, might render it impregnable to sin, and might ready it to become superior to destruction and corruption. Paul in his wisdom knew this when he wrote us, "For God has done what the law, weakened by the flesh, could not do: sending his own Son in the likeness of sinful flesh and for sin, he condemned sin in the flesh, in order that the just requirement of the law might be fulfilled in us, who walk not according to the flesh but according to the Spirit."[11]

2. And in fact the Word from God the Father, in indicating to us the long-desired time of the Incarnation, or rather in speaking as though already arrived in our state, has already cried aloud, "I who speak am here, as a season of beauty upon the

4. Is 25.8; cf. Rv 21.4.
5. Cf. Ps 8.3.
6. Is 54.4.
7. Is 43.25.
8. Gal 4.4.
9. Cf. Heb 2.16.
10. Cf. Heb 2.17.
11. Rom 8.3–4.

mountains, as the feet of one preaching glad tidings of peace, as one preaching good news."[12] "For in many and varied ways God spoke of old to our fathers by the prophets; but in these last days he has spoken to us by a Son,"[13] through whom we have all sprouted afresh unto incorruptibility and life. For he has come to us like "a season of beauty upon the mountains."[14] Now what does that mean?

The plants on the mountains and in parks, when winter induces condensation in them and prevents the sap from the roots from coursing upwards abundantly, all but wither and do not bear fruit, suffering as they do from lack of foliage. But when the season of beauty shows itself, when, that is, springtime laughs and warms everything with the sun's hot rays, then what was shut opens up, and, with the sap that had been lying deep now having its course free to run everywhere, the twigs, quite drunk on it, throw out the fresh verdure of their leaves and so are crowned at once with their own fruit. Our Lord Jesus Christ has become for us, then, "as a season of beauty upon the mountains." This too may become clear to us through other passages of sacred Scripture. In the Song of Songs, for instance, the person of the bridegroom is introduced crying out to the Church as to a bride, "Rise up, come, my companion, my fair one, my dove! For behold, the winter is past, the rain is gone, it has departed. The flowers are seen in the land; the time of pruning has arrived."[15]

In addition, he has been "as the feet of one preaching glad tidings of peace, as one preaching good news."[16] For it happens sometimes that enormous armies of the most savage barbarians, yearning to devastate a city or a countryside, use their insatiability as a pretext for war. But when their plans come to naught, then beautiful indeed are the feet of the one who brings the news of peace[17] to those who were in danger. It is in something of this fashion that one may view our own situation as remedied

---

12. Is 52.6–7.   13. Heb 1.1–2.

14. The Sources chrétiennes editor (SC 434, 90, n. 1) notes that Cyril frequently refers to the arrival of spring as a metaphor of Christ's defeat of the devil.

15. Song 2.10–11.   16. Is 52.7.

17. Cf. Rom 10.15; Is 52.7.

through Christ. Rather, it is quite easy to understand, without any trouble, that the Father has sent the Son to us from heaven as Savior and Redeemer.

A boastful tyrant waged war not on a single people or upon one city or countryside, but, seeking wickedly to subject to himself the whole earth, he placed man beneath his own yoke. Alienating him from the love of God, and dissociating him from true knowledge of God, he soiled him instead with many kinds of sin and rendered him a thrall of the horde of demons, according the name of God to the creature rather than to the Creator.[18] In giving their veneration, some to the sun and others to the moon, they deprived the nature that is sovereign over all of the prerogatives that are most fitting to it, and to it alone. Still others, who offered their worship to earth, water, air, and fire, descended quickly to such a degree of stupidity that they arrived at the final measure of evil and presented the honor and glory of divinity even to insensate pieces of wood.[19]

The murderous dragon, luxuriating in such deceptions that we suffered, never ceased to boast, and thought that his contentment would be unshakeable. It was of him that the blessed prophet Jeremiah said, "Woe to him who multiplies to himself the possessions which are not his! How long? And who heavily loads his yoke."[20] For he wanted to gather to himself man, who belongs to God, thus always making more grievous the punishment prepared for him. But God the Word, seated with God the Father, announced to us in advance the time of salvation when we were behaving godlessly and dangerously, saying, "The Spirit of the Lord is upon me, because he has anointed me; to preach good news to the poor he has sent me, to proclaim release to the captives, and recovery of sight to the blind, to proclaim an acceptable year of the Lord."[21] Now since the time of the promised aid had arrived, he set his own self on our behalf to oppose the devil's misdeeds; he subdued that murderous tyrant and laid him beneath the feet of the faithful, saying clearly, "Behold, I

18. Cf. Rom 1.25.
19. Cf. *Letter* 6.3–4, FOTC 118, 104–8, for a similar discussion.
20. Hab 2.6.
21. Is 61.1–2; Lk 4.18–19.

have let you walk upon snakes and scorpions, and on all the power of the enemy, and no one will harm you."[22]

All of us, then, who have come to love piety toward God, and yearn to share the splendor of the saints, let us thirst to arrive at the city above, and let us take this matter to heart. The kings on earth who constantly punish the barbarians for their attacks, and keep safe the cities in each region, are richly honored with the names of "saviors" and "redeemers" and every other sort of title. And while boasting of their own brave deeds, they subject to themselves those they have saved, and, placing upon them, as it were, the yoke of statutes and laws, they lay them under tribute, making this a sort of acknowledgment of the duty of submission. Let us, therefore, who have been redeemed through Christ, removed from the error of polytheism, enriched through him by kinship with God, and gone over to the hope of the saints, devote our own life to him. For as the blessed Paul writes, "One has died for all, that those who live might live no longer for themselves but for him who for their sake died and was raised."[23]

This has been recorded for us as well in the older Scriptures, as it were in shadows and figures still.[24] For the law is a shadow, and is pregnant with the shape of truth.

3. God, then, spoke of old to Moses, the teacher of sacred truths:

If you take the computation of the children of Israel in the surveying of them, and they shall give everyone a ransom for his soul to the Lord, then there shall not be a destruction in the visiting of them. And this is what they shall give you, as many as pass the survey, half a didrachma which is according to the holy didrachma—twenty obols the didrachma—but the half of the didrachma is the offering to the Lord. Everyone that passes the survey from twenty years old and upwards shall give the offering to the Lord. The rich shall not give more, and the poor shall not give less than the half didrachma in giving the offering to the Lord, to make atonement for your souls.[25]

22. Lk 10.19.
23. 2 Cor 5.14–15.
24. Cf. Heb 10.1. For a discussion of Cyril's approach to biblical interpretation, see the introduction in FOTC 118, 9–12.
25. Ex 30.12–15.

For the stater or didrachma is a genuine coin, stamped with the imperial imprint. It was brought to the Lord by those accustomed to pay the tribute, not for one person only, but for two. And tribute-collectors were appointed, according to the law, who traveled up and down the territory of the Jews, and ordered the ransom to be delivered in equal measure by rich and poor alike, God thus ordaining that the figure should be preserved as an accurate manifestation of the truth.[26]

And in fact once when Christ our Savior had gone to Capernaum, the collectors of the didrachma went to Peter and said, "Your teacher does not pay the didrachma." But he said, "Yes, he does."[27] He did not thereby subject the freeman to the law,[28] nor rank the Son with the slaves, but he knew that the Legislator had come under the law in order to rescue us from the curse of the law, and, transforming the form of slavery into something better, had rendered us conformed to himself and made us sons of God, enveloping us in the spirit of freedom as in some splendid dignity. "For we did not receive the spirit of slavery to fall back into fear," as the divinely inspired Paul writes, "but we have received the spirit of filial adoption, in which we cry, 'Abba, Father!'"[29] When Peter then came bursting into the house, the Savior asked him, "From whom do the kings of the earth take tribute or toll? From their sons or from foreigners?"[30] When he answered that it had to be collected of course from foreigners, Christ said further, "Then the sons are free. In order, however, not to give offense to them, go to the sea and cast a hook, and take the first fish that comes up, and when you open its mouth, you will find a stater; take that and give it to them for me and for yourself."[31] You see, then, that the didrachma was paid for two persons.

Now in what does the mystery consist? Or where will we find

---

26. In addition to being centuries of theological development, the fourth and fifth centuries were also centuries of biblical commentary. Cyril participated in this tradition vigorously. His many commentaries on the books of the Old Testament indicate that discovering the enduring truth contained in the older books was a key interest.

27. Mt 17.24.   28. Cf. Gal 4.4.
29. Rom 8.15.   30. Mt 17.25.
31. Mt 17.26–27.

the beauty of the truth hidden in the shadow that is in the law? Well, the true stater, the image of the great king, the Son that is, the imprint and reflection of the Father's substance,[32] gave himself for us.[33] And he gave his own soul in exchange for the life of all, not that he might save Israel alone, even though Israel seemed to be rich in the knowledge of the law, but that he might rescue as well from the devil's greed the innumerable flock of the nations, "who had no hope,"[34] as Paul says, and who suffered from the lack of every good. The divine, heavenly stater was therefore given for two peoples. "For we have been ransomed not with perishable things such as silver and gold, but with the precious blood of Christ, like that of a lamb without blemish or stain."[35] "We are debtors, therefore, not to the flesh, to live according to the flesh,"[36] but to Christ, who ransomed and redeemed us.

When indeed the merciful God finally took pity on the children of Israel, who could not endure the misery of Egyptian domination and who were unreasonably burdened by the yoke of slavery, he called them to freedom. He dealt heavy blows to their adversaries. But when he saw how very unfeeling they [the adversaries] were, he inflicted upon them the death of their firstborn. And they, distraught at these overwhelming evils, and yielding to the enormity of the unexpected calamity, reluctantly bade the oppressed to leave their land. Once this had been done and achieved, God sought from those ransomed a fair compensation, as it were. He spoke thusly to Moses, the teacher of sacred truths: "Consecrate to me every firstborn, the first-produced opening every womb among the children of Israel, both of man and beast: it is mine."[37] Then the blessed Moses clarified the reason for the law to those from Israel: "And it shall come to pass when the Lord your God shall bring you into the land of the Canaanites, as he swore to your fathers—and he shall give it to you—that you will separate everything opening the womb, the males to the Lord."[38] And later he adds, "If your son should ask

---

32. Cf. Heb 1.3.
33. Cf. Gal 2.20.
34. Eph 2.12.
35. 1 Pt 1.18–19.
36. Rom 8.12.
37. Ex 13.2.
38. Ex 13.11–12.

you afterwards, 'What is this?' you shall say to him, 'With a strong hand the Lord brought us out of Egypt, out of the house of bondage. And when Pharaoh hardened his heart, sending us away, he slew every firstborn in the land of Egypt, both the first-born of man and the firstborn of beast. For this reason I sacrifice to God everything opening the womb, the males, and every first-born of my sons I will redeem.'"[39]

It is to God that we owe ourselves, beloved, God who strikes down our enemies and rescues us so marvelously from the dev-il's tyranny, washing away our past failures in good and gentlest waters; we must honor our benefactor in return with gifts of equal value. Come then, let us honor our Savior with the brave deeds of our works, our right and blameless faith shining forth as we make this thing a distinguished offering and a truly spiri-tual sacrifice. For it is written, "Present your bodies as a living sacrifice, acceptable to God, your spiritual worship."[40]

4. While we are at present practicing abstinence from food, therefore, and applying fasting as a bridle, let us join to this a manner of behavior that is moderate and sober. For fasting, alone and by itself, will never suffice for the attainment of virtue; but when the fragrance of good deeds is, as it were, joined and united to it, it will be acceptable to God, and replete with all praise. But someone who is frightened by the accusations of his conscience may perhaps say: What do you mean? I am already suffering compunction for my sins, and the filth of my sins is in-delible. What words can I use in the presence of the universal Judge? Or what manner of behavior will free us from the curse that clings to these things? The sentence is hardly to be avoided; for the Judge knows all and cannot be deceived. Such a person will hear in reply: the curse that hangs over those who love sin, the curse that your sharp eyes have already perceived, you right-ly fear, dear sir. But let Paul release you from the fears connected to these things when he writes, "And he brought us to life when we were dead through the transgressions and sins in which we once walked, following the course of this world, following the

39. Ex 13.14–15.
40. Rom 12.1.

prince of the power of the air, the spirit that is even now at work among those who are disobedient. Among these we all once lived in the passions of our flesh, following the desires of the flesh and our thoughts, and so we were by nature children of wrath, just like the rest. But God, who is rich in mercy, out of the great love with which he loved us, even when we were dead through our transgressions, brought us to life together with Christ."[41] It is just as the Savior himself said, "For God the Father loved the world so much, that he gave his only-begotten Son, so that everyone who believes in him might not perish, but might have eternal life."[42]

For the Word, being God and from God by nature and by reason of his ineffable generation from the Father, equal in strength and operation to the One who engendered him, image and reflection, and "imprint of his hypostasis,"[43] emptied himself,[44] descending to human level and not disdaining the nature that had been so trampled upon, that he might rescue us from sin and, once he had freed us from that ancient curse[45] as God, might render us superior to death and corruption. It was for that reason that the Only-Begotten became a human being, and the one who as God is above the law[46] was born under the law. He was called a slave,[47] he who rides upon the highest powers themselves and who is hymned as Lord Sabaoth by the voice of the holy Seraphim.[48]

But because he became a human being, will we fail to recognize the Master? Will we not recognize the Word engendered from God the Father? Will we not worship Immanuel? Away with such nonsense! For those who have dared to think such things, and who deny the Master who purchased them, will hear the prophet saying, "Walk by the light of your fire, and by the flame that you have kindled."[49] Wisdom, too, will lament over them, saying, "Woe to those who forsake straight ways to walk in ways of darkness."[50] But we will pass by the twisting path to walk in the one that is straight, following the divinely inspired Scriptures.

41. Eph 2.1–5.
42. Jn 3.16.
43. Heb 1.3.
44. Cf. Phil 2.7.
45. Cf. Gal 3.13.
46. Cf. Gal 4.4.
47. Cf. Phil 2.7.
48. Cf. Is 6.3.
49. Is 50.11.
50. Prv 2.13.

Even though we worship him who became a human being because of us and for us, we do not worship him as having come to be in a human being, but as having himself become a human being by nature. For as blessed John says, and as the very nature of the reality bears witness, "The Word became flesh and dwelt among us."[51]

Now we say that the Word became flesh, not that he passed over into the nature of flesh. For that would be a change, and alien to the divine dignity. But [what we say is] that he was born of a woman and became a full human being like us, blended completely in nature, in that union, I mean, in a way that surpasses understanding and expression. For he has been given the title of "mediator between God and humans," connecting through himself those things which for natural reasons were excluded from all kinship with each other.[52]

For as God, he was attached to God the Father's substance, but he also took hold of us, inasmuch as he became man. But he cannot cease to be God because of what is human about him. But it is just in this way that he is God, the divinity which is above all not yielding the victory to the flesh, but rather carrying what has been assumed into its own glory. John in his wisdom, accordingly, even though he understood that he had been born of a woman, did not say that he had come from below or from the earth, but from above: "For the one who comes from above is above all,"[53] he clearly cried.

Casting away as far as possible, then, the silly, vain tales of the unbelievers,[54] we will recognize our own Master, even if he has become a human being. For the Jews, those wretched folk, who did not know the mystery of piety, replied in their ignorance, when Christ asked them for what reason they persecuted and raged against him uncontrollably, "It is not for a good work that we stone you, but for blasphemy, because you who are a human

51. Jn 1.14.
52. Cyril frequently noted that all attempts to describe the drama of the Incarnation must end with an acknowledgment of the limitations of human nature to understand these mysteries. See most famously his *Second Letter to Nestorius* 3.
53. Jn 3.31.
54. Cf. 1 Tm 4.7 and 6.4.

being are making yourself God."[55] That is not the view that we shall take. For it is not that he was a human being who ascended to the glory of divinity, but rather, being God by nature, he became a human being. For how otherwise did he empty himself,[56] according to the Scriptures? Being God, therefore, he became a human being, for in no respect was he a human being who was deified. This is why it is fitting to worship him, even if he is regarded as being with flesh. For blessed David sang, "God will come manifestly; he is our God and will not keep silence."[57] And the divinely inspired Thomas, when he had touched the mark of the nails and finally recognized him as God, worshiped him, saying, "My Lord and my God!"[58] Now of course the divine is intangible and invisible. But he came to dwell manifestly, since the Word is not other than his own flesh and the temple from the Virgin; he is regarded, rather, as one with it, in the union, that is, by which he is even said to have become flesh.

He it is whom the wretched Jews dishonored, even though he said clearly, "Those who believe in me have eternal life,"[59] and "I am the light of the world,"[60] "I am the resurrection and the life."[61] But taking no account of such things, and yielding to anger and jealousy, they ended by crucifying him. The Psalmist, moreover, curses them, caught as they are in their incessant audacities, when he says, "Lord, you will trouble them in your anger, and fire shall devour them. You will destroy their fruit from the earth, and their seed from the sons of men. For they intended evils against you; they devised a plan which they will by no means be able to carry out."[62] For it was not possible for life to be held fast by the bonds of death. For he was raised from the dead, having plundered hell and said "to those in bonds, 'Come out!' and to those in darkness, 'Show yourselves!'"[63] Having made a way for human nature to return to life, shown himself to the holy disciples, appointed them spiritual leaders of the world, and bidden them baptize "in the name of the Father and of the

55. Jn 10.33.
57. Ps 49.2–3 (LXX).
59. Jn 6.47.
61. Jn 11.25.
63. Is 49.9.

56. Cf. Phil 2.7.
58. Jn 20.28.
60. Jn 8.12.
62. Ps 20.10–12.

Son and of the Holy Spirit,"[64] he ascended to the Father, as a kind of first harvest and "firstfruits of those who have fallen asleep,"[65] appearing also to the spirits above, that he might make heaven accessible to ourselves as well. Indeed, he said to the holy disciples, "I will go, and I will prepare for you a place; and I will come back, and I will take you to myself, that where I am, there you too may be with me."[66]

In celebrating the feast for all these reasons, let us purify ourselves by our efforts as we must, and by mortifying the flesh, or rather the pleasure that is in and of the flesh, through our abstinence, in order that, once pure, we may show ourselves worthy of the splendor of the saints when we are joined in purity to the holy God through Christ the Mediator. And in joining to our fasting the honor that comes from good deeds, let us take pity on widows, let us have a care for orphans,[67] let us break our bread for the hungry, let us clothe the naked, let us have a care for those in prison,[68] let us bring into our homes the poor who have no shelter; in a word, let us practice every kind of virtue.

For then it is, then indeed, that we will fast in purity. We begin holy Lent on the thirteenth of Phamenoth, and the week of the salvific Paschal feast on the eighteenth of Pharmuthi. We break the fast on the twenty-third of Pharmuthi,[69] late in the evening, according to the gospel precept. We celebrate the feast on the next day, the eve of Sunday, the twenty-fourth of the month, joining thereto the seven weeks of holy Eastertide, according to the precept of the divine law. For adorned thus with right faith and good works, we will inherit the kingdom of heaven in Christ Jesus our Lord,[70] through whom and with whom be glory and power to the Father with the Holy Spirit, now and always, and for endless ages. Amen.

64. Mt 28.19.
66. Jn 14.2–3.
68. Cf. Mt 25.36.
70. Cf. Mt 25.35.

65. 1 Cor 15.20.
67. Cf. Jas 1.27.
69. April 19, 425.

FESTAL LETTER FOURTEEN
A.D. 426

N TIMES PAST there were sacred words that intoned the signal for our holy feast; they order us to cry out concerning it as loudly and clearly as is fitting, when they say, "Blow the trumpet at the new moon, on the glorious day of your feast."[1] But now that the shadow of the law has been removed, and indeed the letter has shifted to where it shows the realities clearly and more manifestly, let us leave aside as stale and now useless that which was discovered by those of old as something in shadow and figures, by which I mean the inarticulate sound of the trumpets, and let us bring the gospel message, in its precision and harmony, to be of service in signaling the feast. For a new moon has now appeared; that is to say, the new and fresh time of our Savior's Resurrection is coming up. "Anyone who is in Christ is a new creation,"[2] as is written, "and the old has passed away, behold everything has become new." Accordingly (for I think we ought to go straight to what is fitting), "Sanctify a fast,"[3] as the prophet says. Now to sanctify is to consecrate, and, as it were, to present to the all-ruling God something of value. Those therefore who are experienced in warfare, and know how to train others in tactics, run around the ranks of their own men when the time comes for battle, bid them expel fear from their minds, and persuade them in every possible form of speech that it behooves them to show themselves courageous in combat.

Now I, for my part, think that I must once again propose to those who do not neglect virtue—but who are utterly convinced

1. Ps 81.3.
2. 2 Cor 5.17.
3. Jl 2.15.

that the labor bestowed upon it is of the greatest worth—the message that is apt to stimulate them, as a sort of challenge to zeal in its regard. "For it is now time to act for the Lord,"[4] as is written. Act how? Quell the passions. Mortify one's pleasures and attune the mind to all that is holily admired, using the panoply of the saints, on which Paul himself, that best of persons, prided himself for us: "I pommel my body and subdue it, lest after preaching to others I myself should be disqualified."[5] For the effort at asceticism is,[6] all agree, something grievous and hard to bear; but it is rich in fruit for virtue and good conduct, and in the acquisition of that which is incomparably better through the minor loss of that which is worse. The blessed Paul makes this clear when he says, "For even if our outer self is wasting away, our inner self is being renewed day by day."[7] For since this loathsome, pleasure-loving flesh rises up against the thoughts of the spirit, being sick within itself with the law of sin,[8] and ever inciting one toward that which, if one inclines to it, requires one to abandon the glory associated with what is better, let us prefer what is beneficial and honored by divine judgment to what is shameful, and so, in sobriety and moderation, let us lull the untameable movement of the flesh; let us, as it were, make friends of continence and the virtues that border it and are its neighbors, by which I mean courage, justice, and prudence. Thus we may fix upon our heads a sort of crown of spring flowers, wonderfully fragrant, skillfully woven to a remarkable beauty; and, having washed away all filth, we may, once pure, discharge in purity, along with the fast, the service that best suits the saints. For thus it is, thus indeed, that we will share in the heavenly feast, resplendent in bright garments, as it were, the glory that comes from the virtues; we will not hear those terrible words that the Savior spoke to one of those who had been called: "Friend, how did you get in here without a wedding garment?"[9]

For it is wise to adapt to the occasion. For it is written: "There

---

4. Ps 119.126.   5. 1 Cor 9.27.

6. For a discussion of Cyril's approach to the ascetical life, see the introduction in FOTC 118, 12–16.

7. 2 Cor 4.16.   8. Cf. Rom 7.23.

9. Mt 22.12.

is a time for every matter,"[10] and all good things have their own time. In addition, it is worthwhile thinking about the following. If someone of the highest state, distinguished by honors most glorious, were to bid us come to him to take part in a feast that he had decided to celebrate for his acquaintances, would not those invited come to his house splendidly dressed? For they would behave in a way worthy of the dignity of the one who had invited them. Could there be any doubt about it? When therefore those at a feast cannot get away with failing to dress splendidly, then certainly those who disdain the divine invitation must stand convicted and condemned by the apparent lack of brightness in their mind. For those who are still, as it were, filthy and smelly, and who lead lives that are incompatible and irreconcilable with what the saints strive for, cannot be numbered with them.

And this even though Christ says clearly concerning the economy that will come in its time: "Then the just will shine like the sun in their Father's kingdom."[11] Away, then, with the unholy defilement of worldly things! Let fornication depart with it, and greed, jealousy, gossip, slander, deceit, and fraud.[12] For it is thus that the atrocious punishment that hangs over the heads of those given to sin will be destroyed, and with it the accusations resulting from wickedness. And there will arise, so to speak, the things in which one might fairly take pride; and we will be with Christ, the Savior of us all. Possessing a glory free from all blame, we will have the contentment of reaping the benefit of what we need when we dwell in the company of the saints.

2. Let us therefore once again welcome the wise John as a sort of governor and guide to what is best, when he says, "Do not love the world or what is in the world. Those who love the world do not have the love of the Father in them. For all that is in the world, the lust of the flesh, the lust of the eyes, and the pride of life, is not from the Father, but is from the world. And the world is passing away, and so is desire. But those who do God's will re-

---

10. Eccl 3.1.   11. Mt 13.43.
12. Cf. 2 Cor 12.20; Rom 1.29–30.

main forever."[13] You see how the saints have chosen to live with a wise and irreproachable attitude, and how they spring up courageously into a sort of observation post with a view of the realities of our situation, measuring nicely the distractions of the present life, and indicating which of them may, with difficulty, be found useful, and to what degree and for what purpose. "For all that is in the world," he says, "is the lust of the flesh, the lust of the eyes, and the pride of life."[14]

For is it not true that the pleasures and luxury of those who have fallen into worldly indolence extend to the pleasures of the table and of the belly? For delicacies of every sort, spices, pretentious preparations of savory dishes, and the gourmet table: this is what they value most of all.

As for "the lust of the eyes," this, I think, can also find satisfaction in the beauty of bodies and the splendor of matter, and in those things that usually charm our eyesight with their pleasantness and grace.

Vanity and love of honor: how can I finally describe how far their wickedness reaches? For God counts among his greatest enemies those who are imperious and haughty. For "the Lord resists the proud,"[15] as is written.

Having rejected these things, and reckoned them of exceedingly little account, and having made the holy choice to value the honor that goes with better things, let us live according to the Gospel, making it our noble concern to show that we have, as it were, even died to the world by refusing to live in a worldly way. This is what Paul too hints at when he says, "For I through the law died to the law that I might live to God. I have been crucified with Christ. It is no longer I who live, but Christ who lives in me."[16] In remembering, I think, what [Christ] himself says, "You received without paying; give without pay,"[17] he urges us ourselves to have the same outlook when he says, "Do you not know that all of us who have been baptized into Christ were baptized into his death? We were buried therefore with him by baptism into death, so that as Christ was raised from the dead by the

---

13. 1 Jn 2.15–17.   14. 1 Jn 2.16.
15. Prv 3.34.   16. Gal 2.19–20.
17. Mt 10.8.

glory of the Spirit, we too might walk in newness of life."[18] I will therefore say something necessary to your advantage, and once again I will make use of the words of the saints: "Who among you are the wise and understanding ones? By their good conduct let them show their works in the meekness of wisdom."[19]

Now it is worth your while to reflect that admirable conduct is none other than that by which certain folk may be guided aright, and may choose to live in the best way and to be sincere in their faith. For to give the appearance of approaching the faith, while looking elsewhere and hating to plant oneself firmly, is, I must confess, to reach the last degree of evil. Against those in fact who have corrupted their mind in this way, who have chosen to think and act thus, the divine words themselves immediately level their curse: "Woe to fearful hearts, and faint hands, and the sinner that goes two ways!"[20] For it is truly a paralyzing sickness of mind to be readily distracted from one's course and willing to love what one has decided to hate, a crime that may be charged to a faint and unnerved spirit. For suppose one were to ask someone of at least moderate sobriety, to say nothing of someone of immense strength, the following question: "If you had the choice, dear sir, of being healthy or sick, and you could easily have whichever you liked, would you choose to be ill, rejecting the other state, or would you hasten to take the choice which is obviously better, dismissing the very question as ridiculous?" Is there any human being so insane as not to cry out how pleasant it is when the body is healthy? And that the last thing one would choose is to experience the contrary? It is indeed impossible that we should say that that person has not judged wisely. For it is unsafe to disparage as unsound that which intrinsically and obviously abounds in glory, even if no one chooses to defend it. If, then, we reckon bodily health as one of the best things, and include it as among the most desirable, how can it not be absurd not to appear to have the same attitude toward the soul? Or rather, not to deem it worthy of a zeal that is more useful? For the degree to which souls are superior to bodies is, I think, the degree to which we should bestow upon them a fuller concern.

18. Rom 6.3–4.   19. Jas 3.13.
20. Sir 2.12.

While ointments, therefore, and food and the sufficient use of other treatments that are not excessive drive illness from human bodies, I would say that the health of the soul, and the incomparable sobriety of a mind looking to be firm, consist in bringing the mind to a longing for virtue, in considering sin an impure corruption, and beyond this in desiring tenaciously to be vanquished by love for God, and in honoring the Creator of all with an integral faith. For the divine law itself reveals to us that those of old had to have this attitude. For the first and admirable commandment is: "You shall love the Lord your God with your whole soul, and with your whole mind, and with all your strength."[21] That, I maintain, is to choose to honor the Maker with an integral faith.

Consider the matter thus: take, for instance, those in attendance upon those in power on earth, and those who are appointed their guards: does it behoove them to think as they do? And when they choose to do so, will we consider them worthy of the highest praise, and pay them the highest marks of honor? Or, rather, would someone perhaps think it better, and preferable, if they were to pretend to be loyal by their speech, while being caught infected with a barbarian outlook and enslaved to the most shameful evils? I am sure that anyone with good sense would say that it would and will befit the evil man to perish evilly, "who says one thing while hiding something else within his thoughts," as the Greek poets say.[22] For I think that one must preserve completely irreproachable one's loyalty toward those in power, while hating with all one's heart anything barbarian. If, however, at least in these parts, one's good reputation is conspicuous and worth having, then obviously we will consider it necessary that those who are united to God and have firmly professed their faith in him, and that in the presence of many holy witnesses, should prefer to rely upon him uniquely, crying out in the words of the Psalm, "My soul holds fast behind you."[23] For it is only thus, and

21. Mk 12.30; cf. Dt 6.5.
22. Homer, *Iliad* 9.313. According to the editor of the Sources chrétiennes edition, references to the *Iliad* are relatively rare in early Christian literature; SC 434, 142, n. 1.
23. Ps 62.8.

not otherwise, that they may be counted among the true worshipers.[24] For to confess with the tongue that he is the God of everything, while not yet departing once for all from the error of demons, can only be, to judge fairly, nothing else than that of which I just spoke: to pretend in speech to be loyal, while being barbarian in mind. It might be said that he who is crowned with the highest glory could justly rebuke them, saying: "O soldier, who bear my arms, are your sympathies with the barbarians? You like only to seem to be mine, while belonging to others completely." Now God too, I think, might say of those who are not firm in faith: "This people honors me with their lips, but their heart is far from me. In vain do they revere me, when the teachings they observe are human precepts."[25]

Now our topic offers the opportunity to speak of something practical. What I mean is that some of those who are reckoned as among us have reached such a point of ignominy as to give over their minds to attending to deceptive spirits and the false and idle chatter of oracle-mongers.[26] The latter imagine that they know what is beyond heaven and under the earth; but the wretches do not realize that they fool themselves, and with their own selves they ruin others as well. For they persuade them to believe that knowledge of the future is available for those who want to get it, and, in attributing to the movement of the stars what is peculiar to the divine excellence alone, they draw away from sound and right doctrine those who are easily led astray and prone to be carried off by deception. They in fact gather together crowds of wretched crones, whispering what they like, as though they themselves were divine. These return home, having been stupidly taken in by the falsehoods and bilked of their money collected with such difficulty. For their whole art consists in wooing vain and unholy dirty money, and of their drawings upon the lethal tablet they make a sort of shop of falsehoods.

This is what some of the people of Israel used to do, neglecting piety toward God and not heeding their proper pursuit. But what does the prophet Ezekiel say? "And the word of the Lord

24. Cf. Jn 4.23.
25. Mt 15.8–9; cf. Is 29.13.
26. See *Letter* 6 in FOTC 118 for a similar critique of astrology.

came to me, saying: Son of man, prophesy against the prophets of Israel who prophesy; and you shall speak to the prophets who prophesy from their heart, and you shall prophesy and say to them: Hear the word of the Lord. Thus says the Lord Adonai."[27] "Because your words are false, and your prophecies are vain, therefore, behold, I am against you, says the Lord Adonai. And I will stretch forth my hand against the prophets that see false-hoods and that utter vanities."[28] And because there were some horrible women who used to pretend to knowledge of the future, God speaks again to the prophet, "And you, son of man, set your face firmly against the daughters of your people, who prophesy from their heart; and prophesy against them, and you will say: Thus says the Lord Adonai: Woe to the [women] who stitch together cushions on every wrist and make coverings for every head of every age, to pervert souls! And the souls of my people have been perverted, and they have preserved souls and have profaned me before my people for a handful of barley and a piece of bread, to kill souls that should not have died, and to preserve souls that should not have lived, when you speak to a people who listens to vain utterances."[29]

For that is the truth. Without ever being inspired by God, they transmit to others things that are beyond the mind according to our customary way of prophecy. When they themselves have composed replies that seem plausible to each of those who like to question them, they send them forth from their shops of deceit. But while they say that they are skilled and wise, and suppose that they are so far advanced in their art and accuracy that they can effortlessly and unerringly understand the affairs of others, one finds that they err so badly about their own concerns that, after they have blundered, they say they would never have expected to suffer what occurred. Indeed, since it is easy for those who know things in advance to protect themselves, and they have the means to escape what they already know will hap-

27. Ezek 13.1–3.
28. Ezek 13.8–9.
29. Ezek 13.17–19. The editor of the Sources chrétiennes edition notes that this use of Ezekiel in arguments against astrology is unique to Cyril; SC 434, 146, n. 1.

pen, and how it will occur, why are they not the first to avoid calamities, convinced as they are that they do well at their art? Their inventions are, then, vain quackery, as we have proved by the facts themselves.

But, they say, some of what has been said has turned out true. Just so, dear sirs: and that is precisely the charge upon which your censure must rest. Does then a defendant, and someone accused, make the indictment his defense? It is not because some of what has been said has turned out to be true that we are being foolish in pouring out our accusations concerning something that is not shameful. It is rather the fact that not all of them are true: that is the clear proof of your disgusting character, and shows as well how erroneous is your trade, how very foolish your art, and laughable your science, even though what comes from God does not prove false. For the divine mind in its purity knows completely and fully what will be, and if it chooses in advance to tell it to certain ones, and those then to others, the narrative will not be false. The inventions of human thought, by contrast, will have the reputation of conjecture rather than of truth.

Each of these folk seems to me to resemble someone who has lost his sight to some disease and no longer has the faculty of vision, and who would do better to remain quiet and yield to the constraints of his handicap, but who then thinks he can practice archery, and is quite serious about it. Is this not madness, and a kind of crime against the art? It is easy to perceive what will happen to him. He will send forth a hail of arrows, most of which will be lost and doubtless miss the mark. But there is nothing to prevent them from heading somehow straight for it, however difficult this may be. He will then boast of this one shot, and rebuff the ridicule that results from the others! The man with healthy vision, however, will not take pride in one successful shot and think well of himself; far from it. On the contrary, if he had set out to receive our praise, he would be ashamed of all of the missed shots, for fear lest his art fail of its beauty.

Let them then choose: they may, on the one hand, acknowledge that they produce what they say from an intelligence that is blind, and they may claim the applause they can get from that. For those without sight will not incur much ridicule for their fail-

ure, and their one lucky success will be put down not to skill but
to chance. Or, on the other hand, if they say that they can see,
and insist that they know the truth clearly, they will then find
that their failure is quite inexcusable, and their method of divination so much mental froth.

There have been holy prophets among us, whose habit was
not to measure the movement of stars, who did not meddle in
the use of the elements and force human nature into what does
not behoove it, and who did not put their trust in worthless
quackery. They rather perceived the future in advance, from the
Holy Spirit's revelation, and told us of it long before it happened. Nothing of what they said has failed, but the course of
events proceeds through their due times until they are at hand;
or rather it does so exactly in the footprints of what has been
foretold. For it is God who has spoken. One is therefore able to
hear these men clearly as they spared no words in declaring how
lethal is this deceitful and money-grubbing juggling with astrology; for I think for my part that one must be extravagant in inventing names for this art.

They say, accordingly, "Thus says the Lord: Do not learn according to the ways of the nations, and do not be alarmed at the
signs of the sky, for they are alarmed at them in their faces, for
the laws of the nations are vain."[30] The stars that adorn this sky
with their multifarious positions, and crown it with their harmonious brilliance, have indeed been made for illumination and
for marking times.[31] But they submit to the laws of their Maker,
you see, and indicate the changing of seasons to those on earth,
rising and setting each at different times.

We must attend, accordingly, not to the ribaldry of these folk,
but to the voices of those divinely inspired, and we will concede
to God the possession of the glory that is beyond all things; we
will not grant it to the nature of the stars. For is not the possession in abundance of the knowledge of the future a dignity and
superiority that befits God? Can there be any doubt of it? For

30. Jer 10.2–3.
31. For a discussion of the early Christian thinking about the influence of
the stars, see Alan Scott, *Origen and the Life of the Stars: A History of an Idea* (Oxford: Oxford University Press, 1994).

just as the bringing of things with ease from non-being into being will be ascribed to him alone, and to no other being, so also, I think, will be the knowledge of everything past and present, and even of the future. But that the devotion to worthless and false divination does not go unpunished, is what the blessed Moses declares, or rather the God of all through Moses: "When you enter the land which the Lord your God gives you, you shall not learn to act according to the abominations of the nations. There shall not be found in you one who purges his son or his daughter with fire, one who practices divination, interprets omens, and performs augury, a sorcerer, enchanter, ventriloquist, observer of prodigies, or necromancer. For everyone who does these things is an abomination to the Lord, your God."[32] And he adds, "You shall be perfect before the Lord, your God. For the nations whom you shall inherit, they shall listen to omens and divinations. But the Lord your God has not allowed this to you."[33] False divination, then, and attention to omens, are the worst of crimes.

And what is paradoxical is that God sometimes allows these folk to say something true, using the event as a sort of test of the firmness of the faith of his own worshipers. He speaks as follows through Moses: "If there arises in you a prophet or one who dreams a dream, and he gives you a sign or wonder, and the sign or wonder comes to pass which he spoke to you, saying: 'Let us go and serve other gods whom you do not know,' you shall not listen to the words of that prophet or of the one who dreams that dream, because the Lord God is testing you, to see if you love the Lord your God with all your heart and with all your soul."[34] When therefore the beauty of loyalty towards God is counterfeited, if someone thinks that those engaged in such filthy lucre are divinely inspired, then even if it happens that they say something true, we will not yield our attention to their claptrap. But as for those folk, let them go their own way, "deceivers and deceived,"[35] as is written, for such is their choice; we, however, will follow the sacred words, remembering the one who writes: "You shall make straight paths for your feet, and order

32. Dt 18.9–12.   33. Dt 18.13–14.
34. Dt 13.1–3.   35. 2 Tm 3.13.

your ways aright."[36] Now the straight and undeviating path is to head directly toward all that is good, to bid farewell to false divination, and to know, and that simply, who it is that is naturally and truly God and Lord. For the law given through Moses prescribed of old that this must be our attitude: "The Lord your God shall you adore, and him alone shall you serve."[37] "For there is in us one God, the Father, and one Lord Jesus Christ, through whom are all things."[38] "For in the beginning was the Word, and the Word was with God, and the Word was God. All things were made through him, and without him not one thing was made."[39]

But now we certainly do not say, since in fact everything was made through him according to the Scriptures, that he has a subordinate and instrumental rank, as though implying that the Father has some need when he creates everything. That would be froth from an unholy doctrine, and the inventions of the folly of heretics.[40] But since he himself is the wisdom and power of God the Father,[41] it is through him that all things are called into existence, and, once called, are preserved and maintained in well-being. "For God did not make death, nor does he delight in the destruction of the living."[42] For thus is it written: "Nor is the dominion of Hades upon earth."[43] "For he created all things that they might exist, and the generative forces of the world are wholesome";[44] "but by the devil's envy death entered the world."[45] For human nature slipped when it disregarded the reverence due to God, and it was delivered to sin. And along with the accusations concerning sin, there entered in, as it were, the necessity of dying and of submitting to the power of corruption.[46] For it at once heard the words: "Earth you are, and off to earth shall you go."[47] But the Creator of all, being good by nature, decided to

---

36. Prv 4.26.   37. Mt 4.10, quoting Dt 6.13.
38. 1 Cor 8.6.   39. Jn 1.1–3.
40. This is a reference to the fourth-century Trinitarian debates. See the introduction in FOTC 118, 26–27.
41. Cf. 1 Cor 1.24.   42. Wis 1.13.
43. Wis 1.14.   44. Wis 1.14.
45. Wis 2.24.
46. Salvation as liberation from corruption is an important idea in Cyril's theology. See *Letter* 5.2, FOTC 118, 85–86.
47. Gn 3.19.

refashion the living being unto incorruption, and, by transforming him unto piety, to restore him completely to the unspoiled
beauty that he had at first.

Thus did the only-begotten Word of God become a human
being; and while he put on the form we have, he retains the fact
of being God as something he cannot lose. For the nature that is
beyond all mind, and is the highest of all, knows no alteration.
He remained therefore what he was, even with the flesh, and,
lowering himself to his providential [self-]emptying, he "dwelt
among human beings,"[48] as is written, reforming him who approached him and justifying him by faith, opening the gate of
the kingdom of heaven, introducing what is beneficial, and
showing the truth. And both by the illumination of the divine
light and by the magnificence of his deeds, he made it clear to
those of good sense that he is God by nature, even if he became
flesh. He said accordingly, "If I do not do the works of my Father,
do not believe me; but if I do them, even if you do not believe
me, believe my works."[49] For the word was what drew [people] to
assent; and the <power>[50] of working miracles was quite sufficient to show clearly that he is God by nature.

But those from Israel decided not to think aright. For they
spent a long time insulting the Savior and Redeemer of the universe by their enormous incredulity, and finally they crucified
him, repaying him evil for good,[51] as is written, and executing
the devil's commands without delay. Did he therefore remain
among the dead, and, having suffered human death with us, was
he caught fast in the snares of adventitious corruption? By no
means. For he was by nature life, and he revived on the third
day, becoming even here a beginning and door and way for the
human race. And when he revived, having plundered hell, he ascended to God the Father in the heavens. And he will come in
due time, as we believe, with the holy angels, will sit upon the
throne of his glory, and will repay each according to his works.[52]

Let us celebrate the feast, therefore, since death has been ban-

---

48. Bar 3.37.   49. Jn 10.37–38.
50. The noun δύναμις has been inserted in brackets by the Sources chrétiennes editor; SC 434, p. 162, ln. 340.
51. Cf. Ps 35.12.   52. Cf. Mt 16.27.

ished, corruption destroyed, sin abolished in advance by faith, and the kingdom of heaven set before us, such a bright hope thus awaiting us. But since we are to present ourselves to the Judge to give an account of our own life, let us give thought to moderation. Let us practice justice, charity, mutual friendship, gentleness, temperance, and, in a word, every virtue. Let us care for widows, let us have pity for orphans,[53] let us assist those with bodily ailments with every possible remedy, let us care for those in prison.

For it is thus, thus indeed, that we will celebrate the feast in a pure manner when we have rid ourselves of every stain, and when we distinguish ourselves by a right faith. We begin Lent on the fifth of Phamenoth, and the week of the salvific Paschal feast on the tenth of Pharmuthi, breaking the fast on the fifteenth of Pharmuthi, late in the evening, according to the gospel precept. We celebrate the feast on the following day, the eve of Sunday, the sixteenth of this month.[54] We join thereto the seven weeks of holy Eastertide. For it is thus, thus indeed, that we will enjoy the holy words, in Christ Jesus our Lord, through whom and with whom be honor, glory, and power to the Father with the Holy Spirit for all ages. Amen.

53. Cf. Jas 1.27.
54. April 11, 426.

FESTAL LETTER FIFTEEN

A.D. 427

OME ONCE AGAIN, let us exult in the Lord.[1] For the time has now come to hold festival, beloved, to betake ourselves without delay to the spiritual banquet, and all but to cry out with the Psalmist's noble lyre: "Delight in the Lord, and may he give you all the requests of your heart."[2] We will carry out what has been commanded, not battening on savory dishes, nor clouding our minds with cup after cup beyond measure; but luxuriating rather in sacred and divine words, widening the eye of our mind unto a sobriety that is still better and ever superior to that which is ours at present, and proceeding in some sense to the lofty heights themselves of the vision of God. For the result will be, with God's generous assent, that we will be able to conquer our obstacles and show ourselves superior to the most revolting passions.[3]

Now the words that befit perfectly those who keep festival thus splendidly, are those which encourage us to seek to desire that admirable way of life, which is in Christ: the divine Singer will, I think, offer sufficient proof of that when he testifies in saying to us, "Blow the trumpet at the new moon, on the glorious day of your feast."[4] And as the clearest evidence I will add to this an ancient oracle. For he says to that holiest man, Moses, "And if you shall go forth to war in your land against your enemies that are opposed to you, and you sound the trumpets, you will be held in remembrance before the Lord, and you will be saved

1. Cf. Ps 95.1.
2. Ps 37.4.
3. For a discussion of Cyril's approach to the ascetical life, see the introduction in FOTC 118, 12–16.
4. Ps 81.4.

29

from your enemies. And in the days of your gladness, and on your feasts, and on your new moons, you shall sound the trumpets at your holocausts and at the sacrifices of your altars, and there shall be a remembrance for you before your God. I am the Lord your God."[5]

It is not without purpose that the law has revealed this to us. It leads one by analogy through figures and riddles to the truth, and, in providing as a sort of coarse image the things that meet the sense of sight, it establishes the subtle eye of the mind above what is sensible. You will understand what I mean if you give the fullest attention to what we have just said. Those of old, that is, were engaged in war against blood and flesh. For Moabites and Midianites,[6] and in addition countless other nations of the most belligerent sort, who bordered the land of the Jews, used to make frequent incursions by surprise. It was necessary for those who were concerned for their reputation in battle to keep resisting and repelling them on their own behalf and for their children and women. We will reckon, then, that the sound of the trumpet was not found by those of old to be without benefit for the waging of war.

So it was for them. But for us whose reputation is based on faith in Christ, the war is not against blood and flesh, nor does it entail a demonstration of bodily strength. "For the weapons of our warfare are not carnal,"[7] as Paul says. A sacred and holy war is now undertaken, rather, against the very ones who were victorious of old, and against every passion that is in us. Let the spiritual trumpet give the signal, then, which means the piercing proclamation of the holy and divinely inspired Scripture; let it incite those able and experienced in war to show great strength; and let it announce that it behooves them to relinquish cowardice. God says this clearly through a prophet's voice: "Proclaim this among the nations: Sanctify a war, rouse the fighters, advance and go up, all you men of war; beat your plowshares into swords, and your sickles into spears. Let the weak say: I am strong."[8]

You see how he says that the battle is holy, and does not allow

5. Nm 10.9–10.
6. Cf. Nm 22.3–4.
7. 2 Cor 10.4.
8. Jl 4.9–10.

what is inglorious and feeble to be weak, knowing as he does how indelible are accusations of unmanliness for those upon whom they are charged. But what does the prophetic message mean to indicate to us, in urging us so strongly to beat the plowshares into swords, and the sickles into spears? Let us consider. Plowshares and sickles, swords and spears:[9] the former would be the most useful implements for agriculture, while the latter are precisely those suited for war. Shall we therefore say that the law removes us from a quiet and industrious life, and bids us choose in place of it, when it is so worthy of reverence, one which is savage and bellicose? It is repugnant even to entertain the thought. The charge is ridiculous, I think, and the idea perverse. For God's law educates us for all that is admirable, and is the last thing that would turn us aside to choose to commit a transgression. Let us therefore consider, if you please, what is meant by transforming the plowshare into a sword, and the sickle into a spear.

The law appears to suggest to us, deftly, that the time has come for those who are justified in Christ[10] and sanctified in the Spirit,[11] and who have undertaken the war against passions and sin, to stop dwelling upon earthly concerns and letting themselves be persuaded to dally there, so that they seem slow to take up the duty to achieve what is better and more fitting. They are rather to redirect the effort spent on earthly affairs, as it were, to the achievement of virtue, even if victory is to be had only after a battle, to tame the passions within themselves, to prefer to appear superior to indolence, and to arm themselves with the full spiritual panoply. For thus does Paul in his supreme wisdom equip for us the best and mightiest fighter when he says, "Stand therefore, having girded your loins with truth, and having put on the breastplate of justice, and having shod your feet with the gear of the gospel of peace; besides all these, taking the shield of faith, with which you can quench all the flaming shafts of the Evil One. And take the helmet of salvation, and the sword of the Spirit, which is the word of God."[12] The best fighter, then, will take pride in his duty to equip himself splendidly, and will win

9. Cf. Jl 4.10.
11. Cf. Rom 15.16.

10. Cf. Gal 2.17.
12. Eph 6.14–17.

the honor worthy of a combatant for this, having chosen to think and act in a way that will show his valor and his complete readiness for the achievement of everything that is excellent. He will be wise, sensible, and docile and obedient to the divine laws.

2. But who are those that lead a life contrary to what I have said, and who are thus rejected from the sacred multitude of the saints? It is once again the God of all who explains it to us in speaking to Moses, the mediator: "Command the children of Israel, and let them send forth from the camp every leper, and everyone suffering from nocturnal discharges, and everyone unclean from a dead body; whether male or female, send them forth from the camp; and they shall not defile their camps in which I dwell with them."[13] You hear how he said that a leper, and someone suffering from nocturnal discharges, and someone unclean from a dead body must be sent from the camp, and he says that it will be an occasion of pollution for the others as well, if they are not separated from the fighters as quickly as possible. Now why ever is that? I at any rate would like to ask this most reasonable of questions. And what is more, I think that anyone would be puzzled, and would ponder for what purpose it was that God made a law that the weak must be subject to punishment.

Would it not be better for the one who is the promoter of holiness and justice to regard those suffering from unwanted illnesses as deserving of gentleness, and, since they have been suffering miserably, to show mercy equally for their condition, and to let no one reproach them at all for their sickness? For leprosy, and the loss of natural seed, and involuntary [menstrual] discharges[14] are things that happen to human bodies, and those suffering from them cannot be blamed for them. One would

13. Nm 5.2–3.
14. The French translator renders καταφοραί as "lethargy," and expresses puzzlement about the meaning (SC 434, 180, n. 1). Lampe notes, however, that elsewhere in Cyril it means "[menstrual] discharge." If that is his meaning here as well, it is easy to see why he would have included it as one of the causes of ritual impurity, especially since the law he quotes mentions females as well as males. It seems likely that Cyril adds it in order to balance the mention of the male seminal discharge.

choose rather, even if one were among those most admired for their wealth, to yield at once all one's possessions to those who promised relief. How, then, can the fact of being a victim of such terrible evils constitute a charge or accusation against the sick? Morals that are thoroughly wicked, and a will that is infected with the tendency to rush headlong into what is shameful, and has chosen to disdain better things, may fairly be punished. But that which is not thus by nature, and which is not chosen by those who suffer it, is not, I think, even to be the subject of jocularity, and does not incur the chastisement contained in the law.

Well, then, what can one say in reply? Has the law been unjust to lepers, or has it pronounced a rigid sentence against the others, neglecting to look for what is fitting? By no means; far from it! For it is written: "The law is holy, and the commandment holy and just and good."[15] But how can we understand this? If someone asks, we shall say: The commandment given through Moses transmitted to those of old the beauty of truth by means of figure and shadow, and the meaning of that which was concealed inside for the mind was represented splendidly by bodily infirmities. For the letter of the law compares to lepers those who, with respect to their morals, are changeable and inconstant in their views, and embroidered with countless evils, while attending only to themselves. It also speaks of someone with an uncontrolled love of the flesh, someone conquered by what is shameful to excess, as one afflicted by nocturnal discharges, as though suffering precisely from the involuntary disease of nocturnal discharge. It execrates as well those who are unclean from a dead body, meaning those who choose to grieve and suffer excessively for the dead.

Retracing our steps, therefore, as it were, and all but guiding our argument back [to its starting point], following the nature of what we are considering, and observing the innermost meaning of what is written, we say the following: If certain folk have chosen to be infected with a variety of vices, they are too weak for battle, and are in no way fit to show themselves superior to passions. This is leprosy and the disease associated with it. Nor will those who are intemperate and yield to inordinate pleasures be

15. Rom 7.12.

enrolled in the ranks of the saints. And in addition, those who lament immoderately the dead who have altogether perished are rejected. For this is to insult God, [to lament] even though he has proclaimed clearly through the voice of the saints, "The dead will rise, and those in the tombs will be raised."[16]

Let us be brave, then, in showing ourselves superior to the passions, as we must; for thus will one be included among those accustomed to a good reputation. And one who is numbered among those selected for merit will truly achieve the glory so deeply desired. Do not be frightened by the effort, even if it seems arduous to reach the life that is commended, and even if the path of virtue is rugged and steep as it lies before one, and labor rears its head before renown. For it is not possible, indeed it is not, for people to abound in the marks of success when they make only slight efforts; it is always in proportion to the labors expended that the results arise and appear.

This is the sort of language the divinely inspired Paul uses to incite us to desire virtue. For he has enjoined as a model, as he likes to do, "Jesus, the pioneer and perfecter of our faith, who for the joy that was set before him endured the cross, despising the shame."[17] In what way and in what circumstances the Word endured the cross for us, lowering himself into his [self-]emptying, even though he is God by nature: let us speak of that, lifting briefly on high our discourse, and bringing it down serviceably to that which is called the voluntary emptying.

3. There has been begotten from God the Father, ineffably and beyond understanding,[18] the Son who is in him and from him by nature. Now when we say "has been begotten," let the mind get beyond the realm of bodies, and the triviality of what the imagination suggests in their regard, leaving it far below; let it consider the Divine as incomparably superior to the nature of body, and let it be firmly convinced that it has a glory which is in-

16. Is 26.19.

17. Heb 12.2.

18. In the lines that follow, Cyril continues to rehearse the major doctrinal conclusions of the previous century. The Christological controversy has yet to begin.

comparable and far above everything created. Without following in any way the laws that apply to us, therefore, we will admit this: that for what is begotten, birth is preceded by complete non-existence, and that the situation of never having been comes before the passage into being, so to speak. To do that [in this context] would be nonsense, and a clear proof of supreme idiocy. For if by chance one were speaking of bodies or of what has to do with us, there would be nothing unreasonable about attributing to bodies what is proper to them, and whatever happens naturally to things subject to generation and decay. For the way into existence is, we all agree, preceded by complete non-existence. They will in addition endure the divisions from the one engendering them, that the offspring may receive its proper endowment.

But when it comes to the substance that is the highest of all, beyond everything created, how can it be anything but sheer madness to admit divisions and severances, and to seek a generation that takes place in time? Away with such nonsense, good fellow! Employ the subtlest possible intelligence in our considerations, and you will see the truth. Or know that you are insulting the divine nature in applying to it what is proper to bodies, and in lowering the lofty pre-eminence, which is beyond everything made, to an estimation of it that is more shameful than that which suits it and which is believed to belong to it.

For since the Father is always Father, and does not pass in time from begetting potentially to begetting in actuality, the one through whom he is Father must always exist with him. For "in the beginning was the Word, and the Word was God,"[19] according to the Scriptures. But of whom "was" is said, when nothing has been cited previously: where will the course of our thought stop [in considering this], and what conclusion will we reach, if our mind chooses to pursue this "was" by some kind of subtle mental intuition?[20] The Word was therefore begotten, and "was

19. Jn 1.1.
20. This language is reminiscent of Cyril's *Second Letter to Successus,* where he discusses human understanding of the division of the divine and human natures in Christ as a "fine-drawn insight or mental intuition." For this translation see Lionel R. Wickham, ed., *Cyril of Alexandria: Select Letters* (Oxford: Ox-

God." But he was not begotten according to a body's nature; that would mean conceiving of a complete otherness between the begotten and the begetter. We have of necessity used the word "beget" from what applies to our circumstances, signifying that the Only-Begotten of God the Father's substance has shone forth in the way of light, and subsists individually, and is regarded as existing in his own right. But it is quite impossible to express this matter in speech. For it is not as one separated at all from his parent's substance, but as one who himself exists in the Father and in his own nature displays his begetter, that he is worshiped and glorified with him. And since he is consubstantial and equal in glory, he is necessarily equal in operation and in power. And since the Holy Spirit subsists for us with them in this way, and is regarded as equally divine and associated with them, the composition of our belief about the holy Trinity will be correct and irreproachable.

He therefore who is supremely distinguished with the dignities pertaining to God the Father, he through whom everything was brought into being, "did not count equality with God something to be grasped," as is written, "but emptied himself, taking the form of a slave, being born in the likeness of human beings. And being found in human form, he humbled himself, becoming obedient unto death, even death on a cross."[21] For even though it was in his power to maintain himself in splendor upon his own pre-eminence, and to enjoy abundantly his equality with the Father, radiant upon the throne of divinity, he descended willingly unto our kind, in no way harming his own nature by assuming what was inferior, but rather adding what was lacking to it. For it would not be reasonable, or rather it would be most dangerous, to think and say that human nature will happen to get the better of the divine and ineffable nature, and will force it into its own ugliness and bring it down from its own pre-eminence. What makes sense, in my view, is to reflect that what pertains to our state will yield before the nature of divinity, and

ford University Press, 1983), 92.14–16. See also John J. O'Keefe, "Impassible Suffering? Divine Passion and Fifth-Century Christology," *Theological Studies* 58 (1997): 50.
    21. Phil 2.6–8.

will take itself off to that which is incomparably superior, vanquished by the renown of what surpasses it.

For it is completely ridiculous, when one sees among God's creatures those not especially beautiful being adorned by the mixture and juxtaposition of those that are superior, to think that when God associates himself with human nature, in a manner that he knows, he does not impress upon it something proper to him, but rather suffers some injury to his own nature contrary to his dignity. The sun itself, when it casts its rays upon the very mud and mire, preserves its radiance quite unimpaired. And the divine, uncontaminated nature, which is above all else and which is quite incapable of suffering any of the things that normally cause distress: how could it be harmed by contact with what is lesser? Will it not rise above the nature that is inferior, and, by illuminating it with its own good things, transport it to what is incomparably better?

But now, instead of admiring unreservedly such venerable things, as they ought, certain folk treat them haughtily and are infected with a supercilious attitude. They think to defend the divine glory by condemning the ugliness of the so-perfect economy. For they do not accept the mystery, but laugh heartily, thinking the matter quite absurd, and claiming that we have ventured upon idle chatter. What they do not realize is that sometimes they place an uncritical trust in their own guides, if in fact they decide to think or say something, and, importing the words, "It was he who said it," then substitute their own thoughts for the divine judgments; they heap upon their own heads that which will be quite hard to escape. Nor do they attribute to the divine nature that by which people have learned to bestow honors.

They think, however, that a brilliant argument has been provided them. How is it, they say, that the uncontaminated mind, free of all quantity and boundary, has made its way into the body of one human being? Now, I for my part commend them when they remove the Divine from corporeal quantity; I agree with this. I do, however, say the following to those who think this way: We do not in fact say that the nature of the Word has been circumscribed, even if he is said to dwell in the body of the Virgin as in a holy temple. On the contrary, he has filled the heavens, the earth, and that which is beneath as God, without omitting anything that is. And with this, he was also a human being. But if you cannot think how or in what way this is, yield to what is above the mind, grant to what is above reason the silence, which is, as it were, from necessity. There is much else that you will admit you do not know:[22] Where is it that the earth is fixed? What base does the sky have? In what manner was the chorus of stars made, and how does it make its way upward to the height? If, however, one chose to speak on each matter, one would, I think, need to say a great deal in composing explanations for you.

They say, however, that it is a shabby thing for the God who is above all to become as we are. Your accusation, then, is that, being kindly and good by nature, he showed a concern for us that was more useful than was fitting. For we may agree that becoming as we are is a shabby thing for him; it is called "emptying."[23] But the account of his clemency toward us will repel the charge. And to level accusations against what should be admired is quite unholy. Speak as follows to those fond of asking questions: Which do you think would be better, and would redound to his glory: to pay no heed to our situation, and take no account of man when he has lapsed into all that is inordinate? Or rather the contrary: to save him, and grant him the care that is fitting? How could anyone accustomed to viewing matters correctly doubt that it would be better and more fitting for him who is good by nature to distribute the good things coming from his own kindness to the beings produced by him? Where, then, is there matter for accusation? And how is it that certain folk prattle on about the faultlessness of the economy?

We will, however, leave it to the physicians to discover how to tame the savagery of their passions; but will we censure God for not being ignorant of the path to care for us? Will we be so senseless as to be convinced that he has failed in reasoning properly, and that human intelligence has seen things in a more fitting way? Come now, shall we not rid ourselves of this ridicu-

22. This is probably an echo of Jb 38.4–7. A similar appeal to the limits of human knowledge appears in Gregory of Nazianzus' *Oration* 28.22–31 (*Second Theological Oration*).

23. Cf. Phil 2.7.

lous insanity? Listen to God, who knows everything, as he clearly says, "For my counsels are not as your counsels, nor are my
ways as your ways; but as the heaven is distant from the earth, so
are my ways distant from your ways, and your thoughts from my
thoughts."[24] For to the extent that he is above our situation by
nature, to that extent is his thought better in every respect. He
does not see by examination the way to each of the things to be
done; he chooses as soon as he thinks, and so accomplishes his
will. "For nothing, nothing at all, fails in God, and he succeeds
in everything," as is wisely sung by those of old.[25] But if it pleases
you and you are eager to learn the reason for the Incarnation, I
will expound it unhesitatingly and briefly.

4. The Creator of all made man imperishable and incorrupt-
ible from the very beginning; he was exempt in this matter by the
laws of his own nature, and hence undisturbed. For that which
comes into existence suffers decay necessarily, and that whose
destiny is to begin to be made proceeds certainly toward having
to cease. But since the Creator wanted him to be thus, he en-
graved in the living thing, in addition to imperishability, knowledge of everything good and indeed an appetite for virtue. Then,
giving him the power to do what he chose, he granted him the
glory befitting beings that are free. For it was necessary, necessary
indeed, that virtue should appear in us as a free choice.

Then, having lapsed into sin through the devil's trickery, and
neglected the laws given him, he was condemned to death,[26] and
joined corruption to his transgressions. But since his Maker decided to refashion the living thing to the manner in which it had
been originally, and to remove it from corruption and sin together, he ordained the law given through Moses; <and> he spoke
through the holy prophets.[27] But the charges against us remained
overwhelming nonetheless. They accordingly besought him final-

24. Is 55.8–9.
25. According to the Sources chrétiennes editor (SC 434, 197, n. 1), Cyril is
paraphrasing an epigram from Demosthenes.
26. Cf. Gn 2.17.
27. Cf. Heb 1.1. With regard to "<and>": the Sources chrétiennes editor has
supplied δὲ; see SC 434, p. 198, ln. 16.

ly to come from heaven in person, saying, "Lord, bow your heavens and come down!"[28] How, then, was God to become visible[29] to those on earth? With glory unconcealed, hidden by no shadow? Who could endure such an august and unbearable sight? I even hear one of the Greek poets, however enmeshed they may be in the error of polytheism, saying, "It is hard to bear the gods' appearing manifest."[30]

But you can tell from the following that it appears evident that to see the glory of the pure nature is beyond the limits of humanity. He descended in the form of fire on the mountain called Sinai.[31] Then he spoke to the sons of Israel, with the all-wise Moses mediating. But Israel, unable to bear the sight, besought him with the words, "You speak to us, and let not God speak to us, lest we die."[32] Since those from Israel had been terrified, then, and had said openly that the need for the mediator would be most pressing for those being instructed, the Legislator made his decision, and, presenting Moses' ministry to those of old as a kind of figure of the one which was to be through Christ, he promised that when the time came he would show him clearly to us. His words: "All that they have said is right; I will raise up a prophet to them from their brothers, like you. And I will place my words in his mouth, and he shall speak to them all that I command him."[33] For he gave the name of "prophet" to the Son, the Lord of prophets, placing him within the limits of humanity due to the ineffability of the economy.

In order, therefore, that he might become as Moses was, a human being, and mediator between God and our condition,[34] he bore the human body. And he took the seed of Abraham,[35] according to the Scriptures, so that that which is by nature life[36] might drive out the corruption that had fallen upon human bodies due to the curse, and might transport all things to the knowledge of God, to continence, courage, perseverance, and to the decision to do and to think the things that render us fervent and fill us with divine gifts.

28. Ps 144.5.
30. Homer, *Iliad* 20.131.
32. Ex 20.19.
34. Cf. 1 Tm 2.5.
36. Cf. Jn 1.4.

29. Cf. Bar 3.38.
31. Cf. Ex 19.18.
33. Dt 18.17–18.
35. Cf. Heb 2.16.

But Israel did not know this economy, even though there were holy prophets proclaiming clearly the mystery that was there. One of them said, "Be strong, hands that are slack, and palsied knees; comfort one another, you who are faint-hearted; be strong, do not fear."[37] "Behold your God! Behold, the Lord comes with strength, and his arm with power. He shall tend his flock as a shepherd, and will gather the lambs."[38] And another of them, Ezekiel, the best of prophets, says,

Behold, I will distinguish between the strong sheep and the weak sheep. You would shove with your sides and your shoulders, and thrust with your horns, and crush what was left. And I will save my sheep, and they will be fodder no longer; and I will judge between ram and ram, and I will raise up one shepherd over them, and he will tend them, my servant David. And he will be a shepherd for him, and I the Lord will be a God to them, and David a ruler in their midst. I the Lord have spoken, and I will make with David a covenant of peace, and I will destroy evil beasts from the land.[39]

Do you hear how Christ, who is from David's seed according to the flesh,[40] is called David throughout, he who is to be shepherd[41] of those from Israel in his time? Realize that at that time, when the prophet said these things, David was no longer among the living; he had died long before. But just as Scripture customarily calls "Jacob" those from Jacob, and "Israel" those from Israel, so also does it give the name "David" to Christ, who is from David's seed according to the flesh.

In their ignorance, then, they crucified him. But even though, since God cannot be constrained, he could have avoided suffering, he delivered himself to the hands of his murderers,[42] in order that, once raised from the dead, he might give full assurance, and above all to those who had crucified him,[43] that as God he was by nature life. He has descended to our condition, that he might render us superior to death and already conquerors of decay.

Since Christ, then, has suffered for us,[44] abolished death,[45] and

37. Is 35.3–4.
38. Is 40.9–11.
39. Ezek 34.20–25.
40. Cf. Rom 1.3.
41. Cf. Jn 10.11.
42. Cf. Is 50.6.
43. Cf. Acts 2.36.
44. Cf. 1 Pt 4.1.
45. Cf. 2 Tm 1.10.

removed sin with its infamy and pollution, and has been raised, and ascended into heaven, and will come at any moment—for he will come down and "will judge the earth[46] in justice,"[47] as is written—let us rub away every stain of sin, let us embrace continence, let us bear the fruit[48] of love for each other[49] in patience, and let us concern ourselves with showing pity for the needy, which is love for the poor. Let us share the suffering of those in bondage, those mistreated, since we too are in bodies.[50] And above all let us preserve in ourselves the faith that is right and faultless.[51] For it is then, then indeed, that we shall fast in a pure manner. We begin holy Lent on the twenty-seventh of Mechir, and the week of the salvific Paschal feast on the second of Pharmuthi. We break our fast on the seventh of Pharmuthi, late in the evening, according to the apostolic tradition. We celebrate the feast on the next day, the eve of Sunday, the eighth of the month,[52] adding thereafter the seven weeks of holy Eastertide. For thus it is, thus indeed, that we will once again delight in the divine words, in Christ Jesus our Lord, through whom and with whom be glory, honor, and power to the Father with the Holy Spirit for endless ages. Amen.

46. Literally, "the economy."
47. Ps 10.9 or 96.13.
48. Cf. Lk 8.15.
49. Cf. Eph 4.2.
50. Cf. Heb 13.3.
51. Cf. Jas 1.27.
52. April 3, 427.

FESTAL LETTER SIXTEEN

A.D. 428

PROLOGUE[1]

HE TIME AT HAND has gathered us here. We do not present ourselves with the promise of a diffuse and ambitious discourse, for we are of quite modest ability in this regard; it is rather that we have decided to follow an ancestral custom, invented by necessity. You must therefore forgive us if this discourse does not shine with the elegance of worldly speech, and cannot boast of rhetorical adornment. For in this matter I cannot at all boast of a reputation; I would have to say that it befits rather these teachers who are so wise and good.

1. The law used to give the signal to those of old that they were to hold the festivals which were still in figures and, as it were, in shadows. That it was indeed necessary to bestow upon them a fitting care, and that negligence in this matter was not excusable, but chargeable as an offense, is something that the God of all makes clear through the words of Zechariah: "And it shall be that if anyone does not go up to celebrate the Feast of Booths, that soul shall be cut off from its people."[2] For if we ought to rejoice in things so venerable and so very rightly prescribed, why would one neglect their observance? If one had the arrogance to treat with insolence something of outstanding worth and noble renown, yielding oneself to sloth and divisions, one would find oneself subject to holy denunciation and well-founded accusation. Pre-

---

1. This is the first time the word "prologue" (*prologos*) appears in the letters. We find it again in *Letters* 19 and 22. Cyril also uses the word "preface" (*protheoria*) in *Letters* 17, 18, 23, 28, and 29.

2. Zec 14.18; Lv 17.4.

scribing, then, as it were, a well-worn path, we will make our proclamation, remembering the one who said, "Hear, O priests, and
testify to the house of Israel, says the Lord almighty."[3] And it behooves us too to show the highest degree of eagerness in ridding
ourselves of lack of restraint and treating it as a most shameful
thing, in order to hasten to fulfill what the law commands.

For the God of all indicated of old to the divinely inspired Moses the time for our holy feast, and how it was to be celebrated by
us holily and faultlessly, representing it in figure, as it were, when
he said, "Speak, and let the children of Israel keep the Passover
in its season, on the fourteenth day of the first month toward evening; you shall keep it at its proper times according to its law, and
according to its ordinance you shall keep it."[4] We must, in submission to the sacred rites, send forth a clear and resounding
proclamation, and address those who have been justified in
Christ: "Come, let us go up to the mountain of the Lord and to
the house of the God of Jacob."[5] There we will complete the all-
holy feast, and, filled with the highest joy, we will glorify the Savior of all with the prophetic words, "Let my soul rejoice in the
Lord, for he has clothed me with the robe of salvation and the
garment of joy."[6]

Now it would seem a most shameful thing, at least to me, if
merchants were to be overcome by their pitiful gains and find
their enjoyment in them, deem it most important to concern
themselves with them, and spend most of their time gathering
them with considerable effort; and if farmers were to exult in
their fields when they see them heavy with lovely fruit; while we,
whose gains are far beyond anything earthly, or rather are incomparably superior, do not consider them most remarkable
and the source of joy to its fullness! And even though the merchants' business—even when it goes according to the hopes of
those who labor at it—rouses no admiration among those who
have chosen the best life. And as for farmers who have worked
skillfully: what remains for them is some modest enjoyment, not
in some profit they might have made that allows them to live
without misfortune or to be able to rise at last above the power

3. Am 3.13.   4. Nm 9.2–3.
5. Is 2.3.   6. Is 61.10.

of death and decay, but in the necessities of life that let them take care of the needs of the body as they arise. What has been prepared for the saints, however, is beyond all understanding; "for their hope is full of immortality,"[7] as is written.

What the time is, then, when Easter is to be celebrated, and how that is to be done, has been explained by us clearly. For he commanded that it should be held on the fourteenth [day] of the first month, toward evening, in its due time and according to its law.[8] Now I think that one should be anxious to inquire into the reasons why the Legislator said that it should take place in the spring, and in the first month, by distinguishing carefully and skillfully between each of the things prescribed, and subjecting them to the best examination possible. It will not be without profit to speak with precision about these matters. This, I think, is what God meant when he spoke through the prophet, "Seek while seeking, and dwell by me."[9] For it behooves us to try to examine what is written by using suitable means of inquiry, as far as possible: that is what sacred Scripture indicates to us in bidding us avoid, above all, getting away from the correctness of the concepts, when it says, "Dwell by me." For all correctness is with God, by him, and from him.

2. The season of spring, then, suits Easter[10] the best of all the others, since it draws on a tablet, as it were, the meaning of Christ's achievements by means of the things that occur during it. For it arises while warming the earth with the pure and gentlest rays of the sun, and all but saying to winter's assaults: Give leave now, give leave at last to mountains and vales to adorn themselves with thickets of trees with lovely trunks, and to the plains, stripped bare, to bloom with tender grass new-sprung. Let the meadows now show off their lilies, let the laughter of the most fragrant flowers be heard in gardens, let the bee also take off from its hives and buzz around the fields without being bothered by violent winds or its flight cut short by dripping rain. For its frail wing

---

7. Wis 3.4.   8. Cf. Nm 9.3.

9. Is 21.12 (LXX).

10. Literally, *pascha*. Cyril clearly has both Passover and Christian Easter in mind.

is unused to labor. Let the flocks now come forth from the folds, and, yes, let the lambs, bounding around their mothers on tender, newly-formed hooves, dance upon the variegated verdure. Let the craftsman whose skill it is whet the pruning-hook for the vines at last.

And even if our discourse lends a voice like ours to the very seasons, as it were, let no one rebuke us. For we have learned this too from the sacred Scriptures. Indeed, the divinely inspired Psalmist says, "The heavens declare the glory of God, and the firmament proclaims the work of his hands. Day unto day utters speech, and night unto night proclaims knowledge."[11] The prophet Isaiah too conceded that the very seas speak excellently well, and seem all but to give vent to what is strictly speech. For he spoke as follows: "Be ashamed, O Sidon; the sea has said, yes, the strength of the seas has said: I have not travailed, nor have I given birth, nor have I reared youths, nor brought up virgins."[12] Now we certainly do not say that the seasons and the sea partake of speech. That would be sheer idiocy and nothing else. But in our eagerness to hunt out what is both graceful and necessary for the benefit of our listeners, we crown with the use of speech even those things deprived of speech by nature. Come, then, let us proceed in just the proper way in adducing the meaning of the concepts when we show what has been achieved through our Savior's visitation by means of the good things of spring. Let us contemplate the beauty of the divine grace as all but pictured in what is sensible.

3. Everything was held fast in mist and darkness, and the many-headed dragon, Satan, had spread a wintry gloom, as it were, over the whole earth under heaven. And chilling to death the mind of each person, he rendered those upon earth willing workers of unholy deeds. But the winter is passing,[13] and the ancient deep and gloomy darkness has been driven off. Pure beams of light are rising for us, and the Sun of justice,[14] Christ, dazzles everything with intelligible rays,[15] and confers another benefit as

11. Ps 19.1–2.   12. Is 23.4.
13. Cf. Song 2.11.   14. Cf. Mal 4.2 (3.20 LXX).
15. Without being explicit, Cyril implies an allegorical and Platonic reading of the pastoral imagery that follows.

well: he does not let us grow old unto sin any more, but renders us ardent with the Spirit,[16] as the divinely inspired Paul says himself.

And in fact we who were in the same state as the tree-trunks, too feeble to bear fruit and deprived even of blossoms, have revived unto life. Like fertile plains crowned with a variety of verdure, we have been enriched with the gospel proclamations of the holy apostles; the writings that are images of the truth in shadows and figures,[17] those of Moses, that is; the predictions of the holy prophets concerning Christ, through which we are well instructed in grasping the mystery. Let that intelligible and exceedingly industrious bee fly about this abundantly fertile land of ours: let the wise and supremely industrious soul, that is, collect in some way that which will answer its need, by which I mean that which will let it gather in itself, like sweet honey, the knowledge of God which is without falsehood or fault. Into this good and rich pasturage,[18] as the prophet says, let the herds of rational beasts come; and let the lambs with their mothers, those, that is, who are still children, with respect to the desire for virtue and for spiritual strength, with those of stouter condition, nourish their own mind, and thus strive to arrive "at mature manhood, to the measure of the stature of the fullness of Christ."[19] I would say that the lilies laugh as though in gardens, for those whose faith is resplendent and who give forth the sweet fragrance of Christ's glory, sprout up in the churches and yield nothing to the flowers of the sweetest odor.[20]

And the time for pruning is at hand.[21] That one may quite easily see, in what I have just said, what Christ has accomplished, requires no other witnesses for its proof, I think; the very one who speaks to the church from the nations suffices. "Rise up, come, my companion, my fair dove, for behold, the winter is past, the rain is gone, it has departed; the flowers have appeared in the land, the time of pruning has arrived."[22]

God, then, said that the Passover was to be celebrated "in the first month." In the second year, however, of the exodus of the

---

16. Cf. Rom 12.11.
17. Cf. Heb 8.5.
18. Cf. Ezek 34.14.
19. Eph 4.13.
20. Cf. 2 Cor 2.15.
21. Cf. Song 2.13.
22. Song 2.10–12.

children of Israel.[23] But why ever did they not determine the laws
for the festivals at the very outset? Well, it was necessary to introduce a sort of stay or suspension, and to decide upon a delay for
such venerable things. It is obviously worth our while to consider
what the point of the economy was, and to what purpose the
Legislator was looking.

4. The mystery of Christ had, then, to yield in its times to the
prior entrances of the law. For it was necessary for the figures to
appear before the truth, and the exercises to be seen to precede
the contests. The soldier wins approval if he practices the maneu-
vers before the efforts of combat. The one whose business is the
art of the wrestling school wins no fame unless he practices enduring the suffering involved therein. And for ourselves, is not
the learning of the elementary principles like a beginning and a
door to the instructions leading to wisdom and understanding? I
think, however, that the argument is clear and precise.

The divinely inspired Paul will assist us in the form of examples; he says that while milk is best suited to those still in infancy,
bulkier food is to be served to those who are more mature.[24] To
those of old, therefore, who had not yet arrived at adulthood in
the fullness of Christ,[25] and whose way of thinking was still child-
ish,[26] milk had to be apportioned before solid food. The elementary principles had to be established in mind and heart before
the complete teachings, and life in the law to be introduced before that life which is understood to be in Christ. For the law is an
instructor,[27] bringing us, through symbols, into a better and superior understanding.[28] That therefore the delay in the evangelical
decrees was necessary for our benefit is suggested, with great subtlety, by God's prescription that the Passover be celebrated not in
the first year, as God prescribes, but in the second.[29]

The following will also support the argument, I think. The
God of all bade the divinely inspired Moses to fashion and display that ancient tent, prepared not in the way he himself chose,

23. Cf. Nm 9.1–3.   24. Cf. 1 Cor 3.2.
25. Cf. Eph 4.13.   26. Cf. 1 Cor 13.11.
27. Cf. Gal 3.24.   28. 1 Cor 13.12.
29. Cf. Nm 9.1.

but as he had been bidden by God. "See," he says, "you shall make it according to the pattern shown you on the mountain."[30] And when he at once executed the divine decree, and the work fashioned was in the most perfect order, God said again, "On the first day of the first month, on the new moon of the month, you shall erect the tent."[31] And the sacred Scripture adds to this, "And it came to pass in the first month, in the second year of their departure from Egypt, that the tent was erected at the new moon."[32] Do you hear that it was in the second year, and at the new moon of the first month, that he pitched the tent? For it was then, then indeed, that a lamb too was slain, signifying in itself the truly sacred and faultless sacrifice, Christ that is, who has offered himself in an odor of sweetness to God the Father,[33] transforming our condition unto a new age. Now the new moon may be considered, quite clearly, a figure of the new age. For what is in Christ is a new creation, and what is ancient has passed away,[34] according to the Scriptures.

It is, then, in the first month, and the first day of the month, that is, on the new moon, that the divinely inspired Moses raises the holy tent. The shape, however, describes externally the manifestation of the tent that is really truer and holy, the Church, which the Savior himself pitched for us,[35] once those ancient times had passed away in which death prevailed,[36] sin aged those on earth, and the inventor of iniquity threatened to seize by force the entire earth, saying, "I will take in my hand the whole earth like a nest, and I will pick it up like eggs abandoned; and there is none that shall escape me, or contradict me."[37] But his words were an empty boast, a criminal imposture of his greed for us. That he failed of his hopes is proved by the realities. For we have been saved in Christ, as I just said, now that the holy tent has been shown to us at the fitting times, those in which we are [being] transformed unto newness of life,[38] casting off the old man[39] with his passions and desires.

---

30. Ex 25.40; Heb 8.5.
31. Ex 40.2.
32. Ex 40.17.
33. Cf. Eph 5.2.
34. Cf. 2 Cor 5.17.
35. Cf. Heb 8.2.
36. Cf. Rom 5.14.
37. Is 10.14.
38. Cf. Rom 6.4.
39. Cf. Col 3.9.

And the very manner in which that ancient tent was prepared may show quite well the advantage of the time of the law preceding the decrees given through Christ, the time following which it was logical that that time should appear which is better and holier, comprising a deeper intimacy with God. Let Paul, then, who knows the law, having been instructed in it in detail,[40] as he himself says, describe its shape in the words: "A first tent was prepared, in which were the lamp stand and the table and the showbread; it is called 'Holy.' After the second curtain there was a tent called the Holy of Holies, having a golden altar of incense, and the ark all covered with gold in which there was a golden urn holding the manna, and Aaron's rod that budded, and the tablets of the covenant."[41] You see that before the second tent, the one innermost, there was placed the one that was in the first entrances; it was in that one that the sacred nation was accustomed to make its approaches, in symbolic fashion, and to perform the figures of the worship according to the law.[42] But the second was holier than the first. It was, accordingly, named the Holy of Holies.

What, then, was the reason why the first [tent] is situated before the second, and the outer one placed as a sort of entrance for the one innermost? Paul in his supreme wisdom will once again explain. He puts it as follows: "These things being thus arranged, the priests go continually into the first tent, performing the ritual services; but into the second only the high priest goes, and he but once a year, and not without taking blood which he offers for himself and for the oversights of the people. By this the Holy Spirit indicates that the way to the holy things has not yet been manifested, as long as the first tent is still standing."[43] For the first is, as I said, accessible to many. But the second and innermost one, the Holy of Holies, is inaccessible. For he alone could enter once a year who was chief of the sacred orders, and "not without blood," as is written. For it was for us that Jesus as forerunner entered "into the Holy of Holies, having secured an eternal redemption,"[44] not without blood, according to Scrip-

40. Cf. Acts 22.3.
42. Cf. Heb 9.6.
44. Heb 9.12.

41. Heb 9.2–4.
43. Heb 9.6–8.

ture. For he was sacrificed for us,[45] as a faultless victim, an odor of sweetness to God the Father.[46] The position therefore in the first tent of those who then sacrificed was usefully effected, since the law does not allow the entrance into the Holy of Holies. For the way to the holy things has not yet, he says, been manifested, "as long as the first tent is still standing."[47]

What has been said suffices, I think, to show clearly the time at which the Passover might rightly be held. Let us then talk about those who might fittingly eat it, and how that might be carried out suitably, drawing from the sacred Scriptures.

5. The great Moses told us, when he composed the revelation concerning this, that those who ate the pure and sacred lamb would have to use unleavened bread and bitter herbs,[48] and partake of the meat while in the following position: "Let your loins be girt," he says, "and your sandals on your feet, and your staves in your hands; and eat it in haste. It is the Passover of the Lord."[49] But what does the position of the diners mean to me? someone might ask some time, and quite fairly. For the law never says anything in vain, and so one must by all means admire each of the things it prescribes. Would it not be completely ridiculous and foolish, if we, in our desire to think rightly, rejected as unseemly what was vain, and called it disgraceful, rather than choosing to carry it out; while the highest nature, in regulating our condition by law for what is better, regarded as necessary what is of no benefit, and tossed off some vain and foolish words? Stuff and nonsense! It will not be our view that such is the case; far from it.

What, then, is the reason why those who eat the lamb must finally gird their loins, have their feet shod, and take up a staff? Is not the figure evident, and does it not all but cry aloud what the manner of the economy is? For those who celebrate the all-holy festival in truth, and are called to participate in Christ's blessing, will consider the distractions of this life to be vain, and, rejecting the choice to live carnally, will set their thoughts on high from then on,[50] will hasten to the city above, and will pass, as it were,

45. Cf. 1 Cor 5.7.
47. Heb 9.8.
49. Ex 12.11.

46. Cf. Eph 5.2.
48. Cf. Ex 12.8.
50. Cf. Col 3.2.

to another life, the one, of course, which befits the saints and is
removed from the earthly one. The law accordingly clearly as-
signs travelers' garb to those eating, since they are about to depart as never before for what is better and transcendent; for I
say, as I just said, that those who celebrate the feast in purity
must distinguish themselves by such a purpose, called as they are
to unity with God in Christ. For it is through him that we have
this access, "and he is himself our peace,"[51] as the Scriptures say.

But that sluggishness in these matters is not unpenalized, and
that a lapse into laziness does not go unpunished, is what the
Legislator would indicate when he says about Holy Passover:
"and eat it in haste. It is the Passover of the Lord."[52] For it behooves those who lead a reputable life, pleasing to God, to show
themselves to be above hesitation and resistant to procrastination. They are to seize their opportunities, as it were, and not allow the time to slip by that is suitable to industry. For just as
those who set out to sail the seas cannot neglect a fair wind without cost; nor does it befit husbandmen to stay home when the
season calls them to work; so also, I say, procrastination is ignominious for those who are concerned about what is best, and
must bring censure upon them, or rather penalties of every sort,
and be seen as the cause of the offenses proceeding from hesitation and negligence. Let procrastination then be gone, and let
the lapses caused by hesitation be driven far away, for they can in
no way suit those called through faith to the duty of sharing in
Christ's blessing.

Let them rather eat unleavened bread with bitter herbs on
it,[53] for that is what sacred Scripture says. And let us say, as well as
may be, what the deep and ineffable mystery of the prescriptions
of the law is. For the divinely inspired Scripture is accustomed to
liken the different kinds of wickedness to leaven.[54] And it takes
the bitter herbs as a representation and example of things that
are grievous: being persecuted, tempted, and sometimes undertaking hard labor for Christ. For such things embitter the mind,
as it were, and maltreat it with unbearable despondency. If there-

51. Eph 2.14.
53. Cf. Ex 12.8.
52. Ex 12.11.
54. Cf. Lk 12.1; 1 Cor 5.7–8.

fore one happens to come to share in Christ, it says, let one not leave virtue untried, let one distance oneself from all that defiles, and show oneself long-suffering. For I for my part say that those who accomplish well the celebration of the holy Paschal feast must adorn themselves with the language expressive of the uncontaminated Deity, and find their enjoyment there. For while bodies enjoy the foods that suit them, the mind, in my view, should have as its nourishment the divine word[55] and an account of sacred doctrines that is correct and unexceptionable, free from cleverness in thought, captious argument, deceit, and falsehood. Such is the food that is pure and unleavened.

For many there are who often all but deride the correctness of the divine doctrines, and, making sport of the language of truth, hasten to introduce instead impious additions containing wretched ideas, and, in inventing fictions based on worldly deceit, these sorry folk injure the minds of the simple. But Christ cries out to his disciples, "Beware of the yeast of the Pharisees and scribes!"[56] For the old wives' tales produced by their depravity are not far from Jewish sophistry. We will then abstain from such food, and we will bring into our minds the pure language that is from the holy prophets, translating the commandments given through Moses into the true meaning of the symbols. This means above all not treating the salvific gospel teaching, the writing of the apostles, as some do, those whose custom it is to force the meaning of the texts into an unseemly sense, and not dragging it impiously away from orthodoxy, but rather betaking our own selves eagerly in the direction pointed out by the teachings. With this, let us practice patience, not refusing to engage in harsh labor, since we have chosen to live rightly and to follow what has been prescribed.

For it is agreed, it really is, that virtue is not simply accessible to just anyone; its approach is steep and difficult. It is not to be attained by the pleasure-loving and the negligent, nor by those entangled in carnal passions or wholly under their sway, driven without restraint by their impulses toward what is shameful, having let out every reef and set every sail, but rather by those distin-

---

55. Cf. Mt 4.4; Dt 8.3.   56. Mt 16.6.

guished by sobriety, full of boldness for what is good, lovers of good order who are nourished on virtuousness, who think nothing of labor expended on improvement, and who purchase their reputation with the efforts they put forth for it. For it would be impossible for anyone to accomplish anything admirable without acting zealously and choosing to endure the unavoidable hardship.

6. The law therefore gives us an explanation of necessary matters, doing it in figures, as it were, with leaven and bitter herbs. If we refuse to experience these things, putting ourselves far from the divine road and fleeing from the life that best suits the saints, we will do ourselves a great wrong. For if Jesus, the pioneer and perfecter of our life,[57] was made perfect through suffering,[58] as is written, how can we avoid living a life that will be ignominious and held in derision, if we refuse to accept the same circumstances and despise the means of attaining high repute? For let us listen forthwith to Christ crying out to us, "If anyone wants to come after me, let him deny himself and take up his cross and follow me."[59] It is, then, necessary for us to follow the footsteps of Christ, who gave himself for us.[60] And for what reason?

Of old the inventor of sin plundered the human race. And leaving no sort of scheme untried for his villainies, he duped those on earth, and, dreaming of the glory of divinity, bade them build him altars and sanctuaries, and ordered them to honor him with sacrifices of oxen and incense.[61] And, leading those deceived wherever he wanted, he persuaded some to venerate the sun, and others the moon and stars. Not only that, but he proceeded to even worse crimes than these: he brought about the consecration of forms of irrational beasts,[62] insulting the divine dignity, in my view, daring to carry off the glory of the substance that is above all others, and thinking fit in his villainy to liken to it these most worthless things, and those of no account at all.[63] For the beast is always terrible, of boundless audacity. Having led

57. Cf. Heb 12.2.
58. Cf. Heb 2.10.
59. Mt 16.24.
60. Cf. Eph 5.2.
61. Cf. 1 Mc 1.47.
62. Cf. Wis 13.10.
63. Cf. Wis 13.14.

man astray from the true knowledge of God, persuaded him to have no share in the best counsel and sound reflection, and subjected him by deceit to his yoke, he rendered him at once a lover of every kind of wickedness, and, having made virtue quite inaccessible and unachievable to him, rendered him repulsive and detestable to God.

But when we had reached this state of wretchedness, the Creator of all took pity on us at last, and countered the other's misdeeds with men who were able to save us. Through Moses he called ancient Israel, drawing him forth as a kind of first-fruit of his divinity, and indeed, fitting him for an orderly life by the best laws, he kindled his zeal. The other, however, insinuating himself nonetheless into the hearts of the simple, kept swaying them to shameful behavior and unholy decisions. Physicians with the skill to heal illnesses of the soul would appear providentially at times. But they were caught dishonoring the holy prophets themselves in many different ways. God the Father then sent the Son himself down to us of necessity when we had acted miserably, to bring our condition to an incomparably better state than of old and to save those on earth, once sin had been removed, that is, and death, which had sprouted through it,[64] been destroyed, root and all, and in addition the devil's tyranny[65] itself been done away with. Such brilliant, illustrious achievements befitted no created being, but only that nature which surpasses all, and is well crowned with the highest powers and excellence.

The only-begotten Word of God became a human being,[66] therefore, he through whom everything was brought into existence[67] and was preserved, once made. And it will not hurt to concern ourselves with the question of the manner of the economy, or of the union of the Word with what is carnal from the earth. For what is beyond mind and reason is always above any test, and can<not>[68] be subjected to scrutiny. But having become as we are, the only exception being the ability to transgress,[69] he

64. Cf. Rom 5.12.   65. Cf. Heb 2.14.
66. Cf. Jn 1.14.   67. Cf. Jn 1.3.
    68. "<not>": The Sources chrétiennes editor has supplied οὐκ; see SC 434, p. 246, ln. 63.
    69. Cf. Heb 4.15.

showed clearly and evidently that he is God by nature by the extravagance of his miracles. For he ordered the dead to return to life from their tombs[70] when they were already stinking with corruption; he gave sight to those blind from birth;[71] he healed chronic illnesses; he caused astonishment when he rebuked the sea and the winds;[72] and long would be the tale of these things, were each set out clear to view.

Nonetheless, even though those from Israel should have admired him exceedingly for this, and, persuaded by the divine signs themselves, should have proclaimed at last, "You are truly God's Son,"[73] they were caught dishonoring him in many ways, and finally they crucified him. Christ lowered himself to this according to the economy, in order that, having come with us among the dead and preached to the spirits in hell,[74] he might return to life on the third day, having abolished the grim, implacable power of death,[75] and, having dug up corruption, root and all, might thus render heaven itself accessible at last to those on earth.[76] For it was as forerunner[77] for us that he ascended to the Father. And he will come in due time in the glory of the one who begot him, with the holy angels, to render to each according to his works.[78]

As those who are to be judged, then, let us keep the faith,[79] let us behave lawfully, let us live rightly, discrediting the ways of vice, and practicing every kind of virtue: mutual love and love of the poor. Let us care for orphans, let us visit widows,[80] let us take pity on the tears of the infirm, let us visit those in prison,[81] let us practice chastity of body. For thus it is, in fasting thus, that we shall celebrate in purity the feast that is holy and perfectly pure. We begin holy Lent on the sixteenth of Phamenoth, and the week of the salvific Paschal feast on the twenty-first of Pharmuthi, breaking the fast on the twenty-sixth of Pharmuthi, late in the evening, according to the gospel precept, and celebrating

70. Cf. Jn 11.38–44.
71. Cf. Jn 9.1–7.
72. Cf. Mt 8.26–27.
73. Mt 14.33.
74. Cf. 1 Pt 3.19.
75. Cf. Heb 2.14.
76. Cf. Heb 9.24.
77. Cf. Heb 6.20.
78. Cf. Mt 16.27.
79. Cf. 2 Tm 4.7.
80. Cf. Jas 1.27.
81. Cf. Mt 25.43.

the feast on the next day, the eve of Sunday, the twenty-seventh of the month.[82] We add then the seven weeks of holy Eastertide. For thus it is, thus again, that we shall enjoy the divine words, in Christ Jesus Our Lord, through whom and with whom be glory and power to the Father with the Holy Spirit. Amen.

82. April 22, 428.

FESTAL LETTER SEVENTEEN

A.D. 429

PREFACE

E SHALL read once again what is customary, and spread for ourselves a table of the language of the Church, regarding the occasion as a sort of summons to choose to distinguish ourselves by right faith, and to embrace the life that is renowned and faultless.[1]

1. Those who have practiced leading a noble and exceptional life, and have been eager to betake themselves to it with generosity, have been above all hesitancy, I think; and, always casting as far away as possible every obstacle, they have known how to devote the most effective care to accomplishing the projects they have in hand. And I would say that to that end they need both the greatest possible concentration of attention, and someone who can kindle their zeal to the highest pitch, as for instance the voice of the trainer does for the youth who like to wrestle: he is ever rousing them to endure the hardship and all but compelling them to yearn for the glory of winning. I myself, then, have come forward as well, joining with the Psalmists' lyre to cry out to those who love the things in which one may well take pride, "Be of good courage, and let your heart be strengthened, all you who hope in the Lord."[2] For as the divinely inspired David himself says again, "It is time to act for the Lord."[3]

---

1. Although *Letter* 16 was published in 428, the year of the beginning of the Christological controversy, it offers no hint of it. This letter, on the other hand, contains many clear references to the conflict.

2. Ps 31.25.

3. Ps 119.126.

Now, I think that I should speak to you in the language of ex-
hortation, without being concerned about not being able to do
justice to the topic, or at any rate falling short of the eloquence
of some, since the sensible thought has occurred to me that it is
far better to entertain one's acquaintances with what one has
available, and make one's friends at home, than to choose a
harsh life of ill repute out of fear of seeming inferior to the distinction accorded to others.

I also think that there is another way of facing the contest courageously: by reflecting on what follows. What I mean is that I will
recall how the all-powerful God speaks to that best of men, Moses: "Who has given a mouth to human beings? And who has
made the hard of hearing and the deaf? The seeing and the
blind? Is it not I, the Lord God? Now go, and I will open your
mouth."[4] Shadow and figures [constitute] that ancient revelation, even if it was spoken through angels by Moses' mediation.
But it cannot lack any of the concepts that are above the realm of
sense, if one considers it with shrewd vision, and, having accustomed oneself to disregard the shadows of the letter, contem-
plates the deep, innermost meaning.

The law, then, prescribed that the God of all was to be honored in many ways; and it added that it was necessary to consecrate turtle-doves to him.[5] And yet, with all the countless flocks of
birds there are in the world, some of which are the glory of lofty
flight by the law of their nature, while others are also aquatic, size
and shapeliness and beauty they have none. Nature[6] paints each
one differently, and by the Maker's arts amplifies their race by the
rich beauty of their colors. Why ever, one might then ask, did the
law, passing over these and skipping the ones that are the best of
all, crown the turtle-dove with all but the highest honors, having
ordered it to be made a sacred offering to God? What is the mystery, what is the wisdom of the law? The one who is beyond all

4. Ex 4.11–12.
5. Cf. Lv 5.7.
6. It is difficult to know how to translate *physis* here and in the previous sentence because the English word "nature" connotes a view of the natural world
unknown in antiquity. The meaning is more akin to "reality" than it is to the
modern "nature."

mind, God that is, accepts the word, as Father of the Word; and those sparrows who customarily sing sweetly he makes acceptable and puts them before the others who nonetheless abound in charm at times. He thereby teaches us in symbols that those who are better than others and most sacred, among ourselves as well, are those entrusted with the use of speech, and are able to admonish those who love the fairest precepts. Come, then, let us charm the Lord's vineyard[7] with the words from sacred Scripture, not emitting a bare inarticulate sound with clarity, but persuading you rather to celebrate the feast with the proper arguments, that things may be as they should, and be done correctly and faultlessly, as the Legislator wants.

2. The divinely inspired Luke says therefore in his own writings,

There came the day of Unleavened Bread, on which the Passover was to be sacrificed. He sent Peter and John, saying, "Go and prepare the Passover for us, that we may eat it." They said to him, "Where do you want us to prepare it?" He said to them, "Behold, when you have entered the city, someone carrying a jar of water will meet you; follow him into the house which he enters, and tell the householder, 'The teacher says to you, "Where is the guest room, where I am to eat the Passover with my disciples?"' He will show you a large upper room furnished; there make ready."[8]

Do you hear that, in searching carefully with the eyes of divinity for a place where it would be worthy to lodge, he said that an upper room would be shown to the holy apostles, large and furnished, and bade them take as a guide thereto the man laden with a jar, carrying water to the master of the house? Proceed, then, with subtlety of thought, as it were, to things yet greater and intelligible.

And if someone intends to have Christ himself dwelling in his mind,[9] lodging there and keeping festival with him when he is already richly endowed with the purification that is by water, let him cleanse the sin from his own soul, and let him rub away the defilement of the ancient symbols.[10] For thus God says through Isaiah's voice as well, "Wash yourselves, be clean, remove your in-

7. Cf. Mt 21.33.
8. Lk 22.7–12.
9. Cf. 2 Cor 6.16.
10. Cf. 2 Cor 7.1.

iquities from your souls before my eyes. Cease from your iniquities, learn to do good, seek judgment, rescue those wronged,
judge for the orphan, obtain justice for the widow, and come, let
us reason together, says the Lord. Though your sins be as pur-
ple, I will make them white as snow; and though they be as scarlet, I will make them white as wool."[11] For I at least say that the
stain coming from wickedness must be crushed out of existence
from our thoughts, as it were, that virtue may then settle there,
renowned and precious as it is and unequaled in worth, to those
of sound mind at least and able to distinguish between what is
unjust by nature and what is not.

For just as it is completely and utterly impossible for things
contrary by nature to coexist together in the same being—"For
what fellowship does light have with darkness?"[12] as is written;
and if the one is removed it will surely let in the other—in the
same way, I think, wickedness and virtue, having an adversarial
quality in their works, are as far separated as may be, and so cannot occupy one and the same mind. And will they not render
those who welcome them unlovely and inconstant, and as
though hobbling on both feet? But the prophet Elijah rebukes
those accustomed to live thus when he says, "How long will you
limp on both hams?"[13] The law as well bars us from such customs
and ways, bidding us in symbols to refrain from what is incompatible and irreconcilable. It says, "You shall not plow with a calf
and an ass together."[14] And also, "You shall not wear wool and
linen in the same garment."[15] You see how it says everywhere to
hate as unlovely and unholy what cannot be combined, as it
were, or joined gracefully, and it cannot honor the combination
of what is dissimilar. Those who have chosen to lead the best life
must then, as I said, scrub away in advance the stains of vice and
rid themselves of defilement. It will befit one who is thereby resplendent to have now the high chamber, and to hold festival as
in an upper story with the glories that come from virtue,[16] and to
dwell with Christ, who for our sake became poor though he was
rich, that we might be enriched by his poverty.[17]

11. Is 1.16–18.
12. 2 Cor 6.14.
13. 1 Kgs 18.21.
14. Dt 22.10.
15. Dt 22.11.
16. Cf. Lk 22.12.
17. Cf. 2 Cor 8.9.

For the Son, being the very image, the impress of God the Father, the reflection of his glory,[18] begotten from him by nature, distinguished by equality in every respect, coexistent and co-eternal, equal in power and activity, equal in renown and sharing the same throne, "did not count equality with God a thing to be grasped,"[19] as is written. For he came into our condition, and underwent a voluntary emptying;[20] and, as John says in his wisdom, "he became flesh and dwelt among us."[21] And the one who before every age and time possesses that birth which is from God who is also Father, the birth that is beyond all mind and understanding: when he became flesh and endured human generation in the economy—he, the Maker and Artisan of all time, as though he had been brought to a beginning of existence when he became as we are—he heard the Father saying, "This day I have begotten you."[22]

Are we then to think of him as having alienated the glory of existing before everything? By no means. Let us have the wisdom to reflect that the Father does not place his own Son outside the natural dignities inherent in him, even when he has come into the flesh. He still acknowledges him, even if he appears in the form that we are in.[23] For the only-begotten Word of God did not become a human being in order to cease being God, but rather in order that, even in assuming flesh, he might preserve the glory of his own pre-eminence. For thus we have been enriched by his poverty,[24] human nature having been brought in him to a dignity befitting the divine, and seated in a place beyond all others. For even though he is always seated with his own Father as Word, and exists from him and in him by nature, he heard him saying once again, even when he was with the flesh, "Sit at my right hand until I place your enemies as a footstool for your feet."[25]

It is thus that we say, too, that he is worshiped both by ourselves and by the holy angels: not that we lower him to a bare hu-

18. Cf. Heb 1.3.   19. Phil 2.6.
20. Cf. Phil 2.7.   21. Jn 1.14.
22. Ps 2.7; Lk 3.22; Acts 13.33; Heb 1.5.
23. Cf. Phil 2.7.   24. Cf. 2 Cor 8.9.
25. Ps 110.1; Mt 22.44; Acts 2.34–35; Heb 1.13.

manity—that would be senseless—but we follow sacred Scripture both in binding into unity with our nature the Word sprung from God, and interweaving into something that is one that which is from both, in order that he may not be regarded simply as a human being who has borne God,[26] but rather as God who has become a human being, and who, in the economic union, that with his own flesh, has put on the birth from the holy Virgin. The sole Christ and sole Lord[27] may be regarded thus and not otherwise, not as being divided into part human being and part God after the ineffable interweaving; even if the nature of those which have come together into a union is regarded as different, he is received and regarded as being only one Son.[28]

It is as with the most precious stones, where some beams of light elucidate the depths when they flash upon them, and if one wished to separate the mixture by thought, one would consider the stone in itself as one thing, and the light swimming therein as another, even though the subject which is from the two is regarded as one. [29] But the act of cutting will quite destroy the principle governing the stone, separating as it does the things gathered into union, with ugliness resulting. And thus we say it is with Christ: divinity and humanity have come together ineffably, in a way that no one can conceive or speak of, into what is henceforth regarded as one, so that he is regarded at once as both a human being as we are, and God who is above us. Thus he is both only-begotten[30] and firstborn.[31]

He was indeed brought forth from the virginal loins, and while still a baby his thoughts were those of God.[32] The blessed

26. This language clearly suggests the anti-Nestorian context of this letter. See anathema 5, Wickham, 30.

27. Cf. 1 Cor 8.6.

28. Cyril here is careful to emphasize that the union of the divine and the human nature did not result in the creation of a mixed or hybrid nature. As always, the point for Cyril is to focus on the united subjectivity of Jesus rather than on the mechanism by which the divine and the human came to be united. Cyril makes a similar argument in his letter to John of Antioch (9).

29. This insistence on the unity of the subject of Christ after the union, even if the natures are different, is central to Cyril's Christology. In Cyril's mind, Nestorius presented a Christ who was not an integrated person.

30. Cf. Jn 1.14.　　　　　　　　　31. Cf. Col 1.15.

32. Statements like this remind modern readers that despite Cyril's insistence

Isaiah will testify about him in the words: "For before the child knows good or evil, he refuses iniquity to choose the good."[33] For as far as the law of humanity is concerned, the time had not yet allowed the baby to be able to distinguish the natures of things. He was also, however, as I said, God in humanity, letting the nature which is as ours proceed by its own laws, while preserving with this the purity of the divinity. It is thus, and not otherwise, both that the one born may be regarded as God by nature, and that the Virgin giving birth may be said to become then mother not simply of flesh and blood, as are of course the mothers we have in our [human] condition, but rather of the Lord and God who has put on the likeness we have.[34] For as the divinely inspired Paul writes, "God sent forth his Son, born from a woman, born under the law."[35] For we do not at all say that the Word of God descended in a human being born through a woman, as he surely was in the prophets too; we will rather give our justifiable approval to John's words, spoken wisely and precisely: "And the Word became flesh, and dwelt among us."[36]

It will be our view that the Word became flesh as having shared in flesh and blood,[37] and that similarly to those who are in blood and flesh, namely, to us. And if he became as we are, how could it follow that he disdains human generation? For he dwelt among us,[38] having, as it were, mixed his own nature with blood and flesh in a divine and ineffable manner. For the generation from God the Father suffices for this divinity of the Word, when the divinity is considered alone and by itself. Having descended economically into the union that is with us, however, and been interwoven with flesh, that is, with the nature which we

on the real and full humanity of Christ, ancient ideas of *kenosis* do not generally include substantial limitations on Christ's knowledge. Cyril was closer to Apollinarian Christology here than he was to many contemporary Christologies that emphasize Christ's human limits.

33. Is 7.16.

34. The editor of the Sources chrétiennes edition points out that Cyril does not use the term *theotokos* here, and that he tends not to use it much at all before the confrontation with Nestorius; SC 434, p. 270, n. 2. After 428, however, the term does appear in these letters: 19.2, 20.3, and 21.4.

35. Gal 4.4.   36. Jn 1.14.
37. Cf. Heb 2.14.   38. Jn 1.14.

have and which is complete according to its own law, then, then indeed, it will receive as well the generation that we have, without the slightest disgrace and without being impaired in any way at all in its being what it is. It is not that it is called thence to a beginning of being (for it always was, and is, and will be, and has an existence older than all time); but rather it wisely allows the laws of humanity to proceed according to their own principles. For just as the precious, perfectly pure flesh from the holy Virgin has become the Word's own, belonging to him who is from God the Father, so also he has everything suiting the flesh, apart from sin alone. And what would suit the flesh especially, and indeed most of all, is birth from a mother. The Divinity itself, therefore, in itself, if considered outside the flesh, will have no mother, quite rightly.

3. With the mystery concerning Christ having been brought to our attention, there is another way in which it is to be spoken of, and that extremely subtle. I mean that it will be our opinion, since we have decided to think rightly and are taking a path quite free from error, that it was not bare divinity, but rather the Word from God the Father become a human being and united to flesh, that the Virgin bore when she was taken to render service in conceiving carnally him who was united to flesh. Immanuel is then undoubtedly God, and she who bore carnally the God who has appeared in the flesh for us may be spoken of as mother of God. And the baby was not as we are, that is not in a pure and simple likeness to us; he was rather in humanity because of the flesh, but was divine because he was above us and from heaven. And in fact the divinely inspired Paul says, "The first human being is from the earth, of dust; the second human being is from heaven."[39] And the blessed prophet Isaiah indeed taught the meaning of the mystery in a kind of prophetic vision. For he says he saw the Lord God of all himself in the holy Virgin well nigh bringing about the propagation of the divine infant. And while the manner of the vision has been represented in human fashion, it is yet understood otherwise, as befits God. For the divine is not as we are.

39. 1 Cor 15.47.

He spoke thus:

And the Lord said to me, "Take for yourself a volume of a large new [book], and write in it, with the stylus of a human being, about making a rapid plunder of spoils; for it is at hand, and take as witnesses for me faithful men, Uriah and Zechariah, son of Berechiah." And he went in to the prophetess, and she conceived, and bore a son, and the Lord said to me, "Call his name 'Despoil Quickly, Plunder Rapidly.' For before the child knows how to call his father or mother, he shall take the power of Damascus and the spoils of Samaria before the king of Assyria."[40]

The volume is, then, new and large, for the mystery of Christ is itself new and admittedly large,[41] as the blessed Paul says. It is, though, written with the stylus of a human being, for the account of the divinity, if the latter is considered again unclad and in itself and outside the flesh, has no need whatever of the reason in us, which cannot express what is above the mind, nor indeed is able to articulate what is beyond all reason. For "the glory of the Lord conceals speech,"[42] as is written. But since the only-begotten Word of God has become a human being and dwelt among us,[43] what concerns him is written with a stylus like ours. But come now, come, let us examine that too.

God, when he had bidden the prophet take the volume and write what is in it with a stylus like ours, went in to the prophetess.[44] And why does it say "went in"? Because it represents the law of intercourse. It also calls the holy Virgin a prophetess, because she prophesied when she was pregnant with Christ.[45] Then it says, "And she conceived and bore a son,"[46] to whom the law also gave a name, not once more a proper name, as to a human being, but one derived from his achievements, as to God. For it says, "Call his name 'Despoil Quickly, Plunder Rapidly.'"[47] For the divine, transcendent infant, just born, was in swaddling clothes,[48] and still in his mother's bosom, because human; but since in addition he was by nature God, an ineffable power plundered Satan's equipment at once.[49] For the magi arrived from the east, seeking him and saying, "Where is the king of the Jews

40. Is 8.1–4.
41. Cf. Eph 5.32.
42. Prv 25.2.
43. Cf. Jn 1.14.
44. Cf. Is 8.3.
45. Cf. Lk 1.46.
46. Is 8.3.
47. Ibid.
48. Cf. Lk 2.12.
49. Cf. Mt 12.29; Mk 3.27.

who has been born? For we have seen his star in the east and come to worship him."[50]

The generation is therefore divine, even if it was done in a human way because of the humanity. But Immanuel is God by nature, and the swaddling clothes are his who is held fast in a human way, while filling heaven and earth and what is beneath in a divine way with his own pre-eminence, and holding fast everything made by him, that it may be and subsist as it should. And even if you hear that he advanced in age and wisdom and grace,[51] do not think that the Word of God became wise incrementally. Recall instead what the divinely inspired Paul wrote: "Christ, the power of God and the wisdom of God."[52] And do not be so stupidly arrogant as to say: We attribute the "advancing in age and wisdom and grace"[53] to the human being.[54] That, in my opinion, is nothing other than dividing in two the one Christ. But as I just said, the Son, who is before the ages, is said to have been designated Son of God in the last times of the age,[55] appropriating the generation of his own flesh economically. Thus even though he is the wisdom of the one who begot him, he is said to advance in wisdom, utterly perfect as God though he is, having understandably taken up into himself what is peculiar to humanity through a consummate union.

But someone may say: Then how could the nature of a human being contain the pre-eminence of the ineffable divinity? And yet I hear the one who is God by nature saying clearly to the blessed Moses, "No one will see my face and live."[56] If the sight is unbearable and its brilliance insufferable, how can the union possibly be explained? My reply would be that the miracle is beyond explanation, and the manner of the dispensation, which is forever, is not to be grasped by our kind of thought. It was nonetheless done wisely, with God rendering his own nature bearable even for the weakest.

50. Mt 2.2.   51. Cf. Lk 2.52.
52. 1 Cor 1.24.   53. Cf. Lk 2.52.
54. Cyril resisted this standard Antiochene language emphasizing the idea that the Word took up a human nature. See J. A. McGuckin, *St. Cyril of Alexandria: The Christological Controversy: Its History, Theology, and Texts* (Leiden and New York: Brill, 1994), 329, 375.
55. Cf. Rom 1.4.   56. Ex 33.20.

The God of all in fact made this august and truly marvelous mystery manifest to the all-wise Moses, using a clear and completely obvious illustration. How the manner of this may be regarded is something that the sacred text itself will teach. It runs as follows:

And Moses was tending the flock of Jethro, his father-in-law, the priest of Midian; and he led the flock toward the desert, and came to Mount Horeb. An angel of the Lord appeared to him in fire that flamed out of the bush. And he sees that the bush burns with fire, but the bush was not being consumed. And Moses said, "I will go up and see this great sight, why the bush is not being consumed." But when the Lord saw that he drew near to see, the Lord called to him out of the bush, saying, "Moses, Moses!" He said, "What is it?" He said, "Do not come near here; undo the sandal from your feet, for the place in which you are standing is holy ground." And he said to him, "I am the God of your father, the God of Abraham, and the God of Isaac, and the God of Jacob."[57]

He therefore declares that the brilliance is unapproachable, signifying then to the blessed Moses himself that if one is satisfied with the education given by the law[58] and with the shadows represented by figures, one will not approach Christ. For the law brings nothing to perfection.[59]

But it is also worth wondering at this: fire was seen in the bush, and it sent forth a voice, saying, "I am the God of Abraham your father."[60] It was the Lord himself therefore in the form of fire, seizing the bush and occupying it completely without burning it at all. Yet what possible explanation could the event have, when matter so fine and easily combustible pays no attention to the fire's ardor? But even more wondrous is the gentleness of the flame, when one sees how it spares the bush. It was, though, a figure, as I said, meant as a clear example of the mystery connected with Christ. For just as the fire became bearable to the shrub, so also does the pre-eminence of the divinity to our nature.

As far, therefore, as we can understand with our mind and reason, divinity and humanity are, understandably, incompatible with each other when it comes to natural unity. It has taken place,

57. Ex 3.1–6.   58. Cf. Gal 3.24.
59. Cf. Heb 7.19.   60. Ex 3.6.

however, as in Christ at least, and Immanuel is one from both. But he who separates, presenting us both with a human being and with another son apart, besides him who is from God by nature, does not understand accurately the depth of the mystery. For it is not a human being whom we worship and whom we learned to adore from the saints who initiated us, but God become a human being, as I said, and regarded as one with his own body: the Word who is from the Father.

It is thus that we say further that Immanuel has been shown to us as king. For God the Father made the proclamation through the prophets' voice, saying about him and about the holy apostles, "Behold, a just king will reign, and rulers will rule with judgment."[61] He himself said indeed through David's voice, "I have been appointed king by him on Zion, his holy mountain, proclaiming the commandment of the Lord."[62] He in fact issued the order to submit to the yoke of his reign, adding clearly, "Come to me, all who are weary and burdened, and I will give you rest. Take my yoke upon you."[63] But if he is king, and regarded as just a simple human being as we are, rather than as the only-begotten Word of God come into union with a nature like ours, then our condition is in no way better than that of old, even though it is said to have been renewed unto that which is incomparably superior precisely through Christ's reign over us.

4. There is another similar matter that applies to our situation. What I mean is that the God of all reigned over those from Israel through holy prophets. The divinely inspired Moses was anointed beforehand for this, and indeed before the others, and then after him those who followed. But when the holy Samuel was administering the government, those from Israel, lapsing into extraordinary folly and giving no heed to the rule exercised by God, I do not know how, approached him, saying, "Behold, you are old, and your sons do not walk in your way. And now appoint a king over us to judge us, as it is with the other nations."[64] And the prophet felt quite bitter about this. But the Lord, it states, said to him, "Listen to the voice of the people, whatever

61. Is 32.1.   62. Ps 2.6–7.
63. Mt 11.28–29.   64. 1 Sm 8.5.

they say to you; for they have not rejected you, <they have rejected me>,[65] from reigning over them."[66] And this was how Saul was
proclaimed, about whom the God of all says in the prophets,
"And I gave them a king in my anger, and held in my wrath a
storm of injustice."[67]

It cannot therefore be doubted at all that it was in anger that
Saul, a human king, was given to those rejecting the rule exercised by the very God of all. For it is incomparably better to be
eager to be subject rather to God himself. But if Christ is a human being as we are, rather than the Word who has appeared in
human form—but has been given as a king and has ruled over
those on earth—then who would be so utterly stupid as to think
and say that he too has reigned as though in the anger of God
the Father, and, since we have committed offenses and sins, has
subjected us as well to the yoke of a human being? Who can
doubt that we have been delivered from all sin through faith?
How then can it be that God is still grieved? How is it that he is
still moved with anger to punish those who are sanctified? I for
my part would say both that we have been delivered from sins,
and that the atmosphere in which we live is quite intoxicated
with the benefactions of God's kindness. It is not, therefore, a
human being who has reigned over us, but rather God who has
appeared in humanity, the Son, who has neither departed from
the glory of his own dignities because of what is human, nor dis-
dained being like us according to the economy.

Besides (I think this must be seen as well), if some of those in
error are accused of exchanging "the glory of the immortal God
for images resembling mortal man,"[68] and are under heavy attack for this, we too must stoutly refuse to range Christ purely
and simply in the nature that is ours, but must preserve the
union inseparable, the union, that is, which human nature has
with the Word from God the Father, in order that he may then
be worshiped as God both by ourselves and by the spirits above.

And if it is truly most grievous to adore the creature instead of

65. The Sources chrétiennes editor has included and bracketed the words
ἀλλ' ἢ ἐμὲ ἐξουθενήκασι; see SC 434, p. 286, ln. 13.
66. 1 Sm 8.7.
67. Hos 13.11–12.
68. Rom 1.23.

the Creator,[69] and we have been ordered to adore Christ, let him be regarded as above created nature as God, even if he is regarded as having been created because of what is human. Possessing in himself this glory, he once addressed those who had decided to disbelieve, all but accusing them of sluggishness. "If I do not do my Father's works, do not believe me. But if I do them, then even if you do not believe me, believe my works."[70] For there were, there were indeed, some senseless folk who thought little of him because of the flesh, rose up against him in their stupidity, and attacked him like dogs, finding pretexts in their sins and saying to the one who accused them, "We are not stoning you for a good work, but for blasphemy, because you, a human being, are making yourself God."[71] But, bidding farewell to the depravity of those so minded, let us honor him with long and unceasing acclamations. Since we have acquired a better way of thinking than the Pharisees' senselessness, we will say to him: "For a good work we are struck with admiration at you, because you who are God by nature have become a human being."

And for what reason? It is that since the Word of God is life by nature, he made a body for himself, a body whose nature it is to perish, so that once he had undone the power of mortality in it, he might transform it unto incorruptibility.[72] For just as iron, when it comes into contact with fire at its hottest, changes its color at once to that of the other and is pregnant with the power of that which conquers it, so also the nature of flesh, once it has received the imperishable, life-giving Word of God, has remained no longer in the state it was in, but has been rendered superior to corruption from then on.[73] And since he is himself the light of the world, he thus sent the rays of true knowledge of God into the intellects of all people, calling them in this way to the light; this he did on the one hand by using faultless teachings and rendering completely wise those who approached him by faith, and on the other hand by working various wonders, in order that, by astonishing the onlookers with deeds beyond understanding, no one might disbelieve that, being God by nature, he had become

69. Cf. Rom 1.25.   70. Jn 10.37–38.

71. Jn 10.33.   72. Cf. 1 Cor 15.53.

73. On the importance of the idea of incorruption in Cyril's Christology, see John J. O'Keefe, "The Persistence of Decay: Bodily Disintegration and Cyrillian

a human being, but had remained what he was even when he descended in the form we have according to the economy.

But the Jews did not understand the mystery, even though it had been announced in advance as fully and completely as possible through both the law and the holy prophets, and so they dared to grieve him in many ways. And when they recognized that he was himself the heir, they expelled and killed him,[74] taking as their accomplice and assistant in this the inventor of sin, Satan. He thought, understandably, that he had gotten away with it, since he had seen him suffer. But he, like those who had carried out the crucifixion, did not realize that he suffered willingly, and that he himself laid down his own soul,[75] not forced by anyone, but willingly, as I said, that he might make proclamation to the spirits locked up in hell, and open the gates of hell[76] to those below. For as Paul writes us in his wisdom, "It was for this that Christ died and lived, that he might be Lord of both the dead and the living."[77] For when he had released those in darkness,[78] he trampled upon the power of death[79] and revived on the third day. Then, after showing himself to the holy apostles and commanding them to make disciples "of all the nations, and baptize them in the name of the Father and of the Son and of the Holy Spirit,"[80] he ascended into heaven and is at the right hand of God the Father.[81] He will come in due time as judge of all, in the power and glory befitting God, escorted by angels, and will sit upon the throne of his glory,[82] judging the earth in justice[83] and rendering to each according to his work.[84]

5. Since, then, we have been bought at a price,[85] and we are not our own,[86] let us serve the one who has purchased us as best

Christology," in *In the Shadow of the Incarnation: Essays on Jesus Christ in the Early Church in Honor of Brian E. Daley, S.J.*, edited by Peter W. Martens (South Bend, IN: University of Notre Dame Press, 2008).

74. Cf. Mt 21.38–39.
75. Or "life." Cf. Jn 10.18.
76. Cf. 1 Pt 3.19.
77. Rom 14.9.
78. Cf. Lk 1.79.
79. Cf. Heb 2.14.
80. Mt 28.19.
81. Cf. Acts 2.33.
82. Cf. Mt 19.28.
83. Cf. Acts 17.31.
84. Cf. Mt 16.27.
85. Cf. 1 Cor 6.20.
86. Cf. 1 Cor 6.19.

we may, and let us be found superior to carnal passions. Having shaken off the defilement of sin and adorned ourselves with all virtuousness, let us fight the good fight, let us finish the race, let us keep the faith:[87] lightening the labors of those in need, consoling orphans, aiding widows,[88] easing the sufferings of those with bodily injuries, visiting those in prison,[89] and showing goodness and mutual affection to all.[90] For then it is, then indeed, that we will fast in purity. We begin holy Lent on the first of Phamenoth, and the week of the salvific Paschal feast on the sixth of Pharmuthi. We break the fast on the eleventh of Pharmuthi, late on Saturday evening, according to the gospel precept. We celebrate the feast on the following day, the eve of Sunday, the twelfth of the same month, adding thereafter the seven weeks of holy Eastertide.[91] For thus we will inherit the kingdom of heaven,[92] in Christ Jesus our Lord, through whom and with whom be glory and power with the Holy Spirit for all ages. Amen.

87. Cf. 2 Tm 4.7.
88. Cf. Jas 1.27.
89. Cf. Mt 25.43.
90. Cf. Eph 4.32.
91. April 7, 429.
92. Cf. 1 Cor 6.9.

FESTAL LETTER EIGHTEEN

A.D. 430

PREFACE

E HAVE gathered here once again to treat of a topic that is both well-known and popular. It requires, though, I think, language that is lavish, and eloquence of speech, so that even that which is beyond speech may be examined with care. Even though I am far from equal to this, however, I come to you once again to tell you of what may be discovered by goodness in thought. But it befits my audience to be forbearing. For the business at hand is not some exhibition of eloquence, but an instruction that is both necessary and suited to the time of our holy feast.

1. The time for our holy feast shines forth again. And it is necessary for us to remember the words of God, who reigns over all: "'Listen, priests, and bear witness to the house of Jacob,' says the Lord God almighty."[1] We will bear witness, then, that the time is at hand in which it behooves us to adorn ourselves splendidly with the virtues that suit holy people, and to abound in the glories of the evangelical way of life. We must also, I think, venerate those who instruct us in the fairest things. For that prophet speaks truly who says, "How beautiful are the feet of those who bring the news of good things!"[2] This of course by no means refers to those good things that are temporary and subject to decay, nor to those which our earthly bodies enjoy, but rather to those which are the achievement of our Savior's grace, and which render those who receive them thrice blessed, and make

1. Hos 5.1.
2. Is 52.7; Na 1.15.

them appear superior to passions of both soul and body. For "a good name is more desirable than much wealth,"[3] as Solomon says. For the virtuous, then, there is no time when it does not behoove them to appear as such. And if in fact the occasion arises of having to make efforts willingly on behalf of virtue, it is precisely then that, stiffening their resolve against all hesitancy, and hastening at top speed in the direction of everything that is held in admiration, they consider their efforts to be sheer enjoyment, battening as they do on the expectation of the good things to come, which cheers them. For when husbandmen are hardy and industrious, and the season reminds them that they have to till the earth, and sow the seed as well, then, even though great and lengthy labor is entailed in getting a generous crop from the land, they make nothing of the matter, and quite wisely. The husbandman puts the yoke on the ox, but what he sees is the field ripe with grain. He casts the seed into the soil, but exults in the reapers, and with the eyes of hope already marvels at the crop falling to the iron, and imagines his threshing-floor full. Or someone with a bent for sea-faring, and a merchant by trade, who sees the sea laughing in the spring breezes, does not brook delay: he ventures to set sail, even though he realizes that at times he will have to brave the waves and the ferocity of the winds. But he does not fear this at all, on account of the gains involved and the profit.

Now I think it most shameful that while they want to prove superior to all the labor entailed in corruptible, earthly business, we whose gains are divine and beyond understanding do not consider the time before our holy feast to be sheer enjoyment; it separates us from food and drink that is superfluous, but fills us with spiritual gifts. Since, then, the season invites us to courage, let no one shrink back, but go readily rather to whatever God has chosen. And I think that I must repeat what we find Jeremiah saying: "Take up arms and spears! Draw near to battle! Harness the horses! Mount, you horsemen, and stand ready in your helmets! Spears forward! On with your breastplates!"[4] For we must be wont to resist the pleasures that lead to wickedness, and

3. Prv 22.1.
4. Jer 46.3–4.

do so quite vigorously, and to battle against the passions once we have strapped on the armor of the Spirit.[5] For as the divinely inspired Paul writes, "The desires of the flesh are against the Spirit, and the desires of the Spirit are against the flesh; for these are opposed to each other."[6] When the flesh has the upper hand, however, the one who is defeated lives in shame and wantonness, more repulsive than any kind of filth; but when it is conquered and yields to the spirit, the victors' crowns are bright and attractive. For they will be at once beyond reproach, far from wickedness, and distinguished by the prestige resulting from virtue.

Now we must, I think, bend every effort to keep clear of what is injurious, and despise what is wicked, while striving for what is held in admiration. For I do not think that anyone at all would deny that bodily fitness is highly desirable.[7] If we fall prey to some illness, we are eager to summon immediately someone who knows how to get rid of it, and to resist the attacks of the disease with the skill that comes from his art. And bidding farewell to culinary delights, we block up the sources of the illness, so to speak, avoiding satiety itself and stopping our pain with our meager fare. Such is our diligence when it comes to the flesh! But if what is incomparably better is seen to be ill, the soul that is, and the method of curing it is sought, and it cannot be otherwise than through continence: how can we possibly not welcome fasting joyfully, if indeed we are in our right minds, and regard good health as better than illness? Let us therefore cleanse ourselves of every stain of flesh and spirit, as is written,[8] recalling what God says through the prophet: "You will be holy, because I am holy,"[9] and the words of one of the holy disciples: "Beloved, I beseech you as aliens and sojourners to abstain from the passions of the flesh that wage war against your soul."[10] People are admired, then, and thought worthy of all praise, when they choose to suffer even death, if necessary, risking themselves without hesitation for their children and wives. And if those who customarily

5. Cf. Eph 6.11.

6. Gal 5.17.

7. For a discussion of ascetical references in these letters, see the introduction in FOTC 118, 12–16.

8. Cf. 2 Cor 7.1.   9. Lv 11.45.

10. 1 Pt 2.11.

pillage countrysides or cities should come ravaging the farms and cut off the sources of livelihood, remaining inactive will contribute nothing to the renown of those afflicted; it is better to fight against evil, and to be seen to prefer to fall courageously, than to live miserably.

Since, then, our situation is such (and I do not think that anyone would find fault with what has been said), then striving on behalf of the soul for its benefit can only be something necessary, since it is all but pillaged by the flesh; and we will strive on its behalf by our labors, overthrowing the concerns of the flesh in order to require it to be subject to the will of the Spirit.[11] We will thus walk straight toward what is fitting, taking the path to everything that is of most renown, in possessing ourselves of the hope of eternal life. For all of us are aliens and sojourners in this world;[12] and short indeed is the time of the life with the body, but long and unending that which follows. It behooves us, therefore, while staying clear of the temporary things of the present, and firmly rejecting involvement with carnal pleasures as an ignominious profanation, to thirst for what is to come, and to consider beyond all reckoning and wonder what God has made ready for the saints. "For eye has not seen, and ear has not heard, nor has it entered the human heart, what God has prepared for those who love him."[13] Let us then explain, as well as we can, the method by which those who have loved him have acquired their reputation, using the topic as a sort of incitement to your enthusiasm for what is good.

2. The divinely inspired David, therefore, even though he governed the kingdom and had subject to him a countless multitude accustomed to distinguishing itself in battle, and so would order his military force to stand to arms and receive the attacks of the foes if ever any of the nations bordering on the Jews took the road to war, he would also, fortifying himself with assistance from above along with that from elsewhere, offer extended prayers and beseech the Lord of Powers to take his part, grant victory to him, and render him superior to his enemies' perver-

11. Cf. Gal 5.16.   12. Cf. Eph 2.19.
13. Is 64.4; 1 Cor 2.9.

sity. And he did not fail of his hopes, as you may hear from his words: "But I, when they troubled me, put on sackcloth, and humbled my soul with fasting, and my prayer shall return to my bosom."[14] You hear that he fasted and donned sackcloth; that is, he resembled a sojourner, downcast and in tears, not living in luxury and merriment nor battening on delicacies, but burdened with the labor of abstinence. And what was the fruit? What benefit did he chance to derive therefrom? We have just heard him say, "My prayer shall return to my bosom."[15] For those who give gifts to others, and demonstrate the generosity they have, place them in their bosom, showing that their hands are too small. And the God of all, when he gladdens people with the wealth of his favors, acts in the same way as those others, placing them as it were into their bosom, and besting the expectations of those who entreat him by the amplitude of his gifts. David therefore fasted, and what makes him worthy of the highest praise, or rather the object of astonishment, is that, excellent and wise as he was, he who boasted of having the crown of the realm and luxury and wealth in abundance, spent time in mourning and abstinence, that he might win the benevolence from on high. He defeated his enemies accordingly, and won his battles; he was illustrious, the object of emulation to all.

And if one wants in addition to look at those three youths, Hananiah, Azariah, and Mishael,[16] one will find how advantageous continence is in every way. They were born of Jewish stock, and when the Persian leaders captured Jerusalem, and took them off into captivity with the others, their destiny, and as it were special lot, was to be in the halls of the king. And since the Persians were always fond of ostentation, any of their captives who were of choice quality, and superior to the others in comeliness of body and of course in maturity, were groomed for their king. What is more, the greatest abundance of meats was made available to them, that they might always be sleek, and, by showing great charm in their expressions to onlookers, might make a not inconsiderable contribution to the king's renown. What then did the noble lads do in response to this? They scorned the

14. Ps 35.13.   15. Ibid.
16. Dn 1.1–20.

self-indulgent table, and, disdaining the exquisite dishes, embraced fasting as the mother and nourisher of their entire decorum, considering the effort it entailed to be their delight. What was the result? They were admired by their enemies. They were victorious when plotted against and were superior to those who were illustrious among the others, since they had the God of all as their benevolent overseer. They defeated fire, and, placed beyond the power of its flames, danced with the supernal powers, and became the teachers of those under heaven, persuading all of creation, as it were, to crown the Creator with the expressions of praise befitting him.

If, therefore, one chooses to imitate the beauty of the virtuousness of the saints, one will certainly attain to gifts equal to theirs. For one will conquer one's adversaries effortlessly and easily defeat one's enemies in their perversity, and even if those pleasures that entice one to what is shameful should assail the mind like fire or flames, one will prove more powerful than even they, with God's strength. For an angel entered the fiery furnace with Hananiah and his companions, tamed the flames, and unexpectedly persuaded the fire to yield to the human bodies.[17] And when Christ has come into our mind and heart through the Holy Spirit, he will certainly lull the savage flames of perverse desire, and, rendering us illustrious over the demons' schemes, make us citizens of heaven, and widen the path of every virtue for us. For sacred Scripture everywhere makes clear that we will find that the recompense of fasting, and the fruit of good efforts, is that God will prosper our journey. For thus it is written in Esdras: "And there I began a fast for the young men before the Lord our God, to seek from him a prosperous journey, both for us and for our children with us, and the cattle. For I was ashamed to ask the king for foot soldiers and horsemen, and an escort, for safety against our adversaries. For we had said to the king, 'The power of the Lord will be with us, with us who seek him, to support us in all ways.' And again we besought our Lord concerning this, and found him very merciful."[18] You see that he says that they fasted for a prosperous journey, supernal favor,

17. Dn 3.8–30.
18. 1 Esdras 8.50–53.

and the invincible assistance of the one who is able to save, and that they found very merciful the God who accomplishes everything with ease and apportions good things liberally to those who ask him. He will then rescue us too when we fast, will snatch us from every evil, and will render accessible every manner of virtuousness. For he will easily make smooth what seems difficult, and will render the rough way level and ready.[19]

3. But prayer, I say, must be practiced with fasting. For the virtues are neighbors, and are most usefully joined. But when one of them is lacking, the other, I think, is of little benefit, and virtuousness goes lame. For it is when we fast that we will pray in purity.[20] For the power of supplication to God is immense; we will realize this once again from the divinely inspired Scripture itself. For Israel was living in the desert. And when Amalek (a barbarian nation), inflamed with the unholy envy with which it was stricken, armed itself for war, the divinely inspired Moses gave the following order to Joshua: "Choose for yourself powerful men, and go out and set them in battle array against Amalek tomorrow."[21] And the youths were armed, and a large and mighty multitude of those who knew warfare squared off against the enemy ranks. But the divinely inspired Moses himself, standing by on a hill, was engaged in prayer to God. And what benefit was derived therefrom for those in battle may be known from what is written: "And it came to pass," it says, "that when Moses lifted his hands, Israel prevailed; but when he lowered his hands, Amalek prevailed."[22] Notice, therefore, how Moses' hands were better than weapons and cavalry; for as long as he stretched them forth in prayer, Israel was invincible to attack, while if he lowered them, Amalek prevailed. The divinely inspired Paul writes to us about what happened to those of old as follows: "These things happened to them in figure, but they were written down for our instruction, upon whom the end of the ages has come."[23] And this, I think, suffices to show the benefit of prayer.

But it will not hurt if we take up another narrative as well, one

19. Cf. Is 42.16.   20. Cf. Mt 6.16–18.
21. Ex 17.9.   22. Ex 17.11.
23. 1 Cor 10.11.

that contains a meaning close to what has been said. It happened once that the Jews became so confused that they thought
they had to worship stones and wood. And neglecting him who
is the one God by nature, they each worshiped as they chose.
And for that reason they roused the Master against them and
were handed over to some of the neighboring nations, and
served their foes, their land having been captured by them.
Then at last, suffering greatly from their exceeding calamities,
and rejecting utterly their unholy decision, and unlearning their
shameful ways, they sought mercy through repentance and approached the blessed prophet Samuel. He told them at once,
"'Gather every man of Israel to Mizpah, and I will pray for you to
the Lord.' And the people gathered to Mizpah, and they drew
water, and poured it out upon the earth before the Lord, and
they fasted on that day, and they said, 'We have sinned against
the Lord.' And Samuel judged the children of Israel in Mizpah."[24] And further:

And the foreign overlords came up against Israel, and the children of
Israel heard, and they were in fear before the foreigners. The children
of Israel said to Samuel, "Cease not to cry out for us to the Lord your
God, and he will save us from the hand of the foreigners." And Samuel
took a sucking lamb, and offered it up as a holocaust with all the people to the Lord, and Samuel cried to the Lord for Israel, and the Lord
listened to him. And Samuel was offering the holocaust, and the foreigners drew near to war against Israel. And the Lord thundered with a
mighty voice on that day upon the foreigners, and they were troubled,
and fell before Israel.[25]

That fasting, then, when accompanied by prayer, is not unprofitable, and is held in admiration by those of sound mind, is
clearly shown both by what has already been said, and also, and
not least of all, by the narrative we have just recounted. For those
who had conquered Israel of old came up expecting to capture
immediately and effortlessly those who might wish to oppose
them. But it was they who were defeated and fell, not because
they encountered a multitude tried in war and skilled in battle,
nor an infantry with its weapons, nor ranks of cavalry, but an ir-
resistible opposition supplied by God. For heaven thundered

24. 1 Sm 7.5–6.   25. 1 Sm 7.7–14.

upon them with terrible violence, and those who once were of haughty demeanor were crushed by fear and turned to flight. The others were superior to their conquerors through fasting and prayer.

4. Come then, if you will, let us busy ourselves for a time with the question of the way in which they sacrificed. For what we will find are those who are saved and victorious in Christ, and even if what was done was in figures and riddles, it shows eloquently enough the power of the mystery of Christ. It says, then, "The people gathered to Mizpah, and they drew water, and poured it out upon the earth before the Lord."[26] Now what is this about? someone might reasonably ask. Or how can this function as a sacrifice? What is it that they did that was pleasing to God? For the law given through Moses commanded cattle to be sacrificed, and turtle-doves and doves to be consecrated to God,[27] but nowhere does it order, as a manner of sacrifice, water to be poured upon the earth. What was it, then, that those of ancient times did, and with them the prophet, even though he possessed within himself a marvelously comprehensive knowledge of the sacred and divine revelations? Our answer is that being a prophet, and having his mind filled with the Holy Spirit, he doubtless knew the great and august mystery of the Incarnation of the Only-Begotten. And he reasoned that even the very figure of the truth could save those in danger, depicting upon himself, as it were, the significance of the salvation given through Christ. How therefore the truth was effected as though in shadows, let us explain as best we may. The only-begotten Word of God, being life by nature, descended therefore to a voluntary emptying, and became as we are, a human being,[28] not, that is, by undergoing a change from his own nature into the flesh that is from earth—for God's nature is fixed firmly upon its own bounty—but because he put on our earthly body which has the rational soul.[29] This is what the proph-

---

26. 1 Sm 7.6.   27. Cf. Lv 1.14; 5.7.
28. Cf. Phil 2.6–7.

29. There is little polemical content in this letter. The theological language in this section is standard in Cyril and appears to be almost formulaic in these letters.

et Samuel portrayed as in water to those of old when he poured water on the earth. For water is a symbol of life, and the earth of flesh. But the Word became flesh,[30] as John says who speaks of God, and the life-giving divinity and the humanity from earth have joined together in unity in a way that is ineffable and inconceivable. And thus it is that we understand Immanuel henceforth to be one from both: he neither departs from the bounds of divinity through the assumption of flesh, nor was loath to become as we are, due to his inherent kindness and the supremely wise economy that comes from this reality. For since he was going to undergo the death that was for the life of all—this of course being the death that is of the flesh—so that, when raised from the dead, he might as life and God trample upon the power of death,[31] he made his own the body subject to death, meaning the human body or the flesh; this was in order that through it he might do away with corruption, ancient and redoubtable as it was, and thus restore human nature to life.

For he was raised, not achieving the resurrection for his own nature, in which he is regarded as God, as indeed he is, but in order that we might have this reality in him abundantly. For this reason he has been called "the first-fruits of those who have fallen asleep"[32] and "the firstborn from the dead."[33] And when the divinely inspired Samuel showed this very thing to those of old in offering the prayers for Israel, he not only fulfilled for them the figure of the Incarnation in shadow and riddle, as it were, by pouring out the water on the earth; he immediately added the rest: the slaughter done on behalf of the whole world. For it says, "Samuel took a sucking lamb, and offered it up as a holocaust with all the people to the Lord, and Samuel cried to the Lord for Israel, and the Lord listened to him."[34] You hear how he sacrificed the lamb as an image and figure of the true God, the one whom the blessed John, too, all but pointed to with his hand when he said, "Behold the Lamb of God, who takes away the sin of the world."[35] For Christ is the spotless sacrificial victim by whose precious blood we have been saved and sanctified.

---

30. Jn 1.14.
32. 1 Cor 15.20.
34. 1 Sm 7.9.
31. Cf. Heb 2.14.
33. Col 1.18; Rv 1.5.
35. Jn 1.29.

Thus God the Father bade the mystery concerning him to be prefigured for us through all-wise Moses as well. For Israel was in slavery to the Egyptians. But they were pitiless, infected by a cruel harshness. Then they made their life miserable, as is written, with mud and brick-making, burdening them with painful labor.[36] But when God took pity on them in their wretchedness and then decided to rescue them from the arrogance of their rulers, he bade the all-wise Moses tell them that mercy had been granted them, and that they would at once make their way to the land promised their fathers once they had shaken off the unbearable burden of slavery. But since it was likely that they would slip from the hope of better things to come at last, and would then not listen to what Moses said, the God of all ordered him to work miracles. For a miracle always somehow draws one to belief, and has the power to cause even the mind in complete despair to revive unto the hope for good things. And when he bade [him] show two signs, he added, "And if they will not believe you nor listen to the voice of the first sign, they will believe you because of the voice of the second sign. And it shall come to pass that if they do not believe you for these two signs, nor listen to your voice, you will take from the water of the river and pour it upon the dry land, and the water that you take from the river will be blood upon the dry land."[37]

5. For the nature of God the Father and of the Son is likened to a spring; and the Father is sometimes a river and water, and sometimes so is the Son, or the Holy Spirit. For God the Father says of himself through Jeremiah, "Heaven is amazed at this, and shudders deeply, says the Lord, for my people have committed two evils: they have forsaken me, the spring of living water, and have dug themselves broken cisterns that cannot hold water."[38] The Son furthermore says of himself through the prophets' voice, "Behold, I bend down to them as a river of peace, and as a torrent drenching them with the glory of the gentiles."[39] Again, the divinely inspired David speaks of himself to the Father in the

---

36. Cf. Ex 1.14.   37. Ex 4.9.
38. Jer 2.12–13.   39. Is 66.12.

heavens, striking the spiritual lyre for us as he says, "How you have multiplied your mercy, O God! So the children of men will hope in the shelter of your wings. They will be intoxicated with the richness of your house, and you will give them to drink of the torrent of your delight, for with you is the spring of life."[40] Our Lord Jesus Christ furthermore gave the name of "water" to the life-giving Spirit who pours forth through him from the Father, when he was conversing with the woman in Samaria. He said, "If you knew the gift of God, and who it is that says to you, 'Give me to drink,' you might ask him, and he would give you living water."[41] And further, "Everyone who drinks from this water will thirst again; but whoever drinks from the water that I will give him will never thirst again."[42] The Son therefore is the life-giving water as from the spring or river of God the Father. He engenders all things, and "in him we live and move and are."[43] And God acquaints us again with this by showing it through figures, as it were, and so to speak from examples that are still lowly, speaking thus to the all-holy Moses: "And you will take water from the river, and you will pour it upon the earth."[44] For the Father's nature is, as I said, quite aptly likened to a river, and the Son, begotten naturally from him, to water. Now this water from the river has been mixed with the earth. For "the Word became flesh"[45] in the union of the economy. And that, once become a human being, he was certainly and indubitably to die for us in the flesh as well, is what is indicated in the words "and the water that you take from the river will be blood upon the dry land."[46] But the blood in this passage signifies nothing else to us but death. For as long as the Word was not flesh, he had not become blood. For the living and life-giving nature is quite beyond death. But when he became as we are, then, then indeed, he made his own the death of his own flesh, and is said to die for us himself, and with his own blood to acquire the earth under heaven; it is always his, for he is himself the Creator of everything, but it had shown itself restive, through being overly inclined to

40. Ps 36.7–9.   41. Jn 4.10.
42. Jn 4.14.   43. Acts 17.28.
44. Ex 4.9.   45. Jn 1.14.
46. Ex 4.9.

sin, choosing to worship the creature, and venerating the elements of the world.[47]

So it was with the pagans. But the Jews, having little regard for the decree given through Moses, turned to doctrines that were human commandments, and, as the divinely inspired David says, "They have all turned aside, they have together become useless, there was no one who did good, not even one."[48] For this reason the only-begotten Word of God appeared with flesh, "and consorted with human beings,"[49] as is written, and announced to Israel, and indeed before the others, the things that concern salvation and life. As the blessed John says, however, "He came to his own home, and his own people did not receive him."[50] For they did not at all accept the Savior of all; they never stopped insulting him, practicing every kind of wickedness in their cruelty. Their insanity reached such a degree that they nailed to a cross the Author of life, and thought they could conquer by death the one who is greater than death. For he came back to life on the third day, having emptied hell,[51] and, having opened the gate of death to the spirits below and become way, gate, and first-fruits for human nature unto incorruptibility,[52] he ascended to God the Father in heaven,[53] and is enthroned with him, and with him rules all things. He will come in due time "that he may judge the earth in justice,"[54] as is written. Since, then, as Paul says in his supreme wisdom, "we must all appear before the judgment seat of Christ, so that each one may receive good or evil, according to what one has done in the body,"[55] let us fast in purity, rejecting every manner of sin, and dismissing every kind of impurity from our thoughts. Let us in addition be good, mutually affectionate, and merciful; let us take pity on orphans, defend widows,[56] help in treating the infirm, suffer with those in prison,[57] and in a word be eager to practice every kind of virtuousness. For thus it is, thus indeed, that, in distinguishing ourselves by an illustrious life, dear to God, we will celebrate the feast in purity.

47. Cf. Rom 1.25.
48. Ps 14.1–2.
49. Bar 3.37.
50. Jn 1.11.
51. Cf. 1 Pt 3.19.
52. Cf. 1 Cor 15.20–21.
53. Cf. Acts 2.33.
54. Ps 9.8.
55. 2 Cor 5.10.
56. Cf. Jas 1.27.
57. Cf. Mt 25.43.

We begin holy Lent on the twenty-third of Mechir, and the week of the salvific Paschal feast on the twenty-eighth of Phamenoth. We break the fast on the third of Pharmuthi, late in the evening according to the gospel precept. We celebrate the feast on the next day, the eve of Sunday, the fourth of Pharmuthi, adding thereafter the seven weeks of holy Eastertide.[58] For thus will we inherit the kingdom of heaven, in Christ Jesus our Lord, through whom and with whom be glory and power to the Father with the Holy Spirit for all ages. Amen.

58. March 30, 430.

FESTAL LETTER NINETEEN

A.D. 431

T IS TO a slender supper that I see so many and mighty banqueters gathered; and I fear I may fail to satisfy you. But I admire your desire to learn, and commend your love of oratory, even if it is not delivered brilliantly. And since you have been invited here, please, please be tolerant if the speech is not all that you might have hoped for.

1. It is time for us once again to say to you what was sung to those of old by the Psalmist's lyre: "All you nations, clap your hands; shout to God with a voice of exultation";[1] let us, that is, sing victory songs to Christ. For he has conquered the world for us, as he himself certainly says, and "he triumphed over the principalities, powers, dominions, and the world rulers of this darkness, the spiritual hosts of wickedness in the heavenly places."[2] He thus withdrew everyone from their perversity, and removed them from their ancient guilt, "nailing the bond that stood against us to the cross,"[3] in order that, in our joy at this very thing, we might say, "Where, O death, is your sting? Where is your victory, hell? The sting of death is sin, and the power of sin is the law."[4] But through Christ we have been removed even from the punishment in the law. The divinely inspired Paul will testify to this when he writes, "For sin will have no dominion over you, since you are not under the law but under grace."[5] And John in his wisdom writes, "For the law was given through Moses;

---

1. Ps 47.2.
2. Eph 6.12. Cf. Col 2.15.
3. Col 2.14.
4. 1 Cor 15.55–56.
5. Rom 6.14.

grace and truth came through Jesus Christ."[6] For one man died for all, acquiring by his own blood the earth under heaven, "so that those who live may live no longer for themselves, but for him who for their sake died and was raised."[7] We will live for him in being eager above all to think and act in a way pleasing to him, and in choosing to follow the gospel precepts.

Now every time is fitting and opportune for those whose concern is excellence, in my opinion, aiming as they do at fulfilling the salvific commandment; but that is especially true of the present time, which all but cries out through the prophet's voice, "Send forth the sickles, for the vintage has come; go in, treaders, for the press is full, the vats overflow."[8] For I, for my part, say that all of those who have an intelligent and accurate understanding of the way we should behave, and who know how to investigate how they may achieve what will be of most benefit to themselves and to others as well, must seize their opportunities with great zeal. What do I mean? Winter's gloom has dispersed, the season of spring is arising, and the richest fields are shaggy with grain, countless rows of which wave in close ranks above the earth; and then it is, then indeed, that no one who knows how to harvest must remain idle any longer. And since the time at hand brings to the industrious whatever they want to obtain, let idleness depart and sleepless endurance be esteemed above all else. For it is thus, and not otherwise, that the highest praise as well will be given them abundantly.

Since, therefore, "Christ your Passover has been sacrificed,"[9] as Paul testifies to us too in his supreme wisdom, "let us cleanse ourselves from every defilement of flesh and spirit, and make holiness perfect in the fear of God,"[10] lest, taking hold of the sacred mysteries with unwashed hands and dishonoring his divine sacrament in our carelessness, we draw upon our own heads the punishment befitting the impious. For the divinely inspired Paul in fact writes something of the sort to those accustomed to behave in this way: "That is why many of us are weak and ill, and quite a few are asleep. For if we judged ourselves, we would not

6. Jn 1.17.
8. Jl 4.13.
10. 2 Cor 7.1.

7. 2 Cor 5.15.
9. 1 Cor 5.7.

be judged. But when we are judged, we are chastened by the Lord, that we may not be condemned with the world."[11] Collecting therefore from the sacred writings the things that serve our purpose, let us explain the manner in which we may celebrate the feast in holiness and perfect purity, and so come then to the spiritual participation in Christ, the Savior of us all.

2. Those of Israel's blood sacrificed the lamb in Egypt as Moses instructed them. They were in fact bidden to eat unleavened bread with it, and bitter herbs as well. For thus it is written: "Unleavened bread with bitter herbs shall you eat for seven days."[12] Tell me, then, shall we ourselves preside over what is in figures and shadows?[13] Then whatever is Paul about when, supremely wise as he is and truly versed in the law, he says, "We know that the law is spiritual"?[14] Who can doubt that he is plain-spoken and, having Christ in him as he does, would not speak falsely? How then can we fulfill that ancient law, Christ saying clearly, "Do not think that I have come to abolish the law or the prophets; I have not come to abolish but to fulfill them. For I tell you, not an iota, not a dot, will pass from the law until all takes place. Heaven and earth will pass away, but my words will not pass away"?[15] The true Lamb who takes away the sin of the world has therefore been sacrificed for us as well who have been called through faith to holiness. We will make our spiritual, all-beautiful, and truly sacred meal from it, a meal described as being of unleavened bread, according to the law, but understood in a spiritual sense. For leaven is always used by the divinely inspired writings as a figure of wickedness and sin. Our Lord Jesus Christ for that matter bade his holy disciples beware, saying, "Beware of the leaven of the scribes and Pharisees."[16] Paul, too, in his supreme wisdom writes as follows to remove those sanctified as far as possible from the leaven and impurity that infect mind and heart: "Cleanse out the old leaven that you may be a new lump, as you are unleavened."[17]

---

11. 1 Cor 11.30–32.   12. Ex 12.8.

13. For a discussion of Cyril's use of non-literal interpretation, see the introduction in FOTC 118, 9–12.

14. Rom 7.14.   15. Mt 5.17–18; Lk 21.33.

16. Mt 16.6.   17. 1 Cor 5.7.

It is therefore not unprofitable, but rather necessary, since it is of the greatest concern to us to come to share spiritually in Christ, the Savior of us all, that we keep our mind unsullied, rub away stains, avoid sin, and, in short, depart from whatever it is that usually causes defilement. For thus it is that we will succeed in making our approach, one which is in participation, blameless and quite irreprehensible. But let one eat bitter herbs too; let one, that is, make one's way through bitter labors, and value highly the perseverance entailed therein. For it is most absurd for those who love piety to think and suppose that they may abound in virtue otherwise, and be able to boast of the highest glories, except by first contending and making a splendid show of courage. For the way that leads up to it is rough and forbidding, and not accessible to the many; it is easily trodden only by those who take it on the run, fearing nothing, stripped for labor, and resistant to fatigue. And Christ himself urges us to this when he says, "Enter by the narrow gate, for wide is the gate and broad the way that leads to destruction, and many there are who enter by it. But narrow is the gate and strait the way that leads to life, and few there are who find it."[18] For it suits not just anyone to choose and then to achieve deeds that are illustrious and exceptional, but only, as I said, those who are outstanding and are able to overcome nobly the pleasure that beckons to what is shameful. But that the path leading to sin is wide and wondrously smooth, one may observe with no difficulty at all, if one wants, from the realities themselves. For the human mind is quite easily carried away and most readily diverted when impelled by pleasure. And it is borne[19] with the greatest ease toward delicacies, and displays how it suffers from lack of self-control in bodily appetites. And I think that one who has perhaps suffered in this way will have to confirm what I say. For the nature of the flesh often forces even one who is unwilling, incites him with its fearful goads to indulge his innate pleasures, all but seizes him if he is reluctant, and bears him off to involuntary inclinations. But the Lord God of all builds him up with the law, and grants him the weapon of continence. For the prophet spoke truly who said of God, the Savior of us all, "For

---

18. Mt 7.13–14.   19. Correcting Ἵεται to Ἵεται.

he has given a law as a help."[20] And consider for me that most holy man Paul, learned in the law, as he turns his attention to a careful examination of these things, and deftly probes the temerity of the movements that are innate and in us, but shows with it the law offering us sufficient assistance. For this is what he says: "I know that the law is spiritual; but I am carnal, sold under sin. I do not understand my own actions. For I do not do what I want, but I do the very thing I hate. Now if I do what I do not want, I agree that the law is good. So then it is no longer I that do it, but sin which dwells within me."[21]

What are you saying, blessed Paul? You, carnal and sold under sin, do not understand your own actions? You do what you hate? Does not each of us proceed to each thing to be done with the free inclinations of the mind, and choose what is preferred without hindrance, and has not each of us allotted to ourselves the reins of our own will? Yes, he says, but I know that pleasure sometimes bewitches even the reputable mind, lowering it easily to what is improper. I also know that it suffers injury involuntarily. For it does not by any means do what it wants. It yields rather to the attacks of the passions,[22] and, overcome by their superiority, gives way even when unwilling, and one who has suffered this may well say, "So then it is no longer I that do it, but sin which dwells within me."[23] You see that he blames the passions that are innate and in us, admits defeat, indicts avarice, and fears the opposition will be overwhelming? The divinely inspired Paul will himself once again confirm that what I say is true, continuing on and adding the following to what he has said: "For I know that nothing good dwells within me, that is, in my flesh. I can will what is right, but I cannot do it. For I do not do the good I want, but the evil I do not want is what I do. Now if I do what I do not want, it is no longer I that do it, but sin which dwells within me. So I find it to be a law that when I want to do right, evil lies close at hand."[24]

You see, then, how evil rises up to attack savagely each person's

20. Is 8.20 (LXX).   21. Rom 7.14–17.
22. For a discussion of the influence of the ascetical movement on these letters, see the introduction in FOTC 118, 12–16.
23. Rom 7.17.   24. Rom 7.18–21.

soul, lowers the mind that is in us, even against its will, to what this evil wants, and turns its freedom to its own inclinations, as it were. So that what is done appears no longer to be ours, but to belong perhaps to that very evil alone. But the Creator has not ignored us, nor indeed, by leaving human nature quite unassisted, has he handed it over to be plundered freely by the pleasures tending to evil. For the law punishes the propensities thereto, and even if passion behaves excessively, it [the law] resists wisely and frightens it [passion] into a better course, displaying the beauty of continence and causing it to exult in the glories of virtue. Having fixed our thoughts, therefore, beyond profane and utterly loathsome pleasure, and made little account of food and drink, "let us make holiness perfect in the fear of God,"[25] as is written; "let us put to death what is earthly in us: fornication, impurity, passion, evil desire, and covetousness."[26] For thus does Paul write us in his supreme wisdom. For the nature of the body has admittedly been afflicted with the proclivity to desire; yet we do not see the Creator of all unconcerned about our situation, but rather determined to accord it the most salubrious attention.

He in fact gave his only-begotten Son, in order that, having become a human being like us and taken a body from holy Mary, the Mother of God,[27] he might put to death sin in the flesh. For he at once freed the body, which had become the Word's own, from the passions that afflict us, removed the goad of the movements toward wickedness, and transformed it, as it were, unto a purity ineffable and befitting God, once sin was put to death in it and pleasure shaken down to its very foundations, so to speak. For just as it [Christ's body] was superior to death, because it became the flesh of that life which is such by nature, in the same way, I think, it trod upon the power of sin. For it belonged to the One who did not know sin. The divinely inspired Paul declared that these words are true when he wrote to us, "For God has done what the law, weakened by the flesh, could not do: sending his own Son in the likeness of sinful flesh and for sin, he condemned sin in the flesh, in order that the just requirement of

25. 2 Cor 7.1.   26. Col 3.5.
27. *Theotokos.* See note 34 in *Letter* 17, p. 64.

the law might be fulfilled in us who walk not according to the flesh but according to the Spirit."[28]

But one might, I think, ask: What is this "what the law could not do"? What it means is that while the law calls one to continence, the nature of the flesh carries one off to the contrary, always urging one toward the most loathsome appetites. But the God of all condemned sin in the flesh when he sent his own Son, not unclad and bodiless, nor dazzling in the fearsome, unapproachable light of his own divine glory, but lowering himself into our condition[29] according to the economy, and tolerable [to our eyes] because of his similar body. For he was killed, as I said, so that we ourselves, as sanctified, might seem to have gotten out of the flesh and to abound in the divine Spirit. Paul in his supreme wisdom writes again as follows: "But you are not in the flesh, you are in the Spirit, if, that is, the Spirit of God dwells in you. Anyone who does not have the Spirit of Christ does not belong to him. But if Christ is in you, although the body is dead because of sin, the spirit is life because of justice."[30]

3. But since it behooves those fond of the renown from on high, and those who have chosen to live in a way pleasing God above all, to be seen to act in accordance with piety, we will of necessity add to the glory of continence the other modes of virtuousness: mutual love, mutual affection, and the readiness to act compassionately toward those in the grip of unbearable poverty. For Christ said somewhere, "Be merciful, because your heavenly Father is merciful."[31] And the law given through Moses commands, "You will surely open your bowels to your brother who is in need among you."[32] For love of the poor is something special. But if one considers it of little account, if any, and says that it is worthless, one will be wholly commending cruelty and inhumanity, and claiming that there is no need for compassion for those in extreme misery. Now is that not a bestial idea, hateful to God, and repellent to that nature that loves mercy? No one would doubt it. For it is written, "Those who close their ears

28. Rom 8.3–4.   29. Cf. Phil 2.7.
30. Rom 8.9–10.   31. Lk 6.36.
32. Dt 15.11.

so as not to listen to the infirm will themselves call out and find
no one to listen."[33] And one must in any event remember the life
that will be ours after this. Be ready; for the life of each person
will surely and inevitably reach its end. As sacred Scripture says
somewhere, however, "We have brought nothing into the world,
nor can we take anything out."[34] One will go one's way carrying
no earthly goods, but deprived of them all, as it were, even the
body. But those who practice virtue have spiritual wealth, and
the light of the love of the poor as companion. For they will
boast before the divine tribunal, or rather Christ himself will
praise them, saying, "Come, you blessed of my Father, inherit
the kingdom prepared for you since the foundation of the
world. For I was hungry, and you gave me to eat; I was thirsty,
and you gave me to drink; I was a stranger, and you welcomed
me; naked, and you clothed me; sick, and you cared for me; in
prison, and you came to me. For amen I say to you," he says, "inasmuch as you did it for one of these least ones, you did it for
me."[35] Do you see that the nature that is merciful and most gentle says[36] that the compassion shown to the poor has been offered to it? But I have no doubt that people will find praiseworthy[37] the notion that care should be shown to those in poverty
and difficulties, and assistance given to the needy as far as possible. But they will waver and go over to the opposite opinion,
heartless as it is, reflecting and speaking for instance as follows:
If I give what I have to others, I will do an injustice to my own
children. What are they to possess? I am not well off. But, dear
sir, I would reply, you are far from thinking as you should. You
really ought to have reflected wisely that, while you consider affection shown to your children while you are alive to be of the
greatest worth, you do not remove yourself from what you own,
nor do you deprive yourself completely of what contributes to
relaxation and enjoyment. It would therefore be the business of
the mind that is truly of the best sort, to have a concern for the
future life, and to choose to act accordingly. It is not inop_por-
tune to imitate the forethought of sailors, who, when they cross

33. Cf. Jer 5.21.   34. 1 Tm 6.7.
35. Mt 25.34–36, 40.   36. Correcting φύσιν to φησίν.
37. Reading ἐπαινέσει instead of ἐπακούσῃ.

the sea, which is so wide, do not forget about food or other provisions that pertain to the voyage; on the contrary, they stash
away in advance stores that are sometimes more than what is
necessary. Since, therefore, each of us is going to depart from
the things that are ours, we must plan for our spiritual provisions
in advance. You will do your own child no injustice by taking pity
on those in need. You will not grieve your heir by saving yourself
from punishment and fire. "For we all offend in many things;
but by alms and faithful dealings, sins are purged away,"[38] as is
written.

4. Gladdening us with such teachings, the only-begotten Word
of God became a human being.[39] For before the times of the visitation, we went on in the world wrapped in spiritual mist, with
neither the knowledge of piety nor any other of the supernal
goods in our mind and heart. We did not see the way of justice,
nor even recognize the very one who is God by nature and in
truth, but in our error we even worshiped creatures,[40] deprived as
we were of the intelligence befitting even human beings. But
when such was our state, the Creator took pity. He saw Satan
laughing heartily at everyone, easily seizing those on earth, with
no one to help them, subjecting them to his own yoke, and casting them down effortlessly into every sort of depravity. He then
established a law through Moses. It was not possible, however, to
escape from the snares of sin by the law; it was not possible to
wash away the defilement of the transgressions. For the law ex-
hibited the sin, and was established by God as a sort of proof of
the weakness afflicting us all; blessed Paul in his wisdom will
come forward as a witness for us when he says, "For we know that
whatever the law says, it says to those who are under the law, so
that every mouth may be stopped, and the whole world may be
held accountable to God. For no human being will be justified in
his sight by works of the law, since through the law comes knowledge of sin."[41] And further, "Law came in to increase evil."[42]

What are you saying, O blessed Paul? Tell me, are you bring-

38. Cf. Prv 15.27, Tb 12.9, and Jas 3.2.
39. Cf. Jn 1.14.   40. Cf. Rom 1.25.
41. Rom 3.19–20.   42. Cf. Rom 5.20.

ing a charge against the law given through Moses? Are you saying that it was for this reason that it slipped in: that it might increase evil? It would then be a teacher of wickedness, if evil
increased through it. But this is not what the Spirit-bearer says.
For he goes on, "What then shall we say? That the law is sin? By
no means! Yet I would not have known sin if it had not been for
the law. I would not have known what it is to covet[43] if the law
had not said, 'You shall not covet.'"[44] The law, therefore, is by no
means a teacher of sin. But it is, as I said, a proof of the weakness
of those under the law, and an indicator of that which is of a
harmful nature. For just as one would not blame the sunlight
when it shows one holes in the ground, or objects littering road-
junctions, and saves those hurrying along from a fall, so also no
one with good sense, I think, would accuse the divine law of pro-
ducing sin in us, but will rather admire it for declaring clearly
what it is that benefits us. But it was introduced, he says, "that every mouth might be stopped, and the whole world be held accountable to God."[45] For since no one fulfilled the law due to
overwhelming weakness and the enormous propensity to transgression, the whole world was held accountable to God, who all
but drove those on earth to the point of needing finally to thirst
for the grace that comes through faith in Christ. For we are just
"not because of deeds done by us in righteousness, but in virtue
of his great mercy,"[46] as is written. And Paul in his supreme wisdom confirms this doctrine as well when he writes, "But now the
righteousness of God has been manifested apart from the law,
although the law and the prophets bear witness to it, the righteousness of God through faith in Jesus Christ for all who believe. For there is no distinction; since all have sinned and fall
short of the glory of God, they are justified by his grace as a gift,
through the redemption that is in Christ Jesus."[47]

In order, therefore, that he might render us free from punishment and penalty, and from his denunciation, the One who is
above all creation became a human being truly as we are: the
Word from God the Father.[48] He remained what he was: the Free

43. Correcting ἁμαρτίαν to ἐπιθυμίαν.   44. Rom 7.7.
45. Rom 3.19.   46. Ti 3.5.
47. Rom 3.21–24.   48. Cf. Jn 1.1.

One among slaves, the Legislator under the law, the Maker of the ages with us in a birth both carnal and effected in time. For he took of Abraham's seed,[49] and shared in blood and flesh, he who in his own nature is incorporeal,[50] so that, having been called our brother, he might render us sharers in his own glory,[51] and having sanctified us by his own Spirit,[52] he might call us finally brothers and sisters who are free. For thus he says somewhere to the holy apostles: "You are my friends; I no longer call you slaves."[53]

The Jews, accordingly, forgetting all these things and denying the Savior and Redeemer of all, handed him over to Pilate and urged that he be crucified. But he, being God by nature and all-powerful, willingly inserted his own body into death's snares, that he might draw us out when he had broken them. For he came back to life on the third day, having made his proclamation to the spirits in hell,[54] and said "to those in bonds, 'Come forth!' and to those in darkness, 'Show yourselves!'"[55] Then, having shown himself clearly to the holy apostles, and having said openly, "Go and make disciples of all the nations, baptizing them in the name of the Father and of the Son and of the Holy Spirit, teaching them to observe all that I have commanded you,"[56] he ascended to the Father in heaven. He exults upon the throne of his own divinity, and will come in due time in the Father's glory with the holy angels to judge the earth in justice.[57]

Since, then, we are to render our accounts, and to present ourselves before his bench, let us purify our own lives through complete virtuousness, let us keep our faith unwavering, pitying the poor, assisting widows,[58] showing mercy to those in prison,[59] having compassion for those in labors and difficulties, practicing mutual affection, love for God and our brothers and sisters, and chastising our carnal passions. For thus it is, thus indeed, that we will keep festival in purity, beginning holy Lent on the third of Phamenoth, and the week of the salvific Paschal feast on the

49. Cf. Rom 9.7.
50. Correcting σώματος το ἀσώματος.
51. Cf. Rom 8.17.
52. Cf. 1 Pt 1.2.
53. Jn 15.15.
54. 1 Pt 3.19.
55. Is 49.9.
56. Mt 28.19–20.
57. Cf. Ps 96.13.
58. Cf. Jas 1.27.
59. Cf. Mt 25.43.

eighteenth of Pharmuthi. We break our fast on the twenty-third of the month, the eve of Saturday, as usual, celebrating the feast on the following day, the eve of Sunday, the twenty-fourth of Pharmuthi,[60] adding thereto the seven weeks of holy Eastertide. For thus it is that, nourished on the words of truth, we will be benefited by them in Christ Jesus our Lord, through whom and with whom be glory and power to the Father with the Holy Spirit for all ages. Amen.

60. April 19, 431.

FESTAL LETTER TWENTY

A.D. 432

HE GOD OF ALL, in many and varied ways showing forth the truth to us in advance through the shadow of the law, and depicting beforehand through the ancient commandment, as on a tablet skillfully made, the supremely pure beauty of the gospel way of life, said to holy Moses, "Make for yourself two trumpets of beaten work; you will make them of silver, and they will be to you for calling the assembly, and for removing the camps."[1] The trumpets, then, are of beaten work, the fact signifying to us that the meaning of our Savior's mysteries is not limited by and measured within the shadow and riddle in the law; it rather advances little by little toward what is better and truer. For what is beaten always moves forward in some way. And they are silver, because the doctrine concerning him has been resplendent, of the utmost purity, and indeed free of every stain, and is presently such in the churches.

But sacred Scripture explains further who it is that used the trumpets. It says, "And the sons of Aaron, the priests, shall sound the trumpets, and it shall be a perpetual ordinance for you throughout your generations."[2] For it well befits the sacred and chosen race, crowned with the honors of the divine ministry, to speak of Christ's mystery, and always to indicate to the peoples subject to it the means by which they may become worthy of citizenship in heaven: by taking leave of what is earthly, moving to a way of life that is pious and distinguished, fighting courageously against the enemies of truth, squaring off boldly against the enemies of Christ's glory, and celebrating his feasts purely and

1. Nm 10.2.
2. Nm 10.8.

faultlessly, "not with the old leaven," as is written, "but with the unleavened bread of sincerity and truth."[3] This is what the Master of all announced to us himself when he said, "If you go forth to war in your land against your enemies that are opposed to you, you will sound the trumpets, and you will be remembered before the Lord, and you will be saved from your enemies. And in the days of your gladness, and on your feasts, and on your new moons, you will sound the trumpets at your holocausts, and at the sacrifices of your peace-offerings. And it will be a remembrance for you before your God. I am the Lord your God."[4]

For the weapons of the saints are not carnal, but are empowered by God, and the manner of their armament is not in visible and perceptible things, but in the power of the Spirit, and of justice, and holiness, and in correctness and accuracy of doctrines. For they had to have the breastplate of justice and the helmet of salvation, and for that matter the weapon of good will, and the sword of the Spirit, which is the word of God.[5] For this indeed will frighten all enemies, and do so quite easily. This will display those who lift their horn on high, and speak unjustly against God, as miserable, abject, and senseless folk, or rather as people with tongues crowded with every impiety, so that it may be said of them, "The poison of asps is under their lips, those whose mouth is full of cursing and bitterness."[6] Let us therefore use against them the trumpets, that is, the sacred and faultless proclamations of the truth. But by all means, if we offer the spiritual sacrifices to God, the Savior of all, let us sing the songs of victory to him who became as we are for our sake, who descended even unto the form of a slave. For the Word from God the Father, being God by nature, "became flesh,"[7] not having cast away what he was—far from it!—but rather having assumed what he was not, that he might transform us too unto that life that is better and more renowned. For "being rich, he became poor for our sake, that we might become rich by his poverty."[8] Indeed, the Savior of all, the only-begotten Word of God the Father, eminent in his complete equality in every respect with him, of equal

3. 1 Cor 5.8.
5. Cf. Eph 6.14–17.
7. Jn 1.14.
4. Nm 10.9–10.
6. Rom 3.13–14; cf. Ps 140.3.
8. 2 Cor 8.9.

throne and majesty with him, did not refuse to go to the extreme of emptying himself for us in the economy.

But the inventors of unholy doctrines, "the enemies of the cross of Christ, whose end is destruction, whose god is the belly,"[9] considering him of small account, and having a low opinion of him, cast down the glory of the mystery, so as to make it seem ill-fashioned, as far, at least, as they are able.[10] The wretches all but ridicule God's wisdom, as though they were able to set about thinking up something better, and acting like a mouth speaking haughtily,[11] like the son of iniquity, whose forerunners they are confident they are. For they condemn the birth of the Only-Begotten in the flesh; they say that it was not truly God that the holy Virgin bore in the flesh, even though the holy evangelist cries, "The Word became flesh."[12] They claim rather that the Word of the Father dwells in a human being, so that the Savior may be found to be a God-bearing human being ranked among the prophets, or perhaps not even possessing anything more than we do in his condition. For the God of all dwells in our own selves as well, as the wise John testifies when he writes, "In this we know that he is in us, because he has given us of his Spirit."[13] What is it then that Christ is regarded as having more abundantly than do others, if he himself was a human being carrying the God of all dwelling within, and not in very deed and truth the Son of God the Father, and true God even with the flesh? For he underwent the birth in the flesh, and remained God when he became as we are. But the heterodox cannot bear to think so. Spitting out the explanation of the mystery as though it were something stale, and drawing upon their own heads a bitter and inescapable punishment, they assign to Christ the name of son as though by way of participation and grace, and ignorantly separate it off into a human being apart, dividing off the very Word of God, and barely manage to assign to him a mere conjunction,[14] as they please, as though it were in equality of dignity.

9. Phil 3.19.

10. The following Christological observations reflect the conflict with Nestorius that erupted in 428. For a discussion of the Christology of these letters, see the introduction in FOTC 118, 26–31, and *Letter* 17.

11. Cf. Rv 13.5.   12. Jn 1.14.

13. 1 Jn 4.13.

14. Greek: συνάφεια (as opposed to ἕνωσις, union).

But this is not the view that we have been taught to hold, nor will we pay attention to their stupidities and ruin our own minds. For there is, there truly is, as the blessed Paul says, "one God the Father, from whom are all things, and we through him."[15] But this knowledge is not in everyone. Let those therefore who have a faulty belief in Christ, and lack an exact and true knowledge, listen to the following words: "Walk in the light of your fire, and in the flame which you have kindled."[16] For we ourselves will walk the straight and unswerving way of faith, and we will travel the royal road, turning off neither to the right nor to the left. For we confess that the Word, being God, became flesh, a human being, that is, having taken a body lacking neither soul nor mind, but one with both soul and mind,[17] in order that, having become like[18] his brothers and sisters in everything, apart from sin alone,[19] he might offer himself for us to the Father as a spiritual fragrance, and, having died as one man for all, might acquire everyone for himself, and through himself for God the Father. For as the divinely inspired Paul writes, "It was for this purpose that Christ died and lived, that he might be lord of both the dead and the living."[20] And if he is Lord of the earth under heaven, having died to the flesh but given life as God to his own temple, then it is understandable that he will not be regarded as a bare human being honored by a conjunction with God, which is only in the order of dignity, but as true God, even if he became flesh, having all creation under his feet. For he is seated with God the Father, even with the flesh. "Every knee bends to him, and every tongue acknowledges that the Lord Jesus Christ is in the glory of God the Father."[21] And the doctrine of the truth in this matter, and the tradition of the correct and faultless faith, take this path.

In giving heed to deceitful spirits, though, and to men with seared minds,[22] as Paul says in his supreme wisdom, some sense-

---

15. 1 Cor 8.6.   16. Is 50.11.

17. Cyril was always careful in his later Christological statements to insist that Christ has a human mind, to avoid the possibility of charges that he was an Apollinarian.

18. Reading ὁμοιωθείς instead of ἐνωθείς.

19. Heb 4.15.   20. Rom 14.9.

21. Phil 2.10.   22. Cf. 1 Tm 4.1–2.

less folk have made shipwreck of their faith,[23] and have brought up the weapons of impiety against those accustomed to think rightly, hatching a variety of plots and bending the bow of malignity. As the blessed Psalmist says, however, "The arrows of children have become their wounds, and their tongues have been weakened upon them."[24] For the holy multitude of the reverend priests[25] of God in every place did not remain silent, but, gathered together all in one chorus, and taking up the shield of faith, as is written, "having shod their feet with the equipment of the gospel of peace,"[26] of Christ that is, and stretching forth "the sword of the Spirit, which is the word of God,"[27] plundered the ranks of the unholy, crying out in the words of the Psalm, "The Lord's enemies have lied to him, and their time will be forever!"[28]

2. Something like this, we say, happened in past times as well, when Moses was still instructing the Israel of the flesh. They had left Egypt, having thrown off the tyrants' cruel yoke, but when they were dwelling in the desert they did not escape the envy of others, nor did they accomplish their journey to the land promised them without labor and fatigue. It is written that "Amalek came and fought with Israel in Raphidim. And Moses said to Joshua, 'Choose for yourself mighty men, and go forth and set them in array against Amalek tomorrow. And behold, I stand on the top of the hill, with the rod of God in my hand.' And Joshua did as Moses had told him, and going forth he set his men in array against Amalek."[29] And when Joshua had come to grips with him and conquered him together with his chosen ones, the Lord, it says, said to Moses, "'Write this for a memorial in a book, and speak it into the ears of Joshua, that I will utterly blot out the memory of Amalek from under heaven.'"[30]

These things, however, are in shadows and figures, for the law is a shadow. But in the circumstances in which we find ourselves, one may be astonished to look upon the beauty of the truth un-

---

23. Cf. 1 Tm 1.19.
24. Ps 63.8–9 (LXX).
25. Reading ἱερέων instead of ὀρέων.
26. Eph 6.15.
27. Eph 6.17.
28. Ps 80.16.
29. Ex 17.8–10.
30. Ex 17.14.

clad and free from shadows. That accursed Amalek has armed himself once again against the true Israel, the Amalek who fights against the Savior's renown, and tries to overthrow the power of the mystery concerning him. But Our Lord Jesus Christ, having gathered the chosen ones from all Israel, has met him in battle and conquered. And he will utterly "blot out the memory of Amalek from under heaven."[31] For he fights him with hand concealed, and defends those who have believed in him, having established the splendid, genuine knowledge of the mysteries of his own self in the hearts of all.

3. Let us therefore celebrate, since the enemy has been disabled, Satan removed, and the church purified, and no one any longer says that Immanuel is not truly God; everyone acknowledges rather his glory, and with untiring lips ascribes to him the praises of glory. For it is written, "Let all the earth adore you and sing to your name."[32] For he has rendered Satan powerless when in his supreme arrogance he boasted, "I will take the whole earth in my hand like a nest, and pick it up like abandoned eggs, and there is no one who will escape me or gainsay me."[33] And he destroyed the very power of death with him, sin being abolished. For we have been justified not from works of the law through the commandment of old, but through faith in him[34] and through that benevolence which is above law. "For the letter kills, but the spirit gives life."[35] And Moses' [law] has been called the ministry of condemnation,[36] and quite rightly so. For no one is justified by God through the law. The grace that comes through Christ, though, has been held to be the ministry of justice. For the only-begotten Word of God lowered himself to his voluntary emptying, and lived together with those on earth as a human being, having undergone birth in the flesh through the holy Virgin, the Mother of God,[37] so that he might transform for the better those who believed in him by means of the instructions that are above the law, and, having shown them the path of the gospel way of

31. Ibid.			32. Ps 66.4.
33. Is 10.14.			34. Cf. Rom 3.28.
35. 2 Cor 3.6.			36. Cf. 2 Cor 3.9.
37. *Theotokos*. See note 34 in *Letter* 17, p. 64.

life, rendered them genuine worshipers. For "God," he says, "is spirit, and those who worship him must worship in spirit and truth."[38]

Now I maintain that those who are true worshipers, and who genuinely practice that adoration which is in spirit and truth, must rid themselves of all defilement, of soul and of body, that is, and must try to accomplish, with all zeal, that through which they may be freed from all guilt. For it befits them to be holy both in body and in spirit. Let us therefore mortify the pleasures, and let us not have a mind that yields to carnal passions, but one that entertains what is of the spirit, knows how to pronounce unsound every kind of impurity, is inclined toward every good thing, and hastens to put as far as possible from itself the sin that readily besets us. For the pleasures of the body enchant the human mind, and brashly plunder the hearts of some, all but attacking them fiercely like an enemy force.

But those whose armor is the fear of God all but laugh at the attacks of such passions, saying, "The Lord is my help, and I will not fear what flesh may do to me."[39] The all-wise Paul brings them to this point of view, and indeed to the enjoyment of spiritual strength, when he cries, "Put to death what is earthly in you: fornication, impurity, passion, evil desire."[40] And this is achieved through efforts that one might think must be admired, and might well praise above all else. Thus the divinely inspired Paul says again somewhere, "I pommel my body and subdue it, lest after preaching to others I myself should be disqualified."[41] In our joy, therefore, at cultivating every virtue, let us welcome the truly all-pure, holy fast, the nourisher of all good order, the mother of sanctification, and the provider of the benevolence from above. When we afflict[42] our body with abstinence, virtuousness must follow. For thus will we be perfect and entire, lacking nothing. For the honor that comes from good works seems always somehow to follow the efforts at bodily training. This is what will crown the champion in piety with God's approval; this is what will supply the prize of supernal renown to those who endure

38. Jn 4.24.   39. Heb 13.6.
40. Col 3.5.   41. 1 Cor 9.27.
42. Reading κατατήκοντες instead of κατήκοντες.

courageously. "While we have time, therefore, let us do good to all."[43]

4. It was to teach us this that the Only-Begotten appeared in a form like ours. But Israel did not recognize the Savior and Redeemer of all, even though the law displayed in advance the mystery regarding him in shadows and figures, and the holy prophets too shouted it aloud in many different ways. Let, therefore, those infected by ignorance of him hear the words: "Hear, O heaven, and hearken, O earth, for the Lord has spoken: children I have begotten and reared, but they have spurned me. The ox knows its owner, and the ass its master's crib. But Israel does not know me, and the people has not recognized me."[44] For they persecuted him with their accusations, saying, "It is not for a good work that we stone you, but for blasphemy; for you, a human being, make yourself God."[45] But let it be said about them, with perfect fairness, "Woe to the sinful nation, a people full of sin, an evil seed, lawless children! You have forsaken the Lord, and provoked the Holy One of Israel."[46] For even though they should have acknowledged that he is God, and the Lord of all, and indeed, recognizing from his wondrous deeds his unspeakable, divine power, should have said, in the words of the prophet, "Behold, we will be yours, for you are the Lord, our God,"[47] they did nothing of the sort, but waxed bitterly arrogant. Sometimes they were ridiculous enough in their zeal to rail at him, "Samaritan drunkard!"[48] and went so far as to call him a bastard; at other times they drove him with stones from the borders of Judaea, and finally they crucified him. They shook their heads at him, and even said, "You who would destroy the temple and build it in three days, save yourself! If you are the Son of God, come down from the cross!"[49] They did their best to kill the Author of life. But it was not possible for him to be held by death, as the divinely inspired Peter says. For, having descended into the lowest recesses of hell and "preached to the spirits"[50]

43. Gal 6.10.
45. Jn 10.33.
47. Cf. Jer 3.22.
49. Mt 27.40.

44. Is 1.2–4.
46. Is 1.4.
48. Mt 11.19.
50. 1 Pt 3.19.

there, he "brought out the prisoners in might," as blessed David says.[51] And he came back to life on the third day, having given life as God to his own temple, and having become the "first-fruits of those who have fallen asleep,"[52] and the "firstborn from the dead,"[53] that he might render human nature superior to death and decay,[54] and might transform it unto life enduring. And having shown himself to the holy apostles, he ascended to God the Father in the heavens,[55] and sat at the right hand of the throne of majesty in the heights, thenceforth to wait in expectation "until his enemies are placed beneath his feet."[56] He will come in due time from heaven in the glory of his Father with the holy angels to judge the living and the dead.[57]

Knowing this, therefore, let us "purify ourselves of every defilement of flesh and spirit."[58] Let us accomplish our sanctification in the fear of God, cultivating every sort of piety, preserving a faith in him that is correct and sincere, reviving widows, consoling orphans,[59] caring for the poor with our resources as far as we may, condoling with the suffering as those who are in bodies ourselves, and remembering prisoners as their fellow prisoners.[60] For thus it is, thus indeed, that we will fast in purity, beginning holy Lent on the twenty-seventh of Mechir, and the week of the salvific Paschal feast on the second of Pharmuthi. We break the fast on the seventh of Pharmuthi, late in the evening according to the apostolic traditions. We celebrate the feast on the following day, the eve of Sunday, the eighth of Pharmuthi,[61] adding thereafter the seven weeks of holy Eastertide. For thus it is, thus indeed, that we will be esteemed, and we will commit our souls to the God who is over all, in Christ Jesus our Lord, through whom and with whom be the glory and power to the Father, with the Holy Spirit, now and forever, and to endless ages. Amen.

51. Cf. Ps 67.7.
53. Col 1.18.
55. Cf. Acts 1.6–9.
57. Cf. 1 Pt 4.5.
59. Cf. Jas 1.27.
61. April 3, 432.

52. 1 Cor 15.20.
54. See *Letter* 17, note 73, pp. 71–72.
56. Cf. Ps 110.1; 1 Cor 15.25.
58. 2 Cor 7.1.
60. Cf. Mt 25.43.

FESTAL LETTER TWENTY-ONE

A.D. 433

T WOULD have been my great joy, brothers and sisters, in announcing our holy festival once again, to offer you the customary discourse, omitting nothing that would make for your spiritual benefit and confirm your correct and unwavering faith in Our Lord Jesus Christ. For thus I would have reaped the profit from my own zeal, and you would not have been deprived of what can benefit you. But since not all human plans run as smoothly as hoped, nor are their results always and completely as expected, come, let us do our best to speak of what is urgent, as far at least as the severity of the illness that even yet weighs upon us allows.[1] For its attacks upon us have brought us so low that we cry out in the words that the holy disciples spoke to the Savior when they were in danger, "Lord, save us! We are perishing!"[2]

I know, then, that being of eminent intelligence, you have made your own the wise and sensible doctrine of our holy fathers and best of teachers, holding fast in your memories their exhortations, so that there is nothing we need supply; as the blessed author of Proverbs says, "Everything is manifest to those that understand,[3] and right to those that find knowledge."[4] I speak with confidence, therefore, as to those who are knowledgeable.

---

1. This is probably a reference to the illness Cyril experienced late in 432, while in the middle of negotiations with the delegates of John of Antioch in the aftermath of Ephesus. See McGuckin, *St. Cyril of Alexandria: The Christological Controversy,* 112–13.

2. Mt 8.25.

3. Correcting ποιοῦσι to συνιοῦσι after Prv 8.9.

4. Prv 8.9.

2. Behold, therefore, the renowned and salvific season of the holy feast is even now at hand, when, having cast off the intolerable burden of our own sins, we have willingly submitted to the salvific yoke of God the Word who has come down from heaven; no longer laboring and burdened, we are instructed by the gentle discourse of Immanuel, with its ability to save. Rejoicing with one another in the churches, therefore, let us lift up songs of thanksgiving through our common, sacred, united assembly, in Christ the Savior, who has redeemed us all from the stain rubbed into us from of old through the transgression of him who was first formed; let us cry aloud the words spoken wisely of old: "Christ has redeemed us from the curse of the law, having become a curse for us."[5] For through the devil's greed we fell from paradise and its delights, having drawn upon ourselves our Maker's just wrath and heard those frightful, unbearable words: "Earth you are, and into earth shall you go";[6] and thus we appeared as prey to the devil's tyranny, not daring for an instant to lift our eyes on high, wretches that we were.

What way to salvation was left, then, to those who longed for it? What means of gaining forgiveness could be found for those who had transgressed the Master's commandment? Only God's kindness: the compassion and mercy of the power so unspeakable and indescribable. He sent us, therefore, his own Son as Savior and Redeemer, the Son who alone is able to rescue human nature from the devil's power. Such great goodness and kindness did the only-begotten Word of God the Father show toward us, that he who is equal in majesty and glory with the One who begot him, and co-eternal with him, he who is the Creator and Fashioner of heaven, earth, the angels, and human beings, "did not count equality with God a thing to be grasped, but emptied himself,[7] taking the form of a slave,"[8] and took on our likeness, in order that, once he had saved everyone through himself, he might present them to God the Father pure from stain and defilement, having become like his brothers and sisters in everything, except only for sin.[9] He thus suffers hunger and fasts in

5. Gal 3.13.   6. Gn 3.19.
7. Reading αὐτὸν instead of αὐτὸς.   8. Phil 2.6–7.
9. Heb 4.15.

due time, that he may appear as an example of the sinless life and the source of salvation. Among us ourselves as well, therefore, let fasting precede the holy festival: "not with the old leaven, the leaven of malice and evil, but with the unleavened bread of sincerity and truth."[10]

For when we keep ourselves free of fault and stain, and with perfect purity practice the way of life pleasing to God, we will fittingly hear the words addressed to honest slaves: "Well done, good and faithful servant; you have been faithful over a little, I will set you over much; enter into the joy of your Lord."[11] For the fruit of the fasting will not be without benefit to those who hope in him, nor will they ever hear those words of cursing that suit the Jews: "'This is not the fast I have chosen,' says the Lord."[12] For he accuses them, with complete justice, through the words of Isaiah, and says, "You fast, and you strike the lowly man with your fists. Why do you fast to me?"[13] What is needed, accordingly, is that life which is all-good, and in which fasting is accompanied by luminous and unblemished beauty, the splendid provision of incorruption, the lovable pledge of the kingdom of heaven, the solid, invincible bulwark of eternal life. It behooves us, then, "to cleanse ourselves from every defilement of flesh and spirit, and to make holiness perfect in the fear of God."[14] For thus we will present ourselves confident and unshaken at Christ's judgment-seat, clad in white robes and crying out unhesitatingly, "Behold, we will be yours, for you are the Lord, our God!"[15]

3. What the Jewish horde[16] did not want to acknowledge, it heard of old[17] from God speaking through Isaiah: "Woe, sinful nation, people full of sins, evil spawn, lawless children! You have forsaken the Lord, and provoked the Holy One of Israel! Why should you be smitten any more as you add to your iniquities?"[18]

---

10. 1 Cor 5.8.

11. Mt 25.23.

12. Is 58.5.

13. Is 58.4.

14. 2 Cor 7.1.

15. Reference uncertain.

16. For a discussion of Cyril's attitude toward the Jews, see the introduction in FOTC 118, 16–26.

17. Reading πάλαι instead of πάλιν.

18. Is 1.4–5.

For they were not astonished at the deeds accomplished by the Savior himself, nor did they marvel at the divine signs that he worked by his own power; quite the contrary, they insulted him with the words, "It is in Beelzebul, prince of demons, that he expels demons."[19] O God-hating madness, and unspeakable impiety! They have not known, they have not understood, they pass through in darkness and wander, from the least to the greatest of them.[20] If you do not understand what is written about him, nor think about the information given by the holy disciples, why do you boast of being a guardian of the precepts of the law? When did you see fulfilled what was spoken of in advance, of old? "Then shall the eyes of the blind be opened, and the ears of the deaf shall hear. Then shall the lame man leap as a deer, and the tongue of the stammerers shall speak plainly."[21] Will you not go on forever hoping for Immanuel to come, and expecting what you have seen accomplished? Do none of the deeds performed astonish you completely, so that you prefer to hide what has been made known to everyone? Do you shut your eyes, and keep your ears closed to Christ's miracles? You have, then, a recompense worthy of your transgressions. For no longer are the tokens of piety among you, neither city, nor festal sacrifice; but you roam about, scattered around the earth everywhere. Listen to one of those who have chosen to think rightly uttering the reproach made by Baruch: "Why is it, Israel, that you are in the land of your enemies? You have grown old in a foreign land, you are defiled with the dead, you have been reckoned with those in hell. You have forsaken the fountain of wisdom."[22]

You will have, then, no defense against the charges. All straightforward speech deserts you as you contrive[23] to deal cleverly with the truth itself. You will accordingly hear what is fitting from the future judge of all: "Walk by the light of your fire, and by the flame which you have kindled."[24] You have given over to the cross the Lord of glory and Creator of all; you thought that life could be overpowered by death; you did not know nor un-

---

19. Mt 12.24.   20. Cf. Is 44.18.
21. Is 35.5–6.   22. Bar 3.10–12.
23. Reading μηχανωμένῳ instead of μηχανώμενος.
24. Is 50.11.

derstand that it was incorruption itself that was being worked out for human nature. In fact, our Lord Jesus Christ himself, having descended into hell,[25] looted it, and with sovereign proclamation ordered those in fetters, "'Come out!' and those in darkness, 'Show yourselves!'"[26] He came back to life on the third day, and, after ascending from the dead, rejoicing in his achievement, he said to his own disciples, "Go and make disciples of all the nations, baptizing them in the name of the Father, and of the Son, and of the Holy Spirit."[27]

4. Having gained such teachers, accordingly, let us decide to obey and submit to them; having learned the truth from them, and having the sacred Scriptures to perfect our teaching and instruction, let us cry out to our Savior and Redeemer in the words of blessed Moses: "Who is like to you among the gods, O Lord? Who is like to you who are glorified among the holy ones?"[28] And further: "Which God is like you, removing iniquities and passing over injustices?"[29] Let no one who is in error[30] persuade you to depart from the right faith. Let us go by the royal road, turning aside neither to the right nor to the left.[31] Let us keep the right faith simple and unadulterated, recognizing it not as an occasion of sectarian disputation, but as the faith of true piety. Let us acknowledge as consubstantial the Trinity of Father, Son, and Holy Spirit. For this is what the divine Scriptures have transmitted to us from above. Let us acknowledge the Lord who became a human being and was born for us through the blessed Virgin Mary, the Mother of God.[32] Let us say to him, as is written, "My Lord and my God."[33] When we adorn our life in this way, and have rubbed off the stain of old sins by a way of life that is right and religious, then when we are pure and spotless, and completely faultless, let us show a fatherly tenderness to orphans, and a compassion befitting holy people to widows.[34] Let

25. Cf. 1 Pt 3.19.
26. Is 49.9.
27. Mt 28.19.
28. Ex 15.11.
29. Mi 7.18.
30. Reading πλάνης instead of πλάνος.
31. Cf. Nm 20.17.
32. *Theotokos*. See *Letter* 17, note 34.
33. Jn 20.28.
34. Cf. Jas 1.27.

us, in short, love our neighbor, and, dismissing all wrongdoing from our own soul, let us bring the homeless poor into our home. This is so that, when we have treated what God has given for our maintenance as belonging in common to the poor, and we have clothed the naked,[35] and, in a word, we have girt ourselves with complete obsequiousness to God, we may gain the enjoyment of the good things awaited.

We begin holy Lent on the twenty-seventh of Mechir, and the week of the salvific Paschal feast on the twenty-fourth of Phamenoth. We break the fast on the twenty-ninth of Phamenoth, late in the evening according to the gospel precept, celebrating the feast on the following day, the eve of Sunday, the thirtieth of the month.[36] We add thereto the seven weeks of holy Eastertide. Thus will we inherit the kingdom of heaven in Christ Jesus our Lord, through whom and with whom be glory and power to the Father for endless ages. Amen.

35. Cf. Mt 25.36.
36. March 26, 433.

FESTAL LETTER TWENTY-TWO

A.D. 434

HIS SHORT message or letter is not conceived as a display of ostentation in discourse; it is something to which we have once again been called by a custom from of old. It would indeed be fitting for the proclamation of our holy feast to shine out in advance of its arrival as never before. Those therefore who are truly eloquent and trained in the art of speech may enjoy the applause of their listeners if they display this skill with words. We meanwhile will babble some explanations of the divinely inspired Scripture to you as well as we may.

1. Those who are distinguished by the honor of the divine priesthood, and selected especially from the others, have received an appointment from the law to govern peoples, and have also been charged with the duty of proclaiming what is necessary for their benefit. One of the holy prophets said accordingly, "'Listen, priests, and bear witness to the house of Jacob,' says the Lord almighty."[1] Now the house of Jacob would by no means at all be those of Abraham's blood, but would be those justified through faith in Christ,[2] as the all-wise Paul writes, "Not all of those from Israel are [of] Israel, nor are they all children because they are Abraham's seed, but it is the children of the promise who are reckoned as seed."[3] What, then, do the divine and sacred words signify? What do they persuade us to cry out, now that the season once again shines forth upon us when the holy and all-pure festival is celebrated, the one that is in honor

1. Hos 5.1.   2. Cf. Rom 5.1.
3. Rom 9.6.

of Christ, the Savior of us all? "Sanctify a fast, proclaim a service."[4] To choose to exert oneself, then, and to engage vigorously in the brave deeds that make for piety, is, I would say, one of
the most profitable of things. For the thing has a glorious fruit,
and, as the prophet says, "A man who labors, labors for himself,
and drives his own ruin away."[5] What could be of equal value to
that, for those at least who are sensible? Nothing at all, obviously.
The Savior himself confirms this when he says, "What will it profit one to gain the whole world, but to suffer the loss of one's
soul? Or what will one give in return for one's soul?"[6]

Now those who have decided to exert themselves, and who are
accustomed to value above all else the joy they find in the efforts
made to acquire virtue, need, I think, both a steady mind, and a
heart that is firm, one that distinguishes itself in patience and
that aims to hasten toward what is beneficial. One can see the
sort of thing applying to us that happens with those whose business is breaking in horses. If they are to appear properly tamed, it
is not enough simply that they accept the bit; it is always quite
necessary as well, I think, that they learn to step gracefully and be
most skillful and swift of foot. It will be, then, a necessary and
beneficial thing for us too, if, in addition to the duty of deciding
to exert ourselves, it is noticed[7] that what pertains to this is the
wisdom to know the way that leads to each of the things to be
done, or otherwise. For we have used the all-pure fast very like a
bit, checking the propensity of the mind toward what is worse,
and chastening the irrational movement of the flesh. For self-
indulgence in bodies is a sort of root and origin of pleasures
sharp and wild, and resists fiercely the desires for what is good,
moving as it does with licentious impulse toward what is shameful.

But the labors of abstinence rise up vigorously to oppose
the attacks of the passions innate within us, and turn the flesh
around quite firmly toward docility when it bucks away toward
the wrongdoing natural to it. Thus far does fasting assist those
devoted to it. Those, however, who are eager to act skillfully in
approaching the question of what is or is not to be done will
doubtless succeed in arriving at all that is good; for splendid and

4. Jl 1.14.   5. Prv 16.26 (LXX).
6. Mt 16.26.
7. Correcting ἐνορῶ τὸ ὑπάρχον to ἐνορῷτο ὑπάρχον.

admirable are the achievements of a shrewd mind. The all-wise Paul testifies to this when he writes to Timothy, "Train yourself in piety; for while bodily training," meaning that which is by way of fasting and labors, "is of some value, piety is of value in every way, as it holds promise for the present life and also for the life to come."[8] Some of those of olden times fasted, but they would practice a bare abstinence quite unconnected with the brave deeds belonging to the rest of virtue.[9] Then when their affairs did not turn out as they had intended, and God did not grant their requests but rendered fruitless their fast, they grumbled, saying, "Why have we fasted, and you have not seen? We have afflicted our souls, and you have not known it."[10] What does God reply? "In the days of your fasts you do as you please, and all those that are under you you wound. You fast for quarrels and strife, and strike the lowly with your fists. Why do you fast for me?"[11] Notice, then, that what does not at all suit those who fast is holding to their own wills, those, I mean, which tend to vice; what does suit them is in effect bidding them farewell, passing over to what is better, and, as it were, tightly embracing the impulses to virtue, singing as they do, "My heart is ready, God, my heart is ready."[12]

2. Since, therefore, it is the Paschal feast of the Lord, and the season of the salvation and life of us all is dawning, let us gladden the only-begotten Word of God with spiritual adornment, the Word who for us has become like us,[13] a human being, that is, according to the economy, that we might be above ourselves, and beyond the limits of humanity,[14] being called God's children,[15] and having as our brother him who is above all creation.[16]

---

8. 1 Tm 4.7, 8.

9. For a discussion of the influence of ancient ascetical traditions on these letters, see the introduction in FOTC 118, 12–16.

10. Is 58.3.   11. Is 58.3–4.

12. Ps 57.7.   13. Cf. Heb 4.15.

14. Cyril, like most of the Greek fathers, tended to understand salvation as a transformation into a new form of human existence characterized by "incorruption," rather than as a juridical settlement.

15. Cf. 1 Jn 3.1.

16. Cyril refers here to the Nicene doctrine of the full divinity of the Son who has become flesh in the person of Christ.

Come, let us, that is, offer him spiritual sacrifices in thanksgiving. For the Israel of old worshiped by slaying sheep, and offered sacrifices of blood. But it heard God saying clearly, "Who has required these things at your hands?"[17] And the divinely inspired David says as well, "Will I eat the flesh of bulls, or drink the blood of goats?"[18] For the divine is all-sufficient, and gives life to everything, and needs none of these things at all.

We do, however, say that he seeks the giving of gifts from us as something owed, above all when the season calls us to the feast. For he spoke thus through the all-wise Moses: "Command the children of Israel, and you will say to them, 'Observe the offering to me of my gifts, my presents, and my fruit-offerings in my feasts.'"[19] It is necessary, then, to look at what kind of thing the oblation is, and how it is to be performed by us. For he rejects as ineffective and profitless the quality of the worship that is in shadows. Listen to him speaking to those from Israel: "I did not speak to your fathers about holocausts and sacrifices on the day when I brought them out of Egypt."[20] And Paul writes, "A former commandment is set aside because of its weakness and uselessness, for the law made nothing perfect."[21] And God had cried out before then through one of the holy prophets,

Behold, the days are coming, says the Lord, when I will establish a new covenant with the house of Israel and with the house of Judah; not like the covenant that I made with their fathers when I took them by the hand to lead them out of the land of Egypt; for they did not remain in my covenant, and I paid no heed to them, says the Lord. This is the covenant that I will make with them: in those days, says the Lord, I will put my laws into their minds, and I will write them upon their hearts; and they shall not teach every one his neighbor and his brother, saying, "Know the Lord," for all shall know me, from the least to the greatest of them, for I will be merciful toward their sins, and their wrongdoing I will remember no more. And I will be their God, and they will be my people.[22]

The first [covenant] is, then, obsolete, for it brought nothing to perfection;[23] henceforth the new [covenant] of the Gospel

17. Is 1.12.
18. Ps 50.13.
19. Nm 28.1–2.
20. Jer 7.22.
21. Heb 7.18.
22. Jer 31.31–34.
23. Cf. Heb 8.13.

has been introduced. Christ, however, said, "Do not think that I have come to abolish the law or the prophets. I have come not to abolish but to fulfill them. For I tell you that not an iota, not a dot, will pass from the law until everything takes place. Heaven and earth will pass away, but my words will not pass away."[24] Since, therefore, as we have already said, the shadow of the worship according to the law is unacceptable to God, and the doctrines that come through Christ have been introduced, along with the new covenant promised of old in advance, and since Christ himself, furthermore, affirms that he has come to fulfill prophets and law, I consider it necessary and wise to inquire about the fulfillment of the law of old in the new covenant.

Those of Israel's stock, then, used to offer to the all-pure God the sacrifices according to the law, a calf perhaps, or a sheep. But it was unwanted and unpleasing, as I said. For he had no need of meat or blood, and he never delights in savory smoke. In what way, then, will we bring to completion the sacrifices in the law? It will be, I think, by adopting the right attitude: that what was given through Moses was figures, and images of spiritual sacrifices,[25] giving shape in various ways to what is spiritual. It was a calf that was the sacrificial victim for those of old. But see in it with me some one, any one, of the faithful who consecrates himself to God in an odor of sweetness. For it is written, "Present your bodies as a living sacrifice, holy and pleasing to God, which is your spiritual worship."[26] See how he calls the consecration of man spiritual worship, contrasting it with the sacrifices in the law. For what was performed was no spiritual worship; it was the sacrifices of cattle, sacrifices containing the beauty of truth in shadow and figures. We may, then, observe what manner of intelligible consecration it is that is performed by us in the Spirit, and observe it quite easily, by scrutinizing the depths of the sacred Scriptures, and by stirring up the outward aspect of the figures, as it were, and thus[27] by seeing, in a manner of speaking, the bare, unclothed truth that is dearest to God.

24. Mt 5.17, 18.
25. Reading θυμάτων instead of θαυμάτων.
26. Rom 12.1.
27. Reading οὕτω τε instead of οὔτε.

3. It is, then, written at the beginning of Leviticus:

If one of you offers gifts to the Lord, you will offer your gifts from the herd and the cattle, and from the sheep. If his gift is a holocaust, an unblemished male from the cattle, you will bring it to the door of the tent of witness, you will offer it as acceptable before the Lord, and you will place your hand upon the head of the victim, to make atonement for it as itself acceptable. And they will slay the calf before the Lord, and the sons of Aaron, the priests, will bring the blood, and they will pour the blood round about on the altar, which is at the doors of the tent of witness, and having flayed the holocaust, they will dismember it. And the sons of Aaron, the priests, will place it on the altar, and they will pile wood upon the fire, and the sons of Aaron, the priests, will pile the dismembered parts, and the head, and the fat, upon the wood on the fire that is upon the altar. But the entrails and the feet they will wash in water, and the victim is a sacrifice, an odor of sweetness to the Lord.[28]

The sacrificial victim is, then, as I said, a calf. But what it is that the figure expresses we will explain as best we can. It is that we approach God in strength of mind, vanquishing all worldly pleasure. Now the calf is a powerful animal. And they say that it is to be male. For what is feminine and easily crushed does not befit the character and manners of the saints; the mind of those who love virtue is always superior to weakness and to being swayed to what is shameful. It is to them that sacred Scripture speaks, and with full justice, when it exhorts them to spiritual fortitude: "Have courage, and let your heart be strengthened, all you who hope in the Lord."[29]

Now the victim, having been brought to the very doors of the holy tent, was slain before the Lord, as is written. For when we too come to the holy tent, to the Church, that is, then it is, then indeed, that we are granted watchful care from on high; and that the gift is worthy of acceptance is what blessed David confirms when he says, "Look at me and have mercy on me."[30] For he crowns with the highest honors whoever it is at whom he chooses to look. For to those of Israel's stock who definitely shun any concern about anything that is good, who are anxious to show that they have no worry that they offend him, and who in

28. Lv 1.2–9.   29. Ps 31.24.
30. Ps 86.16.

their wickedness give no heed to reverence for the law, the following words come: "When you stretch out your hands to me," he says, "I will turn my eyes from you."[31]

But he delights in those who love him, and attends to those who approach him through faith in Christ. For it is written, "The eyes of the Lord are upon the just, and his ears are open to their prayer."[32] The calf therefore was slain, and the blood poured upon the altar. But this very thing is done, I think, with respect to ourselves as well, in an intelligible and spiritual way, I mean. For by ceasing from our depraved endeavors, and putting "to death what is earthly in us: fornication, impurity, passion, and evil desire,"[33] we die to the world, and pass over to a holy and faultless life; and this is something worthy of all praise in the view of the God who loves virtue. The prophet David sings accordingly, "Precious in the sight of the Lord is the death of his holy ones."[34] The all-wise Paul, having undergone this glorious and admirable kind of dying, writes as follows: "Through the law I died to the law, that I might live for God. I have been crucified with Christ; it is no longer I who live, but the Christ in me who lives."[35] He wrote to others too, or rather to our own selves, as follows: "Do you not know that all of us who have been baptized into Christ were baptized into his death? We were buried therefore with him through baptism into his death, so that as Christ was raised from the dead through the Father's glory, we too might walk in newness of life."[36]

The calf's death, therefore, indicates the situation of having died to the world, while the pouring of the blood on the altar signifies the consecration of a holy soul, and suggests the sweet odor of a holy life, pleasing to God; for in the divinely inspired Scripture, blood is a figure of the soul or of life. It says, for instance, in Deuteronomy, "Take great care not to eat blood, for its blood is soul. The soul will not be eaten with the meat. Do not eat it; pour it out like water upon the ground."[37] It says, however, that "having flayed the holocaust, they will dismember it." Paul,

31. Is 1.15.
33. Col 3.5.
35. Gal 2.19.
37. Dt 12.23–24.

32. Ps 34.15.
34. Ps 116.15.
36. Rom 6.3, 4.

learned as he was in the law, understood this quite well when he wrote, "For the word of God is living and active, sharper than any two-edged sword, piercing to the division of soul and body, and of the thoughts of the heart, and before him no creature is hidden. But all are open and laid bare to his eyes."[38] For the removal of the hide suggests nudity. For nothing that is in us is hidden at all, nor can anything escape the notice of the divine mind in its purity; it reaches even unto "joints and marrow,"[39] which is, I think, the cutting up of the animal from limb to limb. For I hear it clearly spoken: "Who is it that hides counsel from me, and holds back words in his heart, but thinks to hide them from me?"[40] And elsewhere: "I am a God who is near, and not a God afar off; will anything be hidden from me?"[41] For he fills everything, and is not absent from anything.

He ordered in addition that the calf's innards and feet must be washed. And the Savior himself clarifies this when he says, "Blessed are the pure of heart, for they are the ones who will see God."[42] But the feet are figures of the journey in works, as it were, and of the path directed toward virtue, so to speak. For it is written, "Make paths direct for your feet, and straighten your ways."[43] For such feet are quite clean, and lead as well to the duty of executing with the greatest zeal the commandments of the Lord.

He then, in order to set those on earth upon paths so sacred, emptied himself,[44] and this even though he is God by nature, begotten ineffably from God the Father; this he did that he might fill human nature with supernal goods; he humbled himself, that he might grant us to be lifted on high; he was born of a woman in the flesh,[45] that we might be enriched in the rebirth through the Spirit unto newness of life through him. He receives from us a mother on earth, and has given us the Father in heaven. In short, what is ours has become his in the economic appropriation, in order that we too, in what is peculiarly his, might ascend with him and through him, gaining that thing by the kindness that is from him. He said, accordingly, "I am going to

38. Heb 4.12.
40. Jb 42.3.
42. Mt 5.8.
44. Cf. Phil 2.7.
39. Ibid.
41. Jer 23.23–24.
43. Cf. Prv 4.12.
45. Cf. Gal 4.4.

my Father and your Father, and my God and your God."[46] For we
have been named sons of God, having the Only-Begotten as firstborn and brother in the flesh. "The Lord is God, and has appeared to us," therefore, that he might "justify the circumcised
on the ground of their faith, and the uncircumcised through
their faith."[47]

4. For the law given through Moses was imposed,[48] not on everyone on earth, but only on those from Israel, and the family
from Abraham was called God's chosen portion. For it is written:
"When the Most High divided the nations, when he separated
the sons of Adam, he set the boundaries of the nations according to the number of God's angels, and the Lord's people became his portion, Israel the allotment of his inheritance."[49] As
the divinely inspired evangelist John says about the Son, however, "He came to his own, and his own did not receive him,"[50] and
this even though the Scriptures given through Moses announced
in advance the mystery concerning him with the greatest insistence, as did the holy prophets as well. But since they saw the
only-begotten Son of God when he became an incarnate human
being, they have been proven by the facts themselves to be ill-
disposed, contemptuous, and completely senseless. For they
sprang at him almost like dogs, barking at him, "Why is it that
you, a human being, make yourself God?"[51]

Now then, you who are so ready to rush off toward every absurdity: search the divinely inspired Scripture, busy yourself with
the words of the holy prophets, weigh what Moses wrote, the way
in which, according to what he proclaimed, the only-begotten
Word of God would shine forth upon the earth. For if it were as
one incorporeal and intangible, and, as God, beyond what we
could see, you might perhaps have made your disbelief specious
when you approached with the words, "Why is it that you, a human being, make yourself God?"[52] But since through the voice
of the holy prophets he announces in advance the mystery of the
Incarnation as venerable and profound, why do you not rather

46. Jn 20.17.   47. Ps 117.27 (LXX); Rom 3.29.
48. Reading Ἐπετέθειτο instead of Ἐπέθειτο.
49. Dt 32.8.   50. Jn 1.11.
51. Jn 10.33.   52. Ibid.

hasten straight in the direction that suits, and, steered toward the recognition of truth by the proper trains of thought, see from the very deeds performed,[53] or from the wonders accomplished, that he is God by nature, who has appeared from God the Father, even if he became flesh for us in the economy? See him, that is, vanquishing the very fetters of death, and injecting life into those already dead and decayed. See Satan, once terrible and invincible, fallen prone, for he lies beneath the feet of the saints. You will see him superior to every disease and infirmity, giving orders to the elements of the world in a Godlike manner, stifling the force of the wild winds, stilling the sea, rebuking the waves,[54] and effortlessly performing wonders of every sort. Be amazed at the multitude of believers beyond count, and behold thus accomplished what was sung by David: "All the nations that you have made will come and worship before you, Lord."[55]

Now it would be declared to those of the stock of Israel themselves that, once Christ shone forth, the worship that is according to the law, that which is, as it were, in shadows and figures, would lose its meaning, as God confirms by the voice of the saints when he once says, "For the children of Israel will abide many days without a king, without a ruler, without sacrifice, without an altar, without a priesthood, and without revelations."[56] And again, conversing with the multitude of believers, he says, "And it will come to pass when you multiply upon the land, says the Lord, in those days they will no longer say: 'the Ark of the Covenant of the Holy One of Israel.' It will not come to mind, nor will it be visited, nor will it be named, nor will it be done any more."[57]

Now it would have been completely reasonable for Israel, when it understood this, to honor Immanuel with its faith. But their behavior was completely opposite. Their opposition knew no bounds as they were marched off by their unholy temper toward every absurdity, and, their hearts scorched by the flames of envy, dared to slander Jesus when he worked miracles, shooting him down with the arrows[58] of jealousy. The enormity of their

---

53. Correcting δεομένων to δρωμένων.
54. Cf. Mt 8.18, 23–27; Mk 4.35–41; Lk 8.22–25.
55. Ps 86.9.   56. Hos 3.4.
57. Jer 3.16.   58. Correcting μέλεσι to βέλεσι.

madness reached the point where they even sought to kill the Author of life. And kill him they did, but he came back to life, and became "the first-fruits of those who have fallen asleep,"[59] and "the firstborn of the dead,"[60] that we too, having shaken off corruption and escaped the power of death, might say in the words of the prophet, "Death, where is your penalty? Hell, where is your sting?"[61] Having rendered death powerless, therefore, he ascended to God the Father in heaven; and he will come thus in due time in the glory befitting God, and will sit as judge. For he will render to each according to his work.[62] As those, therefore, who are to render an account of our own lives, let us hasten to lay claim to the glories of virtuousness, and let each of us adorn his own life with every virtue. Let us observe bodily chastity;[63] let us cease from every wicked, loathsome pleasure; let us be seen to be above dissension between brothers; let us restrain the impulses to anger; and may it be far from us to swear by God, and, as the all-wise Paul says, "Let your speech always be gracious, seasoned with salt, that it may please your listeners."[64] Let us show ourselves kind and compassionate toward the needy. Let us do good to orphans, let us support widows,[65] let us visit prisoners.[66] Let us remember the infirm, since we ourselves are in bodies. Let our loyalty to Christ, the Savior of all, be firm and unshaken. For thus it is, thus indeed, that we will celebrate the holy, all-pure feast. We begin holy Lent on the ninth of Phamenoth, and the week of the salvific Paschal feast on the fourteenth of Pharmuthi. We break the fast on the nineteenth of Pharmuthi, late in the evening, according to the gospel tradition. We celebrate the feast on the next day, the eve of Sunday, the twentieth of Pharmuthi,[67] adding thereto the seven weeks of holy Eastertide. For thus it is, thus indeed, that we will have words in which to luxuriate in Christ Jesus Our Lord, through whom and with whom be glory, honor, and power to the Father with the Holy Spirit, now and always, and for all ages. Amen.

59. 1 Cor 15.20.   60. Col 1.18.
61. Hos 13.14; 1 Cor 15.55.   62. Cf. 2 Cor 5.10.
63. Reading ἁγνείαν instead of εὐγένειαν.
64. Col 4.6.   65. Cf. Jas 1.27.
66. Cf. Mt 25.43.   67. April 15, 434.

FESTAL LETTER TWENTY-THREE

A.D. 435

PREFACE

THIS SHORT discourse, prepared by us once again, does not have any claim to distinction in language, that not being our purpose; it does, however, have the power to confer a necessary benefit on its audience, and guide it to the paths of well-being. It has been composed for no other reason than that. Let not the niceness of its diction or composition be put to any scrutiny, therefore, but let the writer's purpose be commended.

1. The blessed prophet David, striking the harmonious and melodious lyre of the Spirit, announced in advance the good news of the holy and all-pure feast of our Savior in the words, "Come, let us exult in the Lord."[1] And it seems to be that he used the word "come" wisely and skillfully. For he, as it were, calls those who are distant to come near, those who are departing from God, so to speak, in those aspects of their disposition, at least, in which it may happen that some people distance themselves from familiarity with God. What those aspects are we must investigate. One of them, and the first, is choosing to worship the creature instead of the Creator,[2] and to venerate the elements of the world. One may add unbelief to that, and for that matter wrong belief. One of these may be ascribed to those of the stock of Israel, and the other to the vain verbosity of the heresies. And we will add to these the common illness of everyone on earth, which is sin.

1. Ps 95.1.
2. Rom 1.25.

With a sacred, clarion proclamation, then, he bids those named to cease from what is shameful and choose to pass over to what is better: the pagans, fleeing with all speed from the darkness of the diabolical perversity inhabiting their minds, to hasten to the pure light of truth and acknowledge as God him who is truly and naturally the Creator and Lord of all; the Jews, by however tardy and grudging a recognition of the one announced in so many different ways through the law and prophets, to declare with the holy apostles, "You are the Christ, the Son of the living God";[3] those caught in the snares of the unholy heresies to abandon the tortuous arguments, so cunningly proposed by those who delight in malice, and, racing straight to the truth, to embrace the true doctrine that is free from error and elaboration; those sunk in the pits of sin to extricate themselves from the deadly trap and scrub away the Jewish defilement[4] infecting their minds, since God justifies the impious by mercy and kindness, through faith in Christ, that is. This is what the all-wise Paul taught to those who believed in him when he wrote, "Is God the God of the Jews only? Is he not the God of gentiles also? Yes, of gentiles also, since God is one; and he will justify the circumcised on the ground of their faith and the uncircumcised through their faith."[5]

Since, therefore, "praise befits the upright,"[6] as is written, let us free our souls from every stain and "come, let us exult in the Lord."[7] Now those who want to do this faultlessly must consider how and in what way one may exult in the Lord without failing of one's purpose. For one who yields to carnal pleasures, and refuses no form of depravity, but is determined to prefer above all else that behavior which is most detestable and irreligious, delighting as well in the distractions of the present life and the enjoyment of wealth, having never related exultation and joy to the Lord instead of to temporary pleasures, will not be a religious disciple, nor included in the choir of the saints. For it is written,

3. Mt 16.16.

4. For a discussion of Cyril's anti-Jewish rhetoric, see the introduction in FOTC 118, 16–26.

5. Rom 3.29–30.   6. Ps 33.1.

7. Ps 95.1.

"Praise is not seemly in the mouth of the sinner."[8] But one who is eager to glory in the courage displayed in continence, and to rise above all passion, as far as possible for human nature at least, may fairly claim as most fitting to him the office of offering praise [to God]. The all-wise Paul assists us too in this when he writes,

Now this I say and affirm in the Lord, that you must no longer walk as the gentiles do, in the futility of their minds, their understanding darkened, alienated from the life of Christ through the ignorance that is in them, through the blindness of their hearts. They have become callous and have given themselves up to licentiousness, greedy to practice every kind of impurity. That is not the way you learned Christ, if, that is, you heard about him and were taught in him, as the truth is in Jesus: that you must put off the old self, which belongs to your former manner of life and is corrupt through deceitful lusts, be renewed in the spirit of your minds, and put on the new self, created according to God in true justice and holiness.[9]

Who, then, is the old self? The one that "is corrupt through deceitful lusts." And the new one is the one who is transformed unto the newness of the life in Christ, the mind in that one now renewed and reveling in the bright beams of the true vision of God, and enjoying finally such health that it runs so quickly that it no longer falls prey to depraved propensities, but thirsts for, and chooses to be filled with, that alone by which it can find itself within all that is marvelous.

2. For the law was given through Moses to those of Israel's stock. But it was in shadows and figures,[10] those of that time[11] not being able yet to approach the perfect good, or the knowledge of the good that is perfect. They had need rather of elementary instruction, so that, by meditating on the truth that was still in figures, as it were, they might know rightly the end of the law, which is Christ. "For the end of the law and the prophets is Christ,"[12] as is written. How, or in what way? In that the law given

8. Sir 15.9.   9. Eph 4.17–24.
10. Cyril frequently referred to the Old Testament as a shadow and figure of the New. See the introduction in FOTC 118, 9–12.
11. Correcting τὸ τηνικάδε to τοῦ τηνικάδε.
12. Rom 10.4.

through Moses supports the gospel teachings, if it is understood by us spiritually. For it leads one to Christ's mystery. He himself is witness to this when he says, "If you believed Moses, you would believe me. For he wrote about me."[13] What, then, did Moses write? That Christ would come to assist not only those of the stock of Israel, but also those everywhere on earth under heaven, and every nation. For everyone belongs to God, inasmuch as he is Creator and Lord of all. He therefore ordered the lamb to be slain as a figure of him, but by the side of the altar facing north.[14] But for what reason? someone might fairly ask. What is the deep riddle of the sacrifice that is wrapped in such dark shadows of obscurity? This is how we will answer that person.

The land of the Jews, dear sir, is southernmost. Further north, above the sea, is that of the nations, they say. The lamb, therefore, was sacrificed by the former; but he does not consider the land of the nations [to be] contemptible. For he has turned to it, according to what is sung in the Psalms: "His eyes look upon the nations; let not them who provoke [him] be exalted in themselves. Bless our God, you nations."[15] For Israel offended and provoked [him] not a little; but that the nations were to be received into friendship with God through faith, when [Israel] had been rejected, may be seen without difficulty, if one chooses to scrutinize the words of the holy prophets. For it is written: "Rejoice and be glad, daughter Zion, for behold, I come, and I will dwell in your midst, says the Lord, and many nations will flee for refuge to the Lord on that day, and they will be a people for him, and I will dwell in your midst, and you will know that the Lord almighty has sent me to you."[16] And who is it that is sent, if not certainly Christ, who recreates the two peoples as one new human being, "breaking down the dividing wall of separation, abolishing the law of commandments and ordinances, and preaching peace to those far off and those near,"[17] to gentiles and Jews, that is? He said accordingly, "I have other sheep as well, which are not from this fold; and I must lead them, and there will be one flock, one shepherd."[18]

---

13. Jn 5.46.
14. Cf. Lv 1.10–11.
15. Ps 65.7–8.
16. Zec 2.10–11.
17. Eph 2.14–17.
18. Jn 10.16.

But I will try to prove from the divinely inspired Scriptures, as far as I can, and by means of what one might call one simple image of the fact, that those from Israel who were more learned in the law and intelligent recognized and honored the only-begotten Word of God when he became a human being and incarnate, while the others, swept away by their vain audacity, paid the penalty suiting them when they grieved the Savior and Redeemer of all by their disbelief; while the gentiles who were accepted were themselves to be called by faith. Let me note first that Scripture often calls Our Lord Jesus Christ "David," because he was born from his seed according to the flesh.

3. It is written, therefore, in the second Book of Kings,

And all the tribes of Israel came to David in Hebron, and said to him, "Behold, we are your bones and your flesh. Yesterday and the day before, when Saul was king over us, it was you who led Israel in and out. And the Lord said to you, 'You will shepherd my people Israel. You will be leader over Israel.'" And all the elders of Israel came to the king in Hebron. And the king made a covenant with them in Hebron before the Lord, and they anointed David king over Israel.[19]

You see how they acknowledge openly that they are his bones and flesh. For those who have come to faith in Christ are not ignorant of the manner of the economy with the flesh. No, they acknowledge that, being God by nature, he became a human being. For thus it was that they were his bones and flesh: because of their kinship in humanity. And they add that, even when Saul was king, he was the one leading and carrying Israel. For even before becoming a human being he was vested with power over all things in virtue of his essence, as God, weighing human affairs and preserving in being by his ineffable commands those firmly yoked to his decrees. And they firmly believe that it was by God the Father's good pleasure and will that he ruled over Israel, as they say, "You will shepherd my people Israel, and you will be their leader."[20] Thus says the divinely inspired Peter, "You are the Christ, the Son of the living God."[21] Nathanael likewise, to whom Christ himself offered that sincere, genuine testimony,

19. 2 Sm 5.1–3.   20. 2 Sm 5.2.
21. Mt 16.16.

says, "You are the Son of God, you are the king of Israel."[22] He himself says somewhere through the Psalmist's lyre, "I have been made king by him (by God the Father, obviously) on Zion, his holy mountain, declaring the ordinance of the Lord."[23]

Governance, however, was not something new to him; for since he is God by nature, enthroned with the One who begot him, he has all creation under his feet. But he is said to have been appointed king because he consented to set the yoke of his own rule from then on upon those then situated outside and under another. For Satan in his greed had seized those upon earth. But having professed the faith, they receive a covenant from him in Hebron. But what is "in Hebron"? The word means "union."[24] In Christ everything has become one, and what is above has been joined to what is below, and what is below to what is above. Those of Israel's stock, and those who formerly worshiped idols, have met together in unity and concord through faith.

We will learn as well, however, from the very passage that follows, that some of those from Israel who were haughtily stubborn perished evilly in their malice, as we read,

And David and his men went off to Jerusalem against the Jebusite that inhabited the land. And David was told, "You shall not enter here, for the lame and the blind have arisen, saying, 'David shall not enter here.'" And David took the stronghold of Zion, which is the city of David. And David said that day, "Let everyone who strikes a Jebusite use a dagger against the lame, the blind, and those who hate David's soul." That is why they will say, "The blind and the lame shall not enter the house of the Lord."[25]

Observe, then, observe the multitude of those who rise up against him. Now we remember Christ saying about the scribes and Pharisees, "Let them be; they are blind guides of the blind."[26] [He speaks] of them as well through David, "Sons not my own

---

22. Jn 1.49.   23. Cf. Ps 2.6.

24. Cyril did not know Hebrew, but in this case he is offering a plausible etymological reading of the root Hebrew verb *habar*, which can mean "unite" or "join." Cyril probably got this from Origen's *Homilies on Joshua* 18.3: "Hebron means 'union' or 'marriage'"; *Origen: Homilies on Joshua*, trans. Barbara J. Bruce, ed. Cynthia White, FOTC 105 (Washington, DC: The Catholic University of America Press, 2002), 166.

25. 2 Sm 5.6–8.   26. Mt 15.14.

have lied to me, sons not my own have grown old and hobbled away from the paths."[27] For those who did not know how to walk straight, nor even brought the intelligible and divine light into their minds and hearts, did not make Christ welcome, but fell by the dagger, that is, by the sword. For they have been consumed by war, their land going up in flames together with their temple of renown. But that the multitude of the gentiles came rushing in[28] and was accepted when those from Israel offended him, and that it claimed Christ as Lord and King, is shown once again by what is written. For it says, "Hiram, the king of Tyre, sent messengers to David, and cedar wood, and carpenters, and stone-masons, and they built a house for David."[29] For Hiram was a foreigner, and not from the multitude of the Jews. He was, rather, an idolater, from the herd of those in error. And yet he built a house for David. For the church of Christ has risen not in one place or region, but over all the earth, those, as it were, building it being those who once worshiped[30] the creature, and were wrapped in the devil's darkness, but who later believed and have been enlightened, and have held Christ, of David's seed according to the flesh, in boundless admiration.

Not only that, but consider the following. The house of David was built by Hiram, the foreigner. But it was the divinely inspired David who brought the ark up into it when it was with others, staying outside. "And he went," it says, "and brought up the ark of God from the house of Obededom into the city of David with gladness."[31] Now the ark containing the law given through Moses may be said to signify those under law and shadow. Once they were blind and lame, but when, after welcoming the faith, they worship him, then they too with us will be brought into David's house, Christ's that is. They will take the straight road to every virtue, and with sure and firm stride, as it were, they will charge down the path of the piety leading to him, the divinely inspired Paul calling out to them, "Lift your drooping hands, therefore,

27. Ps 17.45–46 (LXX).
28. Reading εἰσπέπαικε instead of εἰ παίπεκε.
29. 2 Sm 5.11.
30. Reading λελατρευκότων instead of λατρευόντων.
31. 2 Sm 6.12.

and straighten your weak knees, and make straight paths for your feet, so that what is lame may not be put out of joint, but rather be healed."[32]

For all of these reasons, then, as I said at the outset, "Come, let us exult in the Lord,"[33] celebrating the festival in his honor, that is. But tell me then, someone might ask me some time, how is it that this is thought or spoken of as a feast, when he suffered crucifixion and death in the flesh? This, dear sir, is how we shall answer. If indeed he had remained among the dead after letting his own body consort with death, no one should celebrate. But if it is true that, even though he did not have to suffer unless he chose to suffer, nor to fall into the hands of those who plotted against him, he yet "by God's grace tasted death for everyone,"[34] as the sacred minister of his mysteries says, so that he might trample death when raised from the dead, and might win incorruptibility for human nature in this way, having become "the firstborn of the dead"[35] and "the first-fruits of those who have fallen asleep,"[36] then this can only be the source of all good cheer for us. We who were caught in the snares of death because of the sin that held sway over us, hope for eternal life because of the firstborn from the dead, who is from us according to the flesh.

The Jews, then, crucified him, he for his part, as I said, allowing his own flesh to taste death according to the economy; but he came back to life, all but bidding farewell to the very bonds of death, and saying to those imprisoned, "Come out!"[37] and to those in darkness, "Show yourselves!"[38] Then, having shown himself to the holy apostles, and having told them they had to make disciples of those over all the earth, to initiate all the nations, "to baptize them in the name of the Father, and of the Son, and of the Holy Spirit, and to keep all that was commanded,"[39] and to[40] be zealous in practicing scrupulously the approved way of life, he ascended to God the Father in heaven while the holy angels glorified him and the multitude above acclaimed him. And he

32. Heb 12.12–13.
34. Heb 2.9.
36. 1 Cor 15.20.
38. Is 49.9.
40. Reading εὖ τε instead of οὔτε.

33. Ps 95.1.
35. Col 1.18.
37. Cf. Jn 11.43.
39. Mt 28.19.

will come in due time in the Father's glory, as he says himself, to render to each according to his works.[41] "For he will judge the earth in justice."[42]

4. Since, therefore, the Judge and Master and universal King of all is to come, "let us cleanse ourselves from every defilement of flesh and spirit. Let us make holiness perfect in the fear of God,"[43] let us live virtuously, and with our zeal for good works let us adorn our own souls, looking after widows, having compassion on orphans,[44] supporting those in need, offering all the assistance we can to those suffering from bodily infirmity, looking after those in prison,[45] and keeping our faith in him solid, firm, and completely unshaken. We begin holy Lent on the twenty-fourth of Mechir, and the week of the salvific Paschal feast on the twenty-ninth of Phamenoth. We break the fast on the fourth of Pharmuthi,[46] late in the evening, according to the gospel tradition. We celebrate the feast on the following day, the eve of Sunday, the fifth of Pharmuthi,[47] adding thereto the seven weeks of holy Eastertide. For thus it is, thus indeed, that we will luxuriate in the divine words in Christ Jesus Our Lord, through whom and with whom be honor, glory, and power to the Father with the Holy Spirit, now and always, and for endless ages. Amen.

41. Cf. Ps 62.12.
42. Ps 9.8.
43. 2 Cor 7.1.
44. Cf. Jas 1.27.
45. Cf. Mt 25.43.
46. Correcting φαμενωθί το φαρμουθί.
47. March 31, 435.

FESTAL LETTER TWENTY-FOUR

A.D. 436

WILL ONCE again use the words of blessed Paul, and say, "Rejoice in the Lord always; again I will say, Rejoice. Let all people know your forbearance."[1] For the time of our Savior's feast is arising for us. Come then, let us once again issue a challenge for this occasion, as it were, to those especially who value the most outstanding deeds of bravery, saying, "Behold, now is the acceptable time; behold, now is the day of salvation."[2] The divinely inspired David mentions it when he says, "This is the day that the Lord has made; let us exult and rejoice in it."[3] Now the day that is keenly desired and longed for,[4] and the acceptable time, is none other, say those who are Spirit-bearing, than the manifestation of the glory of Christ, the Savior of us all. Because of it, all those upon earth may rightly and fittingly be filled with the joy that is above all others. For through it we have obtained that through which it was possible for human nature to pass over to what [was] in the beginning, and to be transformed in a way, through a holy way of life, unto the one who is beyond all understanding, that it might rejoice and be glad when it possesses in itself abundantly the divine features through sanctification. Christ himself foretold through a prophet that his own advent would be the source for us of such good things when he said, "Rejoice and be glad, daughter Zion, for behold, I come, and I will dwell in your midst, says the Lord, and many nations shall flee for refuge to the Lord on that day, and they shall be his people, and they shall dwell in your midst,

---

1. Phil 4.5.   2. 2 Cor 6.2.
3. Ps 118.24.
4. The meaning of εὐέραστον is uncertain.

and you will know that the Lord almighty has sent me to you."[5] For since the Only-Begotten became a human being and was born in our likeness (for it is thus that we speak of him as having been sent by God the Father), we have to give ourselves over to leaping for joy. Let me explain the matter briefly.

2. There were for us countless reasons for weeping. For the winter of all wickedness and sin was an unbearable presence to those upon the whole earth, pressing fiercely and vehemently upon them, and raising up the death that had been brought in through the transgression committed in Adam as an invincible tyrant over those on earth. Sin in its many forms was a weapon and spear for him, and a redoubtable, impenetrable armor. For through it, [death] reigned over those on earth. Accordingly, as the prophet Isaiah says, "Hell widened its soul, and opened its mouth without ceasing."[6] For all of these reasons it is quite obvious that pleasure and joy had left us, and that there had sprung up in its place, as it were, the need to mourn, with an inescapable disaster looming over us that all but bedewed everyone's cheeks with the tears from their eyes. As the prophet Isaiah says, however, "Death has prevailed and devoured, but God has removed every tear from faces; the reproach of the people he has taken away from all the earth."[7] For sin has been undone and its lethal sting weakened. The evil that grew up from it has, as it were, been destroyed at its very root, which is death. Rejoicing was therefore not only not unfitting for us now, in a way, but suitable and logical. The giver and promoter of all our prosperity says, accordingly, "Rejoice and be glad, daughter Zion."[8]

It would be necessary, however, with the time of the feast so near, to wipe away first the filth from those who have fallen, and to scrub off the stains of soul and body. Having first welcomed fasting as the nurturer and solicitor of all that adorns us, accordingly, as is quite understandable, "let us run with perseverance the race that is set before us,"[9] as is written, decorating our minds with the glories of piety and returning to a completely pure and

5. Zec 2.14–15 (LXX).   6. Is 5.14.
7. Is 25.8.   8. Zec 2.14 (LXX).
9. Heb 12.1.

faultless life. For we remember what God, the Savior of all, said: "You will be holy, because I am holy."[10] Let us therefore be sanctified through a holy way of living and a life in full accordance with the law, wearing the splendor of virtue as a kind of garment most fair, befitting those at a feast, and thus appearing at last with confidence in the sight of the one who furnishes the festival for us. For "the eyes of the Lord are upon the just," it says, "and his ears unto their prayer."[11] When therefore he sees [us] resplendent, he will preserve our happiness unshaken; but if he does not see us thus disposed, he will not let us share in his munificence. This is what the parable in the Gospels clearly teaches. It says that someone furnished a wedding for his son, with quite a few invited. The groom entered after them to see those reclining. And when he noticed, mingling with those elegantly garbed, someone filthy, who did not have a robe befitting those celebrating the feast, he rebuked him with the words, "Friend, how did you get in here without a wedding garment?"[12] And he punished him in the severest manner.

But someone may ask: How, then, did he get in at all when he was so filthy? Those wearing robes in any way unbefitting the festival should never have been allowed in from the outset. Our answer is that the Savior calls everyone through faith; and he wants them to come to share in his supernal munificence, and everyone enters indiscriminately. For the grace that is through faith is upon us all. But those who add to faith the unblemished splendor that comes from good works, and who don the brightness of virtue as a kind of robe, will dine with the groom and partake of the holy and spiritual feast. But those who have added nothing to faith, but have remained in the filth of wickedness and retain the stain of their former guilt, so hard to wash out, will be finally and unconditionally dismissed from the sacred wedding. They will lament their negligence, for they had burst in without a wedding garment.

The fast is, accordingly, most beneficial, for it rubs away dirt, cleanses what is filthy, and with a little work removes us from eternal punishment. For it mortifies pleasure, checks the impetus of

10. Lv 11.45.   11. Ps 34.15–16.
12. Mt 22.12–13.

the desires for the shameful indulgence of the flesh, brings it into orderly behavior as though with rein and bit, produces lovers of every kind of virtuousness, and tames the law of sin in the members of the flesh as though it were a raging savage beast; in a word, it produces those who are concerned for everything that is good, and, by brightening the atmosphere of the mind, introduces the beloved light of the true vision of God, through which alone one may gain the correct and unobtainable knowledge of the sacred doctrines. It is something life-giving and beneficial, and certainly worth getting, if indeed the entrance into eternal life is desirable to us, and reckoned as worth more than all else.

3. That the preference to be firmly established in faith in Christ is the source of the life that is forever, is what he himself affirms when he speaks to God the Father in heaven: "And this is eternal life, that they know you, the only true God, and Jesus Christ, whom you have sent."[13] Faith, however, among those at least who are virtuous and have a heart that loves God, is something simple and true, and in no way perverse. It does not put up with very much in the way of inquiry or tests, for anything like inquisitiveness about that which has been received by faith does not go unpunished.

But this does not seem right to those who are, above all, inquisitive, and who know nothing of the truth, but like to boast of the unsound arguments they discover.[14] "Their paths are crooked, and their courses winding,"[15] as is written. "For they lead away whomever they may to ruin and destruction, diverting them from the straight way."[16] As the divinely inspired apostle writes, therefore, "Out with the evildoers, out with the dogs!"[17]—those who bark at the doctrines of truth, "speaking what is from their heart," as is written, "and not from the mouth of the Lord."[18] For no one will denounce Christ, the Savior of us all, and rashly oppose his glory, dragging it down into unseemliness, as it were, who has not

13. Jn 17.3.
14. The text needs emendation; εὑρὴ may perhaps be corrected to εὑρήματι or εὑρήμασι(ν) if it was meant to complement ἐπαυχεῖν, but this is not certain.
15. Prv 2.15.   16. Cf. 1 Tm 6.9.
17. Cf. Phil 3.2.   18. Jer 23.16.

first borne in himself the inventor and father of falsehood, the devil. For as the all-wise Paul writes, "No one says, 'Cursed be Jesus!' who is not in Beelzebul."[19] Those, therefore, who try to think and say this are to be rejected, those wretches who have brought upon themselves first, before others, an inescapable punishment. "Transgressing against the brothers as well, and wounding their weak conscience, they sin against Christ,"[20] and have weighed down their collar heavily,[21] as the prophet Jeremiah says.[22]

Those, however, whose minds and hearts abound in the intelligible and divine light will not be caught in their deceptions. They will in addition know[23] the virtue that suits each of the things to be done, and the way that is admirable. For one must, I think, proceed here circumspectly,[24] and prefer to reject untouched whatever in these things is wicked and forbidden, and contrary to sacred laws; but to regard as worthy of all zeal, and hasten to achieve with all vigor, whatever contributes to a distinctly admirable way of life. For it is written, "Woe to those who do the Lord's work carelessly!"[25] For just as armor that is resplendent[26] does not suffice to demonstrate the courage of those who wish for renown in battle, nor does the mere appearance of the ability to win, but they need as well the distinction resulting from their deeds; in the same way, I think, one will fail to achieve the beauty of virtue if one continues to be negligent and lack concern. What is needed, in my view, is to embrace the efforts to attain piety with all one's strength and enthusiasm. Those who do so will be worthy of all praise, and will win that glory which is truly exceptional, their reputation secure with God and men.

This is what Moses laid down for those of old through riddles and shadow, and Christ appeared in order to make manifest, being himself the truth. But since it was possible to find clearly neither what was to be done, because of the shadow of the world,

19. 1 Cor 12.3.
20. 1 Cor 8.12.
21. The meaning of στοιβαρῶς is uncertain.
22. Cf. Is 47.6.
23. Correcting Εἴσεται to Εἴσονται.
24. Correcting παρεσκεμμένως to περισκεμμένως.
25. Jer 48.10.
26. Reading παντευχίᾳ rather than πανευτυχίᾳ.

nor cleansing from transgressions—for the law has justified no one, but condemns transgressors rather than releasing them from the charges against them—God the Father provided for the salvation and life of us all. For knowing how we are made, and how easily the mind inherent in us is led to what is unlawful, he has given us the justification in faith in Christ which removes us from the former charges against us, cancels the condemnation of those already fallen, and transports them rather into the newness of life unfamiliar to those of old; for "in Christ everything is new, and the former things have passed away,"[27] as Paul says. The only-begotten Word of God, being God and Lord, has appeared to us, then. Appeared in what way? By lowering himself unto a voluntary emptying, and appearing unexpectedly as a human being on earth. For "he took of Abraham's seed, and became like his brothers and sisters in everything,"[28] apart from sin alone. For it was not possible for the divine and inviolate nature, which is beyond all comprehension, and above reason and wonder, to be caught in the snares of sin. "For he is the true light, and the darkness did not grasp him."[29]

But since he was seen to be a human being like us, in order that he not be regarded as only that by those who did not clearly understand the mystery concerning him, but that he be recognized[30] as the God of all together with that, he showed himself to us as connatural and consubstantial with the Father through the greatest possible number of miracles. He said, accordingly, "If I do not do my Father's works, do not believe me. But if I do them, then even if you do not believe me, believe my works."[31] For he accomplished what surpasses reason by his mere will and pleasure, "upholding all things by the word of power"[32] of the one who begot him, and escorted by the holy angels. For after the devil's temptation, "angels came and ministered to him."[33] And there were times when he rebuked creation; he said to the sea, for instance, "Peace! Be still!"[34] And he ordered the raging winds to be calm, when all the disciples as well crowned him with fit-

27. 2 Cor 5.17.　　　　　28. Heb 2.16–17.
29. Jn 1.10.
30. Correcting γνωρίζεται to γνωρίζηται.
31. Jn 10.37.　　　　　32. Heb 1.3.
33. Mt 4.11.　　　　　34. Mk 4.39.

ting acclamations, saying, "You are truly God's Son!"[35] For it was easy to see from the miracles, as I said, that he is truly God, and Son of the one who is God by nature.

Somehow, though, those from Israel, even though they had been educated through the law, and had read the writings of the holy prophets, were so addled that they did not know him; they rose up in bitter opposition to him, and slandered him wickedly with all that from which they might reasonably have been expected to derive considerable benefit, and to detect without difficulty the supernatural, boundless superiority of the power within him, as from the splendor of his deeds. But they went astray, falling into ungovernable savagery, as it were, and, kindled to uncontrollable anger in their stupidity, the wretches sprang at him, sometimes asking, "Why do you, a human being, make yourself God?" and sometimes slinging stones at him, and, finally, crucifying him, even though the law says clearly, "You shall not kill the innocent and the just."[36]

And for which crimes did they kill Jesus? They could not say. For[37] "he committed no sin; no guile was found on his lips,"[38] as is written. In refuting them as they babbled on, therefore, and seeking to calm them as they broke into furious anger, he said, "Which of you convicts me of sin? If I tell the truth, why do you not believe me?"[39] For he was not convicted by them of any wrongdoing at all, but the wretches condemned him to be put to death all the same when they were roused for no reason, as you may learn from what follows. For they brought him to Pilate and urged that he be crucified. Then when he said, "What has he done wrong?"[40] they charged Christ with the truth, although they did not interpret[41] correctly the nature of the reality. For they said, "He made himself God's Son."[42] The defender of the truth, however, will resist their loathsomeness and say, He did not make himself God's Son; he is such in truth. For that reality is believed by us to belong to him not as something external, nor as something acquired or received by adoption, but as that

35. Mt 14.33.
36. Ex 23.7.
37. Reading οὐ γὰρ.
38. 1 Pt 2.22; cf. Is 53.9.
39. Jn 8.46.
40. Mt 27.23.
41. Reading ἑρμηνεύοντες instead of ἑρμηνεύοντος.
42. Jn 19.7.

which he is by nature. For we ourselves are God's sons by adoption, in comparison to the one who is Son by nature, begotten from him. For if in fact there is no Son who is truly such, then upon whom are we, who are such by adoption, modeled? Whose features do we bear? Is there any possibility of imitation unless we say that the truth subsists? But they knew nothing whatever of the august and salvific proclamation of the Incarnation, nor did they understand what Moses said, nor for that matter the predictions about him made by the holy prophets through the Holy Spirit. For he was not a human being who made himself God's Son; the converse is true: being by nature and in truth Son of the God who is over all, he became a human being, in order that, by giving his own blood in exchange for the life of all, he might rescue all from both death and sin.

4. You have the matter portrayed in the law as on a tablet. Search in what Moses wrote, take away the shadow, enter for a little into what is innermost within the veil. Do not stay in the first tent, which stands where it does. Test the words of blessed Paul. What did he say to us about these things? "A tent was prepared, the first one, which is called 'holy.' But behind the second curtain stood a tent called the Holy of Holies."[43] He says, however, that "into the first tent go the priests when they perform the rites. But into the second, only the high priest, and not without blood, which he offers for himself and for the errors of the people. By this the Holy Spirit shows that the way into the sanctuary has not yet appeared[44] as long as the first tent is still standing."[45] The first tent, then, while standing, may signify the power of the rites in the law, rites which do not bring people into the Holy of Holies, nor send them within the veil. For to us alone has Christ opened this holy entrance, so deeply desired.

But since we have been brought all the way in, and the veil of the understanding of all of us has been removed, let us at last seek what has been hidden with eyes that are sharp and utterly pure, and, having rent the shadow of the law, as it were, let us see the truth. As I said, then, those from Israel, due to their over-

43. Heb 9.2–3.
44. Reading πεφανερῶσθαι instead of πεφανῶσθαι.
45. Heb 9.6–8.

whelming stupidity, thought that they could make life, Christ that is, to be overpowered by death itself. But they failed of their purpose, their attempt in vain, their efforts for naught; as the prophet David says, "They devise a stratagem which they cannot execute."[46] For the Savior and Lord of all, acting most skillfully—since he himself is wisdom entire[47]—made the devil's malicious arrangements into an occasion for salvation and life throughout the earth. For he had his very own flesh taste death, as is written, in order that, once he had shown that it was superior even to death through the resurrection from the dead, he might make available to those on earth the possibility of overcoming both death and decay.[48] For he himself became "the first-fruits of those who have fallen asleep,"[49] and "the firstborn from[50] the dead,"[51] in order that we too, having followed in his footsteps, might be raised with the first-fruits, and might follow the firstborn, all of us, who are called through him to kinship with him. For "to all who received him," it says, "he gave the power to become children of God."[52]

For the fact that in Christ's death we have become superior to decay is something that contentious Israel may learn from Moses' own writings. For they sacrificed the lamb in Egypt. Then, having devoured its meat and smeared the entrances or doorposts of the houses with the blood as well, they did not perish with the Egyptians. Now if there is nothing of what is mystical about this, if it is not a true account of the mystery concerning Christ, an account having its meaning written in shadows still, then why is it that the lamb, when slain, no longer saves anyone, shaming the destroyer with its own blood? For the power of divine mysteries will in no way be exhausted. As the all-wise Paul writes, "The gifts and the call of God are irrevocable."[53] It is therefore clear to all that in Christ, and in him alone, we have gained indestructibility. For he is life, and is life-giving; that consequently which in its own nature is corruptible may itself come to enjoy immunity from suffering, and that quite easily, by being enriched with the garment of incorruptibility, Christ. "For all of

---

46. Ps 20.12 (LXX).
47. Cf. 1 Cor 1.24.
48. Cf. Heb 2.9.
49. 1 Cor 15.20.
50. Reading ἐκ.
51. Col 1.18.
52. Jn 1.12.
53. Rom 11.29.

you who have been baptized into Christ," it says, "have put on Christ."[54] It would be most fitting for each of those baptized to say, in the words of the prophet, "Let my soul exult in the Lord. For he has clothed me in the robe of salvation, and the garment of joy."[55] For having put on, as I said, the garment of joy, which is Christ, we escape the clutches of death.

You have the mystery portrayed in the shadows of the law. For what was given through Moses were figures, and images of realities, containing somehow dimly yet the beauty of the truth. When those from Israel were dwelling in the desert, therefore, God gave them as bread the mystical manna. They gathered what sufficed for the day, as the divine law also bade. For what was kept over, and what was gathered that was superfluous and beyond what was needed, spoiled, and their labor was in vain, and was perhaps an occasion of punishment. Some of them did indeed keep it until the next day, as is written; "and Moses was irritated with them,"[56] it says, since they had spurned the divine ordinances.

That what is naturally corruptible may, however, come to be beyond corruption, as I said, and above the bounds of its own nature, if God wants, is something of which Moses has assured us. For thus it is written in Exodus, "And Moses said to Aaron, 'Take a golden jar, and put into it a full homer of manna. And you shall set it before God for your generations.' And Aaron set it aside before the testimony, to be kept."[57] For sacred Scripture always somehow takes gold as a symbol of the divine and inviolate nature, because of its pre-eminence among materials of its kind. When Christ, then, embraces us, as of course the golden jar does the manna, then we will remain imperishable, with God gazing upon us and, as it were, setting his eye upon all that has to do with us. For having been removed from his presence through the transgression in Adam, and placed out of his sight, as it were, we sank into corruption. For thus it is written through David, "When you have turned away your face, they shall be disturbed, and to their dust they shall return."[58]

But since we have been granted mercy and providential care by him, gaining that together with the other things in Christ, we

54. Gal 3.27.
55. Is 61.10.
56. Ex 16.20.
57. Ex 16.33–34.
58. Ps 104.29.

will be transformed unto life enduring, and we are under the eyes of the Father of all, and will remain to be kept, so that each of us may say in exultation, "O death, where is your victory? Hell, where is your sting?"[59] For the dead will rise, as the prophet says: "And those in the tombs shall be raised. For the dew from you is healing for them."[60] Since then we are to walk unto life enduring, and return to what was in the beginning, let us show ourselves worthy to be with Christ. For it is written, "You will be holy, for I am holy."[61] And as his disciple says, "If we invoke as Father him who judges impartially according to each person's deeds, let us conduct ourselves with fear during the time of our sojourn,"[62] knowing well that the things in this life are petty, wither quickly, are quite easily lost, and hurry past like shadows, while those which are from God are firm and well established, remaining forever with those who have gotten them. While the opportunity presents itself, then, let us rub away the defilements of flesh and soul. Let us set ourselves to behave virtuously, let us take on an attitude of compassion. Let us be distressed at the misery of the needy. Let us show sympathy to those in trouble, let us be compassionate to orphans, let us support widows,[63] let us share the tears of those in trouble, let us show mercy to those in prison,[64] and let us share the suffering of those in infirmity, reviving them with every possible form of care, and, in a word, practicing every form of virtue. For thus it is, thus indeed, that we will fast purely, beginning holy Lent on the thirteenth of Phamenoth, and the week of the salvific Paschal feast on the eighteenth of Pharmuthi. We break the fast on the twenty-third of Pharmuthi, late in the evening, according to the gospel precept. We celebrate the feast on the next day, the eve of Sunday, the twenty-fourth of Pharmuthi,[65] adding thereafter the seven weeks of holy Eastertide, in order that, by following the right way of life, we may luxuriate in the holy words in Christ Jesus Our Lord, through whom and with whom be honor and glory to the Father with the Holy Spirit for all ages. Amen.

59. 1 Cor 15.55. Cf. Hos 13.14.
60. Cf. Is 26.19.
61. Lv 11.45.
62. 1 Pt 1.17.
63. Cf. Jas 1.27.
64. Cf. Mt 25.43.
65. April 19, 436.

FESTAL LETTER TWENTY-FIVE

A.D. 437

COME ONCE again, since the season urges us, to fulfill what is laid down in the divine ordinances; let us take up the sacred trumpet, as it were, and shout out the words, "Exult, you just, in the Lord!"[1] For the only-begotten Word of God proclaims to us a spiritual feast: the power of the economy according to the flesh. He is in no way inferior to the pre-eminence of the one who begot him, but is equal in glory and power, as consubstantial with him. Having appeared from him naturally, conspicuous for his indistinguishable identity—for "he is the stamp of his substance and the reflection of his glory,"[2] according to the testimony of the sacred Scriptures—he lowered himself to our condition.[3] He did not lose the dignities naturally his, but assumed flesh and blood, in order that we in turn might become sharers in the divine nature, gaining spiritually by being joined to him. For we are joined to him through faith, sanctification, and the virtuous deeds that make for piety. This is feast and festival, and the source of the good things that lead to what is above all else. The very Savior and Lord of all, accordingly, suggests the significance of his Advent through a sort of example when he says, "The kingdom of heaven is like a king who gave a marriage feast for his son, and sent his servants to call those who were invited, saying, 'Behold, I have made ready my dinner; my oxen and my fatlings are killed, and everything is ready; come to the marriage feast.'"[4] He has us compare what is distinctive of the spiritual to a wedding on the corporal level. For it is written, "He who is joined to the Lord is one spirit."[5]

1. Ps 33.1.
2. Cf. Wis 7.26; Heb 1.3.
3. Cf. Phil 2.8.
4. Mt 22.2–3.
5. 1 Cor 6.17.

146

Since, therefore, God the Father gathers us together for the spiritual banquet, and sets before us a most bounteous dinner of the divine teachings—for we have heard him say, "My oxen and my fatlings are killed"[6]—come, let us take up the robe befitting those at the feast, put on the crown of virtue in its many forms, woven, as it were, of the flowers of spring, and, with him as our chorus leader in whose honor we keep festival, let us sing, "Come, let us exult in the Lord; let us shout aloud to God our Savior!"[7] There are those who exult in the world, fattening their flesh on an extravagance of foods. They indulge themselves in other ways as well, yielding to unbridled impulses that lead to every form of immorality. But self-indulgence ends in punishment, bringing with it finally a cruel and inescapable penalty for love of the flesh. For "those who sow in the flesh will reap corruption from the flesh."[8]

The divinely inspired prophet Amos as well is moved by love to shed a tear for those who are accustomed to live in this way; he says, "They sleep on beds of ivory, live wantonly on their couches, eat kids from the flocks and sucking calves out of the herds, and clap to the sound of music as though thinking it something abiding, rather than fleeting. They drink strained wine and anoint themselves with the best ointment, and have suffered nothing at Joseph's calamity. For this reason they will now be captives when the rule of the powerful begins."[9] Do you see how a life without value ends? He says that they will be captives, those who think that the fleeting, transitory things of the present life are fixed and abiding, and who value a life that is at odds with the sacred laws.

But we who are in Christ are led away from such shameful endeavors and vain distractions by the words of his disciple: "Children, do not love the world or what is in the world."[10] It is written further: "Do you not know that friendship with the world is enmity with God? Whoever wishes to be a friend of the world makes himself an enemy of God."[11] Leaving behind worldly desires, then, distancing ourselves as far as possible from every concern,

6. Mt. 22.4.   7. Ps 95.1.
8. Gal 6.8.   9. Am 6.4–7.
10. 1 Jn 2.15.   11. Jas 4.4.

and opposing ourselves to profane love of the flesh, we will be holy disciples, and, keeping the all-pure festival for Christ, we will hear the words: "Come, you blessed of my Father, inherit the kingdom prepared for you from the foundation of the world."[12] The works of the saints are, then, trustworthy, and beyond all speech and wonder. For the all-wise Paul writes further: "Eye has not seen, and ear has not heard, nor has it occurred to the human heart, what God has prepared for those who love him."[13]

But we who might enjoy the gifts from God abundantly, once we have chosen the life that is uncontaminated with that which is worse, refuse to act generously and provoke the divine and undefiled mind to anger. Now the Divine is by nature free from anger. But it does not put up with those with unrestrained inclinations toward doing what is wicked. That is what, in its regard, we call "anger," using language appropriate to our own selves. For it would be impossible otherwise to signify to certain folk that which is above us, that which is within the divine, ineffable nature. When, therefore, he sees us inclined to indolence, sunk into the swamp of profligacy, and quite indifferent to the need to be educated by his laws and to hasten to perform every fair and good deed, he then at last imitates those who are the best fathers, and raises the whip. For it would have been easy for some folk to have been presumptuous enough even to suppose that he was not in fact good, if he did not check their indolence by suitable measures, and frighten into better courses those whose purpose it was to depart from what was most beneficial to them, to follow the unbridled propensities of their minds right onto the rocks, as it were, and to leap senselessly into the pit of perdition. We will find the most holy Paul writing along these lines: "If you are disciplined, God is treating you as sons. For what son is there whom his father does not discipline?" And he adds, "Besides this, we have carnal fathers to discipline us, and we respected them. Shall we not all the more be subject to the Father of spirits and live? For they disciplined us for a short time as they pleased, but he disciplines us for our good, that we may share his holiness. All discipline at the time seems painful rather than

12. Mt 25.34.
13. Is 64.4; 1 Cor 2.9.

pleasant. But later it bears the peaceful fruit of justice to those who have been trained by it."[14]

God, then, disciplines out of love. But even here one may be utterly astonished at the surpassing clemency that is in him. For even though he could without hindrance inflict punishment proportionate to our faults, he somehow tempers his measures to the weakness of those who transgress; he disturbs rather than really punishes. So that we may show that what we say is not false, however, let us present as evidence the things that came upon those of old in their times. Let us relate what happened to them. For holy Scripture says somewhere, "These things happened to them symbolically. But they were written for our instruction, upon whom the end of the ages has come."[15]

2. The God of all, therefore, gave to those from Israel through Moses the law[16] which served as a guide to all that is praiseworthy and was able to crown with the glory of justice those who were utterly determined to carry it out as they should. But they failed of its purpose, and, having rejected their instructor, brought upon themselves the charge of disobedience. And God charged them with law-breaking, speaking as follows through Hosea the prophet, "Hear the word of the Lord, children of Israel, for the Lord has a dispute with the inhabitants of the land, because there is no truth, nor mercy, nor knowledge of God in the land. Jealousy,[17] rather, falsehood, murder, theft, and adultery abound in the land, and blood is mixed with blood. For this reason the land will mourn with all of those who dwell in it."[18] And he says further through Micah, "They fell to pondering troubles, and working evils upon their beds, and with the day they carried them out. It was because they did not raise their hands to God. And they coveted fields, plundered orphans, lorded it over houses, and plundered a man and his house, a man and his inheritance."[19] And another prophet cried out, "Woe to them who join house to house, and add field[20] to field, that they may take away something

---

14. Heb 7.7–11.   15. 1 Cor 10.11.

16. Reading νόμον instead of νόμου.

17. Reading φθόνος instead of φόνος.

18. Hos 4.1–3.   19. Mi 2.1–2.

20. Reading ἀγρόν instead of ἀγρούς.

of their neighbor's! Will you dwell alone upon the land? For these things have reached the ears of the Lord of hosts."[21]

For those whose greed is uncontrollable, who are always eager to add to their property not what is theirs but what is their neighbors', are perhaps striving to be the only inhabitants in the land, without putting up with neighbors. This is what some of those of old did, paying no attention to the divine laws. But the Law-giver and Judge was so kindly that he called to repentance, through Jeremiah, those who had caused grief, saying, "Turn to me, house of Israel, says the Lord, and I will not harden my face against you, for I am merciful, says the Lord, and I will not be angry[22] with you forever. Nevertheless, know your iniquity, that you have sinned against the Lord your God."[23]

But since, as the facts themselves reveal, they were deeply infected with contumacy, soiled with ineradicable impurity, and quite given over to wickedness, he finally loosed upon them the brunt of his anger. He hardly did so immoderately, however; he tempered his wrath with mercy. For he said, "And I will give you dullness of teeth in all your cities, and lack of bread in all your places, and you have not returned to me, says the Lord. And I have withheld from you the rain three months before the harvest, and I will rain upon one city, and on another city I will not rain. One part will be rained upon. And the part on which I will not rain will be dried up, and two and three cities will be gathered together to one city to drink water, and they will not be satisfied. And not even so have you returned to me, says the Lord. I struck you with burning and with blight. You multiplied your gardens, your vineyards, and your fig groves, and the caterpillar devoured your olive-groves; and not even so have you returned to me, says the Lord."[24]

Notice how he did not hurl fire from on high upon those who had sinned. Rather, he disturbed them by reducing their necessities of life. He did so as a kind of warning to give up their lawless ways and embrace what was better. And that those to whom these things happened were being punished for their transgressions is what the God of all shows when he says, "Because you

21. Is 5.8–9.
23. Jer 3.12–13.
22. Reading μηνιῶ instead of μηνίων.
24. Am 4.6–9.

have ignored me, says the Lord, your ways and your pursuits have done this to you."[25]

Thus it was for them. Now let us consider what concerns our own selves, if you please. For sometimes the rains fail, even though it is the season when they should be abundant, and grief follows the disappearance of the river-waters; in vain are the plowman's labors. The fields bear no crops, the ripe fruit perishes, and bodily illnesses appear that are severe and incurable. Thence arise the sounds of grieving, lamentation, and wailing, and cities and villages lose much of their population. Come, therefore, let us follow the example of those physicians who are most skilled, and consider diligently what may be the reason for such misfortune.

3. It has, as a sort of evil root, sin in its many forms. It is from there that our hardships spring, and no one who has reached a sound understanding of our situation from a study of what happened to those of old, would assign any other origin to those things that are naturally vexatious. Let certain people explain how it is that, when we have a Master who is good and abounding in generosity, we do not find ourselves enjoying great and lasting prosperity. What is it that prevents this, makes us part company with what we most enjoy, exposes us to grief, and forces[26] us into familiarity with what is so repulsive? Well, it is clear to everyone, I think, that we suffer from a shortage of what we most desire, and this when it is not just at one time that we offend, and have neglected[27] the sacred precepts. For he is incomparably gentle and kind to the human race, as can easily be seen even from this. For he extends his hand to rescue those who have fallen. But he bids them betake themselves to what is better when he says, "Seek what is good, and not what is evil, that you may live, and thus the Lord God will be with you."[28] And to those who choose to do this he promises an abundant supply of good things when he says, "And it will happen in that day, says the

25. Jer 4.17–18.
26. Correcting ἀναγκάζειν το ἀναγκάζον.
27. Correcting καταρᾳθυμήσαντες το καταρραθυμήσαντες.
28. Am 5.14.

Lord, that I will listen to the heaven, and the heaven will listen to the earth, and the earth will listen to the grain, the wine, and the oil."[29] And he says further through another prophet, "'Try me in this,' says the Lord almighty, 'and see if I do not open for you the torrents of heaven, and pour out upon you my blessing, until you are satisfied,'"[30] until, that is, you are filled and have enough.

Therefore, "come, let us adore and fall down before him," as the divinely inspired Psalmist says, "and let us weep before the Lord who made us."[31] Let us ask from him the oil of kindness. Let us move our hearts to where they want to do what is good, for negligence is quite inexcusable. For the Son himself has appeared to us from heaven, and we have received as our instructor him who illuminates the heavens and brightens the very powers above. For the only-begotten Word of God, being God by nature, and having appeared from God, partook of blood and flesh, and became a human being in the economy, that he might render us wise in every virtue, well-versed in the best endeavors, and well established in the true knowledge of God.

For since the divine nature is completely invisible and unseen, possessing a glory that is unapproachable (for "he dwells in light inaccessible," as Paul says),[32] he put on our flesh and consorted with human beings,[33] fitting himself to the dimensions of humanity while remaining what he was, and initiated the sacred revelations among those of Israel's stock, for theirs were the promises. But when they became hard and intractable, and, quite refractory, ended by crucifying him, he abandoned them and bestowed himself upon the multitudes of the gentiles. For it was not impossible for him not to undergo suffering. But since he promised us the resurrection of the dead, he made suffering bearable, in order that, having trodden upon death and risen from the dead, he might become "the first-fruits of those who have fallen asleep,"[34] and we might firmly believe that he will destroy corruption and drive off death's attack upon our bodies, since, being God, he is by nature Life and the Giver of life.

29. Hos 2.21–22.
30. Mal 3.10.
31. Ps 95.6.
32. 1 Tm 6.16.
33. Cf. Bar 3.37.
34. 1 Cor 15.20.

And in order that he might also render the upward path accessible and easy to travel for us, he ascended to God the Father in the heavens, with the flesh united to him that had been endowed with a soul intellectually. And he is in the Father's glory, having all creation under his feet,[35] beyond everything that is made, his lordship something that is natural. And having an unshakeable kingship, he will come in due time "in the Father's glory with the holy angels, to render to each according to his deeds,"[36] as is written. Since, then, we are to render our account to the Judge, let us purify ourselves of every stain of flesh and spirit. Let us practice every form of virtuousness. Let us love justice, charity, continence, mutual affection, and love for the poor. Let us have compassion for orphans, wipe away the widow's tear,[37] and visit those in prison.[38] Let us support the infirm with our thoughtfulness, and, in a word, let us be eager to practice every form of virtue. For thus it is, thus indeed, that we will be pleasing to Christ, the Savior of us all.

We begin holy Lent on the fifth of Phamenoth, and the week of the salvific Paschal feast on the tenth of Pharmuthi, breaking our fast on the fifteenth of that month, late on the eve of Saturday, according to the gospel tradition. We celebrate the feast on the next day, the eve of Sunday, the sixteenth of Pharmuthi,[39] adding thereafter the seven weeks of holy Eastertide, so that we may be granted the companionship of the saints when we have passed this season correctly and piously, in Christ Jesus our Lord, through whom and with whom be glory to God the Father with the Holy Spirit for all ages. Amen. "Greet one another with a holy kiss. The brothers and sisters with me greet you."[40]

35. Cf. 1 Cor 15.27.   36. Mt 16.27.
37. Cf. Jas 1.27.   38. Cf. Mt 25.43.
39. April 11, 437.

40. The first sentence is from several places in Paul (Rom 16.16; 2 Cor 13.12); the second sentence, Phil 4.21.

FESTAL LETTER TWENTY-SIX

A.D. 438

 SHALL ONCE again use the words of the all-wise Paul, and say to those justified in faith and sanctified in the Spirit, "Rejoice in the Lord always; again I say, rejoice. May your forbearance be known to everyone."[1] It is a time for perseverance and patience, a time for exceptional deeds of courage and for spiritual bravery. For the time of our holy feast is once again upon us, preceded of course by the holy and all-pure fast, that by leading a life that is approved and of good repute, and scouring away the stains of sin through good works, we may present ourselves to Christ holy and blameless, all but crying out, "It is good for me to cleave to God!"[2]

Now I think that anyone who understands what the Gospel means by living well, and who longs for the gifts prepared for the saints, must progress toward them when fully roused by desires not to be gainsaid, casting from their minds as far as possible all ineffectual and profitless reluctance, and having bidden farewell, as it were, to senseless idleness. For those inclined to laziness cannot attain those things that are excellent or possess that which comes from God. For virtue likes exertion, and, having been allotted a path leading to itself that is rough and steep, renders it smooth and easy to those who have chosen to suffer, drawing and calling to itself that breed which is most naturally inclined to be highly esteemed, while repelling, as it were, those who are lazy and unaggressive. For it loves the elect, as I said. Such is the way the prophet speaks: "Straight are the ways of the Lord, and the just will walk in them, but the impious will weaken in them."[3]

1. Phil 4.4–5. 2. Ps 73.28.
3. Hos 14.9.

154

As the divinely inspired Paul writes, therefore, "Finally, be strong in the Lord and in the strength of his might. Put on the whole armor of God, that you may be able to stand against the devil's wiles. For we are not contending against blood and flesh, but against the principalities, against the powers, against the world rulers of this present darkness, against the spiritual forces of evil in the heavenly places. Therefore take the whole armor of God, that you may be able to withstand on the evil day, and, having done all, to stand."[4] For[5] just as those who live in a city next to and bordering on barbarian territory, if they are used to warfare and well versed in battle strategy, worry very little about their incursions, but if they cannot accept the need to exert themselves and bravely resist those bent on plunder, they will fall a ready prey to them; so also it is with those who are practiced in the law of life. Their enemies are near; and there are relentless hordes of them. But those who are firm in mind, and have strapped on as a kind of armor their piety for Christ and marched forth to meet them, will prove superior to their perversity. Having kept their hearts sound and unwounded, they will strike up songs of thanksgiving to Christ, saying, "In you will we push down our enemies, and in your name will we bring to naught those that rise up against us."[6]

With Christ therefore supporting those who love him, and rousing to a holy courage those who are determined to follow the gospel precepts, let us vanquish the flesh, and let us cleanse ourselves of every stain. Let us remember what sacred Scripture says: "But fornication and all impurity or covetousness must not even be named among you, as befits saints. Let there be no filthiness, nor silly talk, nor levity, which are not fitting; let there rather be thanksgiving. Be sure of this: that no fornicator, or impure person, or one that is covetous (that is, an idolater), has any inheritance in the kingdom of Christ and of God."[7] And further: "So then, brothers and sisters, we are debtors, not to the flesh, to live according to the flesh—for if you live according to

4. Eph 6.10–13.

5. The meaning of this sentence is clear, but the first clause needs repair; we suggest correcting ἡ βαρβάρων χώρα to οἱ βαρβάρων χώρᾳ and translating.

6. Ps 44.5.

7. Eph 5.3–5.

the flesh you will die, but if by the Spirit you put to death the deeds of the body, you will live. For all who are led by the Spirit of God are sons of God."[8] For we are being numbered among God's children, having brought into our minds the beauty of that way of life which is in Christ, and being quite transformed by our efforts to achieve piety in his regard.

When, therefore, the marks of the uncontaminated nature shine forth for us, and we have been numbered among God's children and been enriched with that brotherhood that is with Christ, the supreme King of all, consecrating our own life to him, let us remain cheerful. For thus we will be real banqueters, with him as the presider at our festival. And if it is most fitting for those keeping festival to be splendidly attired, then it is not unsuitable, in my opinion, to be adorned with the glories of the virtues. On the contrary, it most befits those wanting to enter the Holy of Holies, where Christ "has gone as a forerunner on our behalf,"[9] as the divinely inspired Paul says.

Now the Holy of Holies is, we say, the modes of mystical perfection. Into them no one may enter, or draw near to God, in disposition and sanctification that is, who has not first thoroughly washed away all the filth coming from sin and carnal desires. Now since the revelations given to those of old in figures through the all-wise Moses were written "for our instruction,"[10] and are images of spiritual realities that are most profitable, let us present to our listeners what is written in Exodus as evidence and clear proof of what we have just said. It runs as follows: "And the Lord spoke to Moses, saying, 'Make for yourself a brazen laver, and a brazen base for it, for washing. And you will put it between the tent of witness and the altar. And you will pour water into it. And Aaron and his sons will wash their hands and their feet with water when they go into the tent of witness, lest they die. And it will be for them a perpetual statute, for him and for his generations after him.'"[11]

2. Notice how the divine law commands those who want to enter the Holy of Holies to wash first. And those who fail to do

---

8. Rom 8.12–14.   9. Heb 6.20.
10. Cf. 1 Cor 10.11.   11. Ex 30.17–21.

so it threatens with capital punishment. For it is not possible, by no means is it possible, for us to draw near to God with unwashed feet, or we will always harm ourselves utterly when we suffer the supreme penalty. "For what fellowship has light with darkness," as is written. "Or what has a believer in common with an unbeliever? What accord has Christ with Belial?"[12] The purification, therefore, that we ought to undergo: is it to be regarded as bodily rather than spiritual? But how could there be any doubt that it is spiritual, when God says clearly through Jeremiah, "Wash your heart clean of evil, that you may be saved, Jerusalem."[13]

And countless are the varieties of acts of wickedness: sorcery, sensuality, avarice, slander, perjury, and deceit. But what most provokes the God of all to anger is the habit of filling one's thoughts with what is unlawful in being easily swayed and perverse, and of diverting the mind to what is discreditable, and the decision some people make to follow spirits of error while giving no admission to the accurate, genuine faith. For there are those, there are indeed, who twist the meaning of the truth to their own private views, and accumulate a heap of specious ideas derived from the common herd. To them we must say, "How long will you attack a man, and all of you kill?"[14] And I will add to what I have said that some who have received the name of Christian are no longer in essence and truth what they are said to be, but love the ways of apostasy and have gone over to the deceptions of the demons. Perhaps they think that even he[15] who knows what is hidden does not notice them. We will also say to them, "Understand now, you senseless ones among the people; and you fools, come to your senses at last! He that planted the ear, does he not hear? Or he that fashioned the eye, does he not perceive?"[16] Nothing may escape the notice of the one who has implanted in our own selves as well the very power to hear, to say nothing of seeing.

12. 2 Cor 6.14–15.   13. Jer 4.14.

14. Ps 62.3.

15. Here there is something missing; the Latin translation supplies "... who knows what is hidden does not notice them," and we have included it.

16. Ps 93.8–9.

For sacred Scripture makes it clear that failing to be devoted to God exclusively, and having an intellect that is lame and ineffectual, and this even after one has faith, so that one thinks and says that there are other gods after the one who is so by nature and in truth, is to bring upon oneself ruin and destruction, and the deepest anger from, I say, the God who judges justly. For it was from the law given through Moses that Israel learned piety toward God. For listen to it said clearly, "The Lord your God is one Lord."[17] And, "You shall not make for yourself an image, or a likeness of anything whatever that is in the heaven above or in the earth below or in the waters beneath the earth."[18] But they, although they should have taken the ordinances with the utmost seriousness, made no attempt to behave sincerely; spurning what was naturally of the greatest benefit, they brought punishment down upon their own heads. For they went over to the unholy business of setting a border around the ineffable, supernatural glory of the God who governs all things, and, fashioning images, they set them up in their hearths, as though they were able to escape the notice of the all-seeing God.

What resulted for them, however, was unbearable punishment. This is what the divinely inspired prophet Ezekiel says:

And he brought me to the porch of the court, and I looked and saw one hole in the wall, and he said to me, "Son of man,"[19] "dig in the wall." And I dug in the wall and behold, one door. And he said to me, "Go in and see the evil iniquities that these folk are practicing here today." And I went in and looked, and saw every likeness of reptiles, and vain abominations of beasts. And I saw all the idols of Israel portrayed upon it round about. And there were seven men from the elders of the house of Israel, and Jaazaniah the son of Shaphan was standing in their midst before them. And each held his censer in his hand, and the smoke of the incense went up. And he said to me, "Have you seen, son of man? Is it a small matter to the house of Israel to practice the iniquities which they have practiced here? Because they have filled the land with iniquity, and have turned to provoking me to anger, I will deal with them in wrath; my eye will not spare, nor will I have any mercy."[20]

17. Dt 6.4.   18. Dt 5.8.

19. Something seems to be missing here: ὤρυξον seems to be an amalgamation of ὄρυξον and ὤρυξα. The Latin translation supplies "dig in the wall," and we have added it.

20. Ezek 8.7–11, 17–18.

For it could not be that those who were so inconstant in outlook, so wantonly wicked and rebellious, would not be wholly and completely subjected to the very worst of punishments. For they perished, a prey to the swords of their foes. And they were enslaved to their enemies, every possible calamity befalling them. When, therefore, some people waver and disdain the ways of practicing genuine love for God in their attachment to the worship of idols, then God himself allows countries and cities to be swept by the attacks of their foes, and to experience all that is grievous. One must certainly, then, worship him, keeping one's faith unshaken and one's mind firmly fixed upon his honor and glory. Of those otherwise disposed the prophet Isaiah will say truly, "This people honors me with its lips, but their heart is far from me."[21] And they will hear Christ saying, "Woe to you, for you are like whitened sepulchers, which outwardly seem beautiful to people, but within are full of the bones of the dead and all uncleanness."[22] For if one chooses to live well, the tendency to adorn oneself with that elegance that is simply and only external, while considering love for God of quite little importance, will hardly suffice for obtaining what is essential to true honor. On the contrary, one must embrace with the most ardent zeal the determination to possess true piety and faith unshaken. It is through this, I think, that one may abound in the grace of the supernal benevolence. For the divine nature in its love of virtue rejoices in those so disposed.

But if, in following the unbridled propensities of the mind toward what is unlawful, we proceed to outrage his supreme glory by ascribing it to those who are not gods, "saying to wood, 'It is you who are my father,' and to stone, 'It is you who begot me,'"[23] and worshiping the elements of the world, and this after receiving the name of Christians, then there is no one of those once initiated among us who would doubt that we will draw down upon ourselves wholly and absolutely a harsh and inescapable punishment. It is to us that the sacred words are spoken: "It is a fearful thing to fall into the hands of the living God."[24] Even the laws in vogue among us punish those trained to be soldiers if

21. Is 29.13.   22. Mt 23.27.
23. Jer 2.27.   24. Heb 10.31.

they neglect the loyalty owed to those in power and side with the barbarians. And if they throw away their shields, they will certainly throw away their lives with them. The word we have just heard, therefore, tells us that if we are divided in mind, and prefer to be shaken down from what is better and true to what is shameful and loathsome, we are inviting war; and they add that this brings about the loss of our other good things as well. For God does not send down rain, so that people can neither till nor engage in the work of husbandry, and cities together with country districts wither away from hunger and thirst.

Now observe with me once again how Israel suffered in this way. It was a time when Ahab was king of the tribes that were in Samaria. Completely neglecting reverence and love for God, he sacrificed to idols. And since the multitude subject to him consisted of commoners easily led astray, it contemned him who by nature and in truth is the one God, and they were at once infected with the same madness as was their ruler, even though they had the law that had been established and were being thoroughly educated, through Moses' commandment, about what was chiefly advantageous to them. But since, as the divinely inspired David says, "They all went aside, together they became useless,"[25] the prophet Elijah, coming into their midst, shared the indignation of the all-ruling God at the contempt shown him. He threatened famine and infertility, and a dearth of the blessing from above. He said, "As the Lord of hosts, the God of Israel, lives, in whose presence I stand, there shall not be dews and rain these years, except through the word of my mouth."[26] And when he had said this, those in the fields could not till, nor could husbandry yield anything, nor could grass be seen covering the earth in season (for he who gives the necessities of life did not rain upon the earth). No, the mountains thirsted, and the plains, once[27] flourishing and fruitful, all but mourned their barrenness. And what was the result? The attacks of famine became so severe[28] that some of those in Samaria were reduced to the point

25. Ps 14.3.
26. 1 Kgs 17.1.
27. Reading πρίν instead of πρός.
28. Reading κατατρέχοντος instead of κατατρέχοντες.

where women laid hold even of their own children, completely disregarding the laws of nature, and spurned the rules governing affection. The prophet Jeremiah, accordingly, distressed at those so afflicted, says, "The hands of tenderhearted women have seized their children."[29]

How then did the whole business end? How did they rid themselves of this fearful and inexorable punishment? Those who deceive Israel were removed from its midst, the prophet Elijah sentencing them to death. And when the truth shone forth once again, and those who had lapsed into the worship of demons acknowledged the one who by nature is God, then the merciful God once again gave them the good things of his bounty, and food in abundance.

3. One must, therefore, as I have just been saying, reject what is shameful and adhere to what is of honest worth, beautify oneself with the adornments in which one may take pride, apply oneself with full sincerity to living the life that excels in its subjection to the law, and preserve in addition a sincerity in faith and firm love of the God who is beyond all. "He did not spare his own Son," as the all-wise Paul wrote, "but gave him up for us all, that he might also give us all things with him."[30] For the one who is beyond all thought, the one through whom all things were brought into being, the Word who sprang from the very substance of God the Father, "did not count equality with God a thing to be grasped," as is written, but underwent his voluntary emptying, "and took the form of a slave."[31] And for what reason? The blessed Paul testifies to this when he says, "Since, therefore, the children share in flesh and blood, he himself likewise partook of the same; that through death he might destroy the one who has the power of death, that is, the devil, and deliver all those who through the fear of death were subject to slavery throughout life. For surely it is not with angels that he is concerned, but with Abraham's seed. Hence he had to be made like his brothers and sisters in every way, that he might become a merciful and faithful high priest in God's service, to make expia-

29. Lam 4.10.   30. Rom 8.32.
31. Phil 2.6–7.

tion for the sins of the people."[32] For the Creator of all created everything in incorruption, as is written, "and the productions of the world are healthful."[33] And "hell had no realm upon earth";[34] "but by the devil's envy death entered the world."[35]

But it was necessary that God's plan of old for us not be defeated by the envy of the twisted serpent, prince of evil, but be revealed as mightier than his perversity. For this reason the only-begotten Word of God, being life by nature and himself giving life to all things, lowered himself, as I said, into our situation, and put on our flesh, that he might become the flesh of life and might finally blunt the sting of the perversity of the devil, who had devised sin as the mother of death for those on earth. The only-begotten Word of God, accordingly, achieved two things at once when he became a human being. He drove off from human bodies the death which he himself had not made but which had supervened because of sin. And he also became a merciful high priest for us all.

But how is this? someone may ask. Being God, was he not merciful even before becoming as we are? But how could the one who by essence is the offspring of the highest nature not be regarded, understandably, as good by nature, or rather as the good in himself? Surely he did not proceed from not being good by nature to a transformation in which he became such? But surely someone who maintained this view would merit ridicule. No, he became a merciful high priest[36] for us in the following way. The law that was declared through angels to those from Israel prescribed punishment, immediate punishment, for those lapsing into transgressions. The all-wise Paul witnesses to this when he writes, "Someone who has violated the law of Moses dies without mercy at the testimony of two or three witnesses."[37] Those, then, who exercised the priesthood according to the law were quite unconcerned about showing mercy to any of those whose negligence in behavior came to light.

But Christ became a merciful high priest. For he did not de-

---

32. Heb 2.14–17.
33. Correcting σωτήριον to σωτήριοι, after Wis 1.14.
34. Wis 1.14.   35. Wis 2.24.
36. Cf. Heb 2.17.   37. Heb 10.28.

mand[38] that those on earth be punished for their sins; no, he justified everyone by grace and mercy, and in addition rendered them spiritual worshipers, presenting us with the clear and evident truth: the true manner of living well. That, at least, is quite well indicated through what is declared in the Gospels; and it was not by censuring Moses' commandments or by overthrowing the ancient precepts that he showed the truth; no, what he did was to remove the shadow of the letter of the law and change figures into that adoration and worship which is in spirit[39] and in truth.[40] He accordingly said clearly, "Do not think that I have come to abolish the law or the prophets; I have not come to abolish but to fulfill them. For I tell you, not an iota, not a dot, will pass from the law until all comes to pass."[41] For to bring the figures into the truth is not to abolish them but to complete them, if in fact it is true that when painters paint a variety of colors over their first outlines, they do not destroy them, but bring them rather into clearer view.[42] That is the sort of thing Christ has done in refining the crudeness of the figures unto the truth.

But Israel did not understand the mystery, even though the law and the prophets foretold it in many ways, and Christ himself, the Savior of us all, offered convincing evidence, through his countless miracles, to lead people to realize that, although he appeared as a human being for us in the economy, he is nonetheless, even as such, that which he was, and that is God. He accordingly accomplished things beyond the measure of human capabilities, and engaged in mighty works divine in character, raising the dead from their tombs when they were already stinking and decayed,[43] sending light into the blind as Creator,[44] rebuking impure spirits with authority,[45] and freeing lepers from

38. Reading ἐξήτησεν instead of ἐζήτησε.

39. Reading πνεύματι instead of Πατρί.

40. Cf. Jn 4.23–24. This was a favorite text of Cyril and aided his thinking about the integration of the Old and New Testaments. See the introduction in FOTC 118, p. 20.

41. Mt 5.17–18.

42. It is difficult to translate σκιαῖς in a way that brings out the dual meaning of "shadow" as well as "outline," which is what Cyril had in mind here.

43. Cf. Jn 11.39.   44. Cf. Jn 9.1–12.

45. Cf. Lk 9.42.

their disease with a command.[46] And he accomplished other things, too, which exalt him beyond all speech and wonder. He said accordingly, "If I do not do my Father's works, do not believe me. But if I do them, then even if you do not believe me, believe my works."[47]

But Israel was so stubborn and unyielding, arrogant, headstrong, and completely intractable, that even though they should have believed him unhesitatingly, they remained haughty in spirit, reviled him, subjected him to unceasing insults, and finally crucified him. He could, then, have chosen not to suffer and to escape from the snares of the Jews effortlessly. For how could God be caught and overcome by human force? But since suffering was the undoing of death and decay (for the body of life could not be conquered by death), he willingly allowed the audacity of the Jews to prevail for a little, so that by coming to grips with death and rising from the dead, he might become a way and a door for human nature, that it in turn might at least have the possibility of overcoming it [death]. For he came back to life and ascended to the Father, the first-fruit of a humanity renewed unto incorruption.[48] Having presented himself on our behalf, as it were, he is seated with the one who begot him. And he will come in due time in the Father's glory, that he may judge the earth. "For we must all appear before the judgment seat of Christ, so that each one may receive good or evil, according to what he has done in the body."[49]

4. As people, therefore, who are to present ourselves in due time to the universal judge, let us adorn our souls with every good work, let us renounce sensuality and corporal defilement, let us adopt an attitude of compassion, let us assist those in need, let us take pity on orphans, let us support widows,[50] let us visit the sick and those in prison and in need.[51] Let us practice eventemperedness, showing patience, mildness, and gentleness, and, in short, every kind of virtue. For thus will we celebrate the holy and all-pure feast, beginning holy Lent on the twenti-

46. Cf. Lk 17.11–19.
47. Jn 10.37–38.
48. Cf. 1 Cor 15.42.
49. 2 Cor 5.10.
50. Cf. Jas 1.27.
51. Cf. Mt 25.43.

eth of Mechir, and the week of the salvific Paschal feast on the twenty-fifth of Phamenoth. We cease fasting on the thirtieth of Phamenoth, late on the eve of Saturday, according to the gospel tradition. We celebrate the feast on the next day, the eve of Sunday, the first of Pharmuthi,[52] adding thereafter the seven weeks of holy Eastertide, in order that, considering the time of relaxation to be like an image of the repose enjoyed by the saints in heaven, we may be granted their company in Christ Jesus our Lord, through whom and with whom be glory to God the Father with the Holy Spirit for all ages. Amen.

52. March 27, 438.

FESTAL LETTER TWENTY-SEVEN

A.D. 439

NCE AGAIN the bright company of the saints gathers us to the customary banquet and the all-pure feast, and bids[1] us send up songs of thanksgiving to Christ, the Savior of all, saying, "The Lord has reigned, let the earth exult."[2] For through the all-wise Moses Israel was of old liberated from servitude in Egypt. The other nations from east to west, and everywhere else, being subject to the unholy tyrant, Satan, and held under the yoke of sin, which they could not shake off, were filled with the deepest misery. But now Christ has come to reign over the earth under heaven, crying out to those who believe in him, "Take my yoke upon you!"[3] And so, having been freed from the loathsomeness of the wicked rebel demon, and having fled from the cruel ranks of the demons,[4] they all but cry out to each other in their eagerness, "Let us break their fetters and cast from us their yoke!"[5] Filled to the brim with joy, they bestow upon the author of their salvation and the promoter of their entire weal the acclamations befitting him, saying, in the words of the divinely inspired David, "Sing to the Lord a new song, for the Lord has done marvels; his right hand has saved him, and his holy arm."[6]

Now they call the Son the right hand and the arm of God the Father. For through him he brought everything into existence, and he is the strength of everything, since he is in fact the Lord of powers as well. This great and admirable arm of God the Father, beyond all thought and understanding, saved for him,

1. Reading ἐπιτάττει instead of ἐπιτάττειν.
2. Ps 97.1.   3. Mt 11.29.
4. Reading δαιμονίων instead of δαιμόνων.
5. Ps 2.3.   6. Ps 96.1.

namely, the people upon earth. For through him we have been reconciled, and he himself has presented us to God the Father. He accordingly said clearly, "No one comes to the Father except through me."[7] As those, therefore, who are joined together through him and in him, and have become sharers in the divine nature,[8] been called the people of God, and received the splendid dignity of adoption, let us recall what one of the holy apostles wrote: "If you invoke as Father him who judges each one impartially according to his deeds, conduct yourselves with fear throughout the time of your exile. You know that you were freed from the futile ways inherited from your fathers, not with perishable things such as silver and gold, but with the precious blood of Christ, like that of a lamb without blemish or spot."[9] We must therefore bend the neck of our understanding to the will of this reality, and hasten to follow his salvific precepts, doing so with the greatest alacrity, "cleansing ourselves from every stain of flesh and spirit, and making holiness perfect in the fear of God."[10]

2. Every season is, then, suited for the virtuous, for the purpose at least of undertaking the duty of entering upon the holy and blameless path of justice, and bearing straight for those endeavors which are the best, racing toward them with all sails spread, as it were. But what is most of all fitting, at least for the present time, is, I think, to decorate oneself with the propensities for this, if in fact it is necessary, once we have been adorned[11] as far as may be, and made splendid with the glories of virtue, to push within the sacred curtains and to appear thus to the all-pure God. To miss this occasion, and the things that come from it, is not without penalty for those who do so, in my view at least. For who would praise a husbandman if, when his business is tilling, and the season affords him the opportunity to do so, he is seen taking his ease and preferring a leisure that is unproductive and without recompense? Or who would not find sailors completely blameworthy if, after paying no heed to the winds when

7. Jn 14.6.
8. Cf. 2 Pt 1.4.
9. 1 Pt 1.17–19.
10. 2 Cor 7.1.
11. Reading δι[ακ]εκοσμημένους instead of διεσμιγμένους.

they are fair, and then missing their chance when it is now too
late for navigation, they decide with complete lack of sense to
seek that of which their stupidity has deprived them?

Therefore, as the all-wise Paul writes, "While we have the opportunity, let us do good to all."[12] For laziness is dangerous, and
one would not miss the truth by deciding that it is the thing that
completely and absolutely brings ruin in its train. For it is written: "Woe to those who do the Lord's work carelessly."[13] Now if a
penalty is incurred even when work is done, if it is not carried
out diligently, what kind of punishment will be suffered by those
who simply refuse to do it at all? Come then, as one of the Savior's disciples said accordingly, "Having girt up the loins of your
minds, in sobriety set your hopes fully upon the grace that is
coming to you at the revelation of Jesus Christ, not being conformed to the passions of your former ignorance, but as he who
called you is holy, be holy yourselves in all your conduct. For it is
written, 'You will be holy, for I am holy.'"[14]

For just as those who are closest in the confidence of earthly
rulers, and held in the greatest trust, are those who are the bold-
est and most experienced in battle, and who have achieved the
greatest renown in warfare, so also those who will be called
friends of the all-pure God, and close to the way he is disposed
to them, are not those who are held fast by carnal impurities, or
involved in the distractions of this present life, but those who distinguish themselves by the splendor of their virtues. What, then,
could possibly be better than this, for those at least who are sensible? Someone may say: earthly wealth. But this is insecure, by
no means firmly established; it slips away quite readily. It comes
tumbling down at times, and someone who was the object of
envy yesterday or the day before may be observed reduced to the
most abject misery.

Let us say, though, that it is securely established. Very well; but
in what way does it contribute to the salvation of the soul for
those who possess it? Is it not the occasion for drunken carousals
and profligate displays of exquisitely laden tables, which often
harm the very stomachs of the gastronomes? But someone may

12. Gal 6.10.   13. Jer 48.10.
14. 1 Pt 1.13–16; Lv 11.45.

say: Are you then chastising elegance in dress and the honors that go with wealth? And if there are those who have quantities stored up of valuable things of the kind that are praised to the skies, will you criticize that too, and say that it is nothing? I would reply that the divinely inspired John says enough when he cries, "Do not love the world, nor what is in the world. For all that is in the world is the lust of the flesh and the lust of the eyes and the pride of life."[15] Observe now the supreme philosophical skill with which this sharer in the Holy Spirit limits the enjoyment of what is earthly to three things. For the lusts of the flesh are surfeits of the stomach, and the seasonings of delicacies, and the impurity that then always somehow follows. And the pleasures and delights of the eyes are the variegated spectacle of clothing, and the lovely color and brightness of the materials, which wealth loves. But the pride of life is the name he gives to the preeminence in dignities, and exaltation[16] in honor and glory.

3. Come, then, now that we have measured the length of life, and are fixing the eye of our mind on the end to which each person comes, let us examine where it is that the rich find themselves at the last. One of the saints has said, "Naked I came forth from my mother's womb, and naked I shall go back."[17] Another writes, "We have brought nothing into the world, and we can take nothing out."[18] When the time of life is so contracted and short, and one cannot possess riches when it is over, is it not obviously better to apply ourselves to sacred endeavors, and to have wealth that cannot be lost accumulated in heaven, "where neither moth nor rust consumes, nor do thieves break in and steal,"[19] as the Savior[20] says?

Come then, let us adduce another short passage from the gospel writings that will not be without benefit to our listeners. Christ says somewhere,

The land of a rich man brought forth plentifully; and he said to himself, "What shall I do? I will pull down my barns and build larger ones,

15. 1 Jn 2.15–16.
16. Reading ἡρμένον instead of εἰρημένον.
17. Jb 1.21.   18. 1 Tm 6.7.
19. Mt 6.20.
20. Reading Σωτῆρος instead of Κυρίου.

and I will say to my soul, 'Soul, you have goods stored up for many years; eat, drink, be merry.'" But God said to him, "You fool! This night they will require your soul of you; and the things you have prepared, whose will they be?"[21]

What an incredible thing! Hemmed in by his riches, he is weighed down ever more by his concern for so many things. "What shall I do?" he asks. On his wealth he bestows the sort of language suitable to poverty. Where shall I pile the good things I have? The rich man abounds in possessions. Fields thick with crops have rejoiced him, those who reap them are past counting, and perhaps he also has a vineyard laden with grapes that fills his vats to the brim with wine. So then, my dear rich friend, you have everything in abundance.

Except for life. Who will get what you have made ready? You would have done better[22] "to do judgment and right justice,"[23] as the prophet says. Now right justice is, in our view, compassion for one's brothers and sisters, love, mutual affection, the mercy that triumphs over the unending fire. For the God of all honors the merciful, and accords all reverence to those who bear the marks of his gentleness in their own souls. For he says, "Be merciful, as your heavenly Father is merciful."[24] For just as a father who loves his child rejoices in the one he has begotten when he sees his own form shining forth beautifully in his offspring, and is sometimes incited for that reason to an even deeper love, so also our God, when in his love of virtue he sees a soul that has received the form of the goodness inherent in him, makes sure that that is not without profit to it. He crowns it with hope and grace, and, removing it from all stain, raises it to the company of the saints. For he says, "Alms and fair dealing cleanse away sins."[25]

Let our mind therefore be merciful, tender, and gracious, lest, having been harsh toward our brothers and sisters, we hear God saying from that most fearsome tribunal, "You wicked servant! Should you not have had mercy on your fellow servant, as I had mercy on you?"[26] And let us acquire in addition the other

21. Lk 12.16–20.
22. Reading ἤν σε.
23. Cf. Jer 33.15.
24. Lk 6.36.
25. Tb 12.9.
26. Mt 18.32–33.

virtues: justice, continence, mildness, humility, patience, and even-temperedness. For just as those practiced in painting on tablets embellish their work with a variety of colors to express a clarity of beauty in it, so also whoever is an artist in piety will by all means please the eyes of the godhead by being adorned not with one virtue but with as many as possible. For he [God] sees into the mind and heart, and searches out the beauty of the brave deeds in souls.[27]

4. These things of which we have now spoken to you we have drawn as from the divine wellsprings and evangelical revelations, through which we have been expertly guided toward every one of those brave deeds that are the best of all, even though formerly we had completely sunk into the mire of wickedness and been dominated by the attacks of the passions. For there was among us "no one who did good, no one at all, but all had gone out of the way; together they had become good for nothing,"[28] as the Psalmist says.

Those in so wretched a state were shown mercy by the Creator, who brought all things into existence, and did not make the earth in vain, as the prophet says, but that it might be inhabited. Now the all-wise Paul explains just how he showed mercy when he says, "In many and varied ways God spoke of old to our fathers by the prophets; but in these last days he has spoken to us by a Son, whom he appointed the heir of all things, through whom also he fashioned the ages. He is the reflection of the glory and the stamp of his substance, upholding all things by the word of his power. When he had made purification of our sins, he sat down at the right hand of the throne of the majesty on high, having become as far superior to the angels as the name he has obtained is more excellent than theirs."[29]

For the Word who has shone forth in a way that is ineffable and beyond understanding from God the Father's substance, the Word who is the image, the reflection of his glory, the co-eternal Son who is enthroned with him and distinguished by equality and similarity with him in every respect, became flesh, a

27. Cf. Heb 4.12.   28. Ps 14.1–3; cf. Rom 3.12.
29. Heb 1.1–4.

complete human being that is. He did not surrender what he
was (that would have been impossible, since his being by nature
immutable and unalterable is intrinsic to him), but rather he assumed flesh and blood and took the form of a slave as his own,[30]
he who by nature and in truth is free, since he had sprung from
the substance that is above all others and in which dwells sovereign might over all things (for the things that have been brought
from non-being into subsistent existence are inferior to their
Maker's glory). He became a human being; he did not come
into a human being or join to himself a human being, as some
have rashly claimed;[31] and in this he remained nonetheless[32] in
the pre-eminence of his own divinity. He dwelt all the same with
those on earth, as one of us,[33] for it was impossible for anyone to
encounter the naked, untempered glory of the divinity. As he
says, "No one will see my face and live."[34] For if no one can take
in the brightness of the sun's rays with the eyes of the body
(since the power of the sense of sight is thwarted and overcome
by the overwhelming assault of the light), how would it be possible to bear it if the Son came to us in the naked glory of his divinity?

Thoroughly cloaking, therefore, in a way known to himself,
the unapproachable light of the brightness that is in him, and
adopting the likeness that is ours, he shared our poverty, in order that, by subjecting himself to his own laws, he might persuade us to hasten straight to every sort of virtue, and might join
to himself in holiness those who had washed away the filth of
their former faults by the grace that comes from him. The legis-
lation he gave was, accordingly, not as were the laws given by Moses formerly, which were in figures and shadows. Having rather
fashioned those toward greater clarity, and brought over to the
truth what had been declared in riddle to those of old, he called
people to the grace that is through faith, and Israel indeed before the others. They should have accepted the benefit of the

30. Cf. Phil 2.7.
31. This Christological expression is consistent with Cyril's mature position.
Compare the *First Letter of Succensus* 5–6, in Wickham, 75.
32. Reading οὐδέν instead of οὐδείς.
33. Bar 3.37.
34. Ex 33.20. Omitting ἰδεῖν.

messages brought by him, decided to follow him, seized the chance to share in the gifts coming from him, and by their faith honored him who for our sake became as we are, but the wretches did none of this; they sprang at him like wild beasts, directing at him from their addled minds language vile and senseless. They said, "It is not for a good work that we stone you, but for blasphemy; because you, a human being, make yourself God."[35]

Senseless Pharisee, were you not persuaded when one of the holy prophets said, "Behold, the Virgin will conceive and bear a son, and they will call his name Immanuel"? That means "God with us."[36] For he came to be with us when he appeared as we are. Do you not know what the divinely inspired David cried, "The God of gods, the Lord, has spoken, and called the earth from the rising of the sun unto its setting. Out of Zion comes the excellence of his beauty. God will come openly, our God, and will not keep silence"?[37]

How, then, could it be possible for God to be seen openly by those on earth, when he is not visible? He was, nonetheless, seen with the flesh when he shone forth in divine fashion, even though he is true God (since he is beyond all things), and, having been born in the last times of the age, he did not come to be in a human being, as I said, nor for that matter did he join a human being to himself, as some folk like to babble. No, he really became a human being in a way unexpected and beyond understanding, and came to be in the form of a slave; the one who fills everything lowered himself unto an emptying; the one who is the highest of all, unto our lowliness; the one who is above every Principality and Dominion, and all Thrones and Powers, and every name that can be named,[38] into the limits of humanity. Do not therefore say accusingly, "Why is it that you, a human being, make yourself God?"[39] On the contrary, accept the extraordinary miracle, and with the highest acclamations applaud the economy, so skillfully devised, saying, "How is it then that you who by nature are God became a human being while remaining God?"

For it was possible then to find the prophet Habakkuk shar-

35. Jn 10.33.
36. Mt 1.23; cf. Is 7.14.
37. Ps 50.1–3.
38. Cf. Eph 1.21.
39. Jn 10.33.

ing what he had to say on the occasion of this miracle, and indeed crying out, "Lord, I heard the report of you and was afraid. I considered your deeds and was amazed."[40] Know, therefore, that even if you see a human being in poverty like yours, for your sake, he is nonetheless God even so, begotten from the Father divinely and from the holy Virgin according to the flesh, in a strange and unexpected way.[41] For even his birth according to the flesh had to be seen as novel. While he was calling people to salvation, therefore, some of the unbelievers hurled stones, censure, and abuse at him. In addition to this, as though giving quite free rein to their arrogance and audacious acts against him, and proceeding to the ultimate wickedness, they "crucified the Lord of glory."[42] It was the leaders of the Jewish gang who set the snare. For they thought that by removing the heir from their midst they themselves would still govern the assembly. But they erred, and what happened to them was the converse of what they had expected. For those evil folk perished evilly, having done no harm to the one crucified. He came back to life not long after, having bidden farewell to the bonds of death, opened the gates of hell to the spirits below,[43] and refashioned the nature of man in himself, the first of all, unto incorruptibility and life enduring.

For just as he died in Adam, the punishment in his case spreading to the whole race that is from him, so also we have lived in Christ. For since he is a second root of humanity, and a second Adam, he will transmit his own life to all human beings. And just as there was in Adam the nature on which was inflicted the curse and the penalty of death, so also there is again in Christ the human nature blessed by God the Father and through him rendered superior to death. He suffered willingly in his own flesh, accordingly, and has remained impassible in his own nature.[44] But his, we say, is the suffering. For it was his own body that has suffered, that he might release us from suffering. For

40. Hab 3.2.
41. Cf. the *Second Letter to Nestorius* 2, in Wickham, 5.
42. 1 Cor 2.8.
43. Cf. 1 Pt 3.19.
44. Cf. the *Second Letter to Succensus* 2, in Wickham, 87.

"by his bruise we have been healed,"[45] as is written. And having trodden upon death's power, won life for the world, destroyed the power of sin, and overthrown the prince of this age and the evil powers in him, he ascended to God the Father in the heavens and is resplendent upon the highest throne, having returned to that innate glory that attends him always, and he will come in due time to judge the living and dead, for "he will render to each according to his works."[46]

5. Since, then, we are to stand in due time before the divine bench, where there will be an exacting scrutiny of each person's life, "let us cleanse ourselves of every defilement of flesh and spirit, and make holiness perfect in the fear of God,"[47] adding to this mercy towards the needy, love for the brothers and sisters, and, in a word, everything suitable to be the boast of saints. We begin holy Lent on the tenth of Phamenoth, and the week of the holy and salvific Paschal feast on the fifteenth of Pharmuthi. We break the fast on the twentieth of Pharmuthi, late in the evening, according to the gospel tradition. We celebrate the feast on the next day, the eve of Sunday, the twenty-first of Pharmuthi,[48] adding thereafter the seven weeks of holy Eastertide, in order that, in considering this season itself to be a kind of image of the repose of the saints in heaven, we may be granted their company, in Christ Jesus Our Lord, through whom and with whom be glory to God the Father with the Holy Spirit, now and always and for all ages. Amen.

45. Is 53.5.
47. 2 Cor 7.1.
46. Mt 16.27.
48. April 16, 439.

FESTAL LETTER TWENTY-EIGHT

A.D. 440

UR TOPIC is proper morals; it concerns the conduct befitting those who are devoted to good order and who are concerned to live a life of excellence. But the author's purpose is not to seek praise, but to benefit those who are gathered.

1. The blessed prophets, who transmitted to us the messages of God from on high, speak as follows somewhere: "How beautiful are the feet of those who bring good news!"[1] For it is not unpleasant to tell people that they are to come into immediate possession of what they are hoping to receive, when that is something to their good.[2] For when it is already present and visible, it will fill us with good cheer, but when delayed, it grieves those who long for it. And since that is how you view the matter, and you prefer the participation in spiritual goods to everything else, come, let us announce to you in addition that our holy and all-pure festival is soon to shine forth, hurrying to overtake our speech. It will come, then, it will come, and it will not be long. And there arises for us, as a kind of harbinger of the holiness befitting it, the season of fasting, which all but cries aloud in the words of one of the holy apostles, "Who is wise and understanding among you? By his good life let him show his works!"[3] For what we must do, once we have washed away the filth of all wickedness, risen above shameful pleasure, and left behind that life which is condemned by the

---

1. Is 52.7; cf. Na 1.15; Rom 10.15.
2. παρέσονται is probably to be corrected to πάρεσται.
3. Jas 3.13.

laws, is to persevere in laying claim to every virtue, and, in distinguishing ourselves by the splendor of our excellence of life, present ourselves in purity to the God who is over all.

He spoke to us accordingly through the all-wise Moses: "Three times a year all your males shall appear before the Lord your God, in the place which the Lord your God shall choose: on the Feast of Unleavened Bread, and on the Feast of Weeks, and on the Feast of Booths."[4] One would not, then, treat lightly the favor of being watched over from on high, but would rather regard it as of the highest value, if one were sound of mind. For what could be of equal worth to being watched over by God? The divinely inspired David sings, accordingly, "Look upon me and take pity on me!"[5] For being pitied must always follow those accorded the favor of being watched over.

If we in fact examine the reasons for each of the feasts, we shall gather a store of ideas not without benefit for our own souls. The reason for the Feast of Unleavened Bread is the redemption of those of the stock of Israel, when, having sacrificed the lamb as a figure of Christ in the first month of the Hebrew calendar, eating unleavened bread with it, they cast aside the yoke of the Egyptian perversity, and, throwing off the bitter, intolerable burden of their unaccustomed servitude, they left behind their labors in earth and bricks, and, fleeing from the tyrant's cruelty, hastened to worship God in freedom of heart. The festival of Weeks is held at the harvest of wheat and other crops, with which the husbandmen rejoice to fill the threshing-floor, gathering the yield of the fields and enjoying a most generous recompense for their labors at the plow. The third feast, that having to do with tents, the Feast of Booths, was celebrated with joy at the conclusion of all the labors, as though an abundance of every crop had already been heaped up in store. As though they had finished all the labor impending upon those engaged in agriculture, they would take palm-branches, and the fruit of a lovely tree, and thickly-leaved tree branches, those of the chaste-tree and the willow, and then, weaving tents, would dwell in them for seven whole days in relaxation and luxury.

4. Dt 16.16.
5. Ps 86.16.

Such are the accounts of each feast. But since the shadow of the law has departed, and what was revealed in figure to those of old has passed over into the truth (for in Christ all is new),[6] come, let us contemplate something spiritual with the eyes of the mind, and let us show how the feasts are arranged most excellently, as we have just mentioned. But the account will everywhere follow the things that happened in figures, representing the truth from them as far as may be.

2. Pharaoh was, then, a figure of the devil's perversity. For he tormented those of the stock of Israel with labor in mud and bricks, and, laying upon them the inescapable yoke of slavery, did not let them sacrifice to the God who is over all. But the inventor of sin, Satan, that frightful, haughty robber of the supreme glory, who spews forth arrogant words as though from a savage mind (for he dared to say, "I will be like the Most High"),[7] placed the yoke of his perversity upon those over the whole earth, and ordered them to worship himself,[8] and bade them become absorbed in unrewarding, unprofitable distractions, a sort of mud and brick-making: the pursuits that have to do with this flesh. For he knew that concern for the things upon earth always ends unfailingly in ruin and destruction.

But upon the world shone Christ, through whom and in whom is complete redemption, the true Lamb who takes away the sin of the world. We have accordingly been rescued through his sacrifice from the tyranny of the former prince, and we keep festival for the universal King and God of all, having washed away the filth of the ancient deceit as though it were some mucus in the eyes of the mind. But since, as I said, we have all been redeemed in Christ, "we have sown ourselves for justice, we have reaped the fruit of life,"[9] as the prophet says; we devote ourselves henceforth to fruitful endeavor. We have valued that labor which has a recompense, applying ourselves to accomplish that through which one may win the approval of God and men.

6. Cf. 2 Cor 5.17.
8. Correcting αὐτῷ to αὑτῷ.
7. Is 14.14.
9. Hos 10.12.

3. This, we say, is the Feast of Weeks, and of the wheat harvest. And when we finally arrive at this degree of splendor, endowed with an abundance of every virtue, amass a wealth of fair fruit for our souls, and lock it away in store, as it were (for it is written, "You shall eat the fruit of your toil"),[10] then it is, then indeed, that we will lodge in the tents above, receive from God the delights in paradise, and ascend to that ancient and truly desirable weal, living the life that is without toil and quite separate from all labor. Its figure is the third feast, that with tents, when they would take the branches of palms and of the other trees, the figure representing, I think, the delights in paradise.

I shall therefore return to what I said at the outset: God said that three times a year every male had to appear before him. Is it not, then, worth our while to examine the reason for this divine and sacred precept? The God who is over all is the Creator of all things, and at his command both the female and the male genders have been brought into existence. How is it then that he has forbidden the female gender to appear before him, while granting the male gender such a splendid and distinguished favor? Our reply is that the power of the commandment in the law conducts us through shadow and figures to the power of the truth. The things, accordingly, that are clearly visible receive images of what is intelligible, and thus introduce us to subtle and refined[11] considerations. What I mean is that the female race is always in some way weak both in mind and body,[12] while the male race is well regarded in both, and looked upon as superior. That race, then, is honored as masculine which excels in spiritual courage and wisdom of thought,[13] and it indeed appears in God's sight, and is granted the watchful care that he exercises. For it is written, "The eyes of the Lord are upon the just, and his ears to their petition."[14]

Whatever God considers of account, however, is considered worthless by the devil and his angels, and will not be spared the

10. Ps 128.2.
11. Correcting ἀπεξεμμέναις to ἀπεξεσμέναις.
12. See *Festal Letter* 10, n. 60, FOTC 118, 185.
13. Correcting ἐζοφωμένη to ἐσοφωμένη.
14. Ps 34.15.

experience of their cruelty. For he attacks every holy person, and leaps savagely at those who possess spiritual courage. But his attempts fail, and all that his innate perversity can devise falls wide of the mark. But that he finds what is spiritually masculine highly offensive, and that its good repute grieves him deeply, is made clear to us from what the all-wise Moses writes. Pharaoh in his madness, that is, plotted against those of the stock of Israel. But when their numbers increased finally beyond all count, he was stung by this, and quite badly. Summoning the midwives of the Hebrews, it says, he gave them this order: "Throw into the river every male baby born to the Hebrews, but keep every female baby alive."[15]

Now if we again place the mask of Pharaoh upon that power which fights God and is opposed to him, on Satan that is, we can say that the race that is strong, and intelligent to boot, is hated by him and most hostile to him. For it will not bear his yoke[16] nor bend its neck to his unholy plans. It rises in opposition and battles vigorously, possessing as it does the spiritual armor and ever adorning its own life with its efforts to achieve virtue. What is female, by contrast, is soft, as I said, unwise and feeble, and unused to war, with hands that are slack; it cannot shoot or strap on the weapons of justice. This he likes and welcomes, and is wholly taken with it; for, as I said, he honors the unmanly race that avoids fighting. As the divinely inspired Psalmist says, therefore, "Take courage, and let your heart be strengthened, all you that hope in the Lord."[17] And in what way we may achieve this is shown by Christ's disciple when he says, "Having girt up the loins of your mind, in sobriety set your hopes fully upon the grace that is coming to you at the revelation of Jesus Christ; as obedient children, do not be conformed to the passions of your former ignorance; but as he who called you is holy, be holy yourselves in all your conduct; for it is written, 'You shall be holy, for I am holy.'"[18] For it is not possible for those who are soiled and defiled to approach the all-pure God. For "what fellowship has light with darkness?"[19] as is written.

15. Ex 1.16.
17. Ps 31.24.
19. 2 Cor 6.14.

16. Reading ζυγῶν instead of ζυγόν.
18. 1 Pt 1.13–16; Lv 11.45.

4. You have Moses, the teacher of sacred truths, as an image of this reality. While he was herding flocks of sheep on Mount Horeb, a blazing fire appeared to him unexpectedly in a bramble-bush, and while the flame devoured the bush, it did it no harm at all (for it was nowhere burned), thus causing a great and extraordinary marvel. Moses approached, then, wondering what the curious spectacle could be. For God was sitting in the bramble-bush in the form of fire. Then, says sacred Scripture, the Lord called the man from the bramble-bush, saying, "Moses, Moses, do not come near here; loose the shoe from your feet, for the place where you are standing is holy ground."[20]

Now someone might, I think, reply to this: What kind of defilement may it be thought to be if one has one's feet shod? How is it that Moses is unclean because of sandals and hides? What can we say in reply? There is no pollution that can come to the human soul from shoes. But since Moses was in Egypt, and the natives thought that one might not carelessly enter the precincts of the idols while wearing shoes, which are from animals, and that is a defilement, and that was the only restriction they had, the God of all showed himself in this way implacable[21] to those not yet purified, making use of the Egyptian custom, as it were, and thus calling the holy Moses to a spiritual purification with the words, "Loose the shoe from your feet, for the place where you are standing is holy ground."[22] For in this way those who worship the all-pure[23] God must, I say, abandon dead works and thus,[24] once freed from those concerns which lead to corruption and pollution, draw near to him, in the sense of spiritual familiarity. Dead works may be listed[25] as acts of carnal sensuality, carousals and drunkenness, a life devoid of all religion, attempts at shameful gain, acts of robbery and avarice, outbursts of temper and what results from this, slander and contempt, and, in short, the things through which one loses eternal life, caught in the

20. Ex 3.5.

21. The word is ἀπροφάσιστον. The context tempts one to correct this to ἀπρόσιτον, "unapproachable," but that would be the *lectio facilior*.

22. Ex 3.5.

23. Reading παναγνῳ instead of παναγίῳ.

24. Correcting ὄυτε τε to οὔτω τε.

25. Reading νεκρὰ ἐννοηθεῖεν instead of νεκρῶν θεῖεν.

snares of sin and liable to accusations of a great variety of wickedness.

Christ's disciple leads us away from such illnesses when he
says, "Do not love the world or what is in the world. For all that is
in the world is the lust of the flesh and the lust of the eyes and
the pride of life. And the world is passing away, and the lust for
it. But the one who does the will of God remains forever."[26] The
all-wise Paul writes as well to those determined to lead the way of
life that is honored, "But fornication and all impurity must not
even be named among you, as befits saints, but rather thanksgiving."[27] The way to this sort of purified and exceptional life was
prefigured of old by Moses' law as well, which describes Immanuel for us in advance through shadow and figures: describes,
that is, the pure, salvific light of the revelations given through
him.

But now the truth has shone forth in its purity. He, that is, who
is above all creation has become as we are, that he might make
the divine light flash upon us, and, having taught us how to make
straight toward every virtue, might render us God's sons. For he
lowered himself, as I said, unto what is ours, that we might gain
what is his, since we have been enriched in a certain way by his
poverty.[28] For if he had not shared our poverty, lowering himself
into our condition,[29] neither would we have had his wealth, gaining through him and from him that sonship which properly befits him, and him alone.

Israel, however, was witless.[30] It did not recognize the Redeemer present with the flesh, even with the all-wise Moses prefigur-
ing that very mystery in so many ways. Christ accordingly charged
them with overwhelming stupidity and disbelief when he said,
"If you believed Moses, you would believe me. For it was of me
that he wrote."[31] Having therefore insulted with their disobedience the law that was their guide, they have remained in dark-

26. 1 Jn 2.15–17.   27. Eph 5.3.
28. Cf. 2 Cor 8.9.   29. Cf. Phil 2.8.
30. The strong anti-Jewish language that follows is quite common in the early letters. For a discussion of Cyril's relationship to the Jews, see the introduction in FOTC 118, 16–26.
31. Jn 5.46.

ness, completely deprived of the divine light. And this was what
had been said of them by the prophets. While they were awaiting
light, darkness fell upon them. Having expected brightness, it
was in pitch darkness that they walked.[32]

But we will find the Lord crying out to them again and again,
saying, "I am the light of the world; those who follow me will not
walk in the darkness but will have the light of life."[33] And again,
"I have come as light into the world."[34] And that he might render
their ignorance inexcusable, even though he appeared a human
being as we are, he gave everywhere a godlike, supernatural
demonstration of the power in him. Is there anything he may be
seen accomplishing that is not beyond both reason and wonder?
He said to them, accordingly, "If I do not do my Father's works,
do not believe me. But if I do them, then even if you do not believe me, believe my works."[35] For the divine is by nature invisible. For it is written, "No one has ever seen God."[36] But he is
known by us, as far at least as that is attainable, from his mighty
works, his unspeakable power, and his supreme pre-eminence.
Creation proclaims him as well; David sings accordingly, "The
heavens tell of God's glory, and the firmament declares the work
of his hands."[37] Not only that, but the all-wise Paul writes about
him, "Since the creation of the world, what is invisible about
him, his eternal power and divinity, has been clearly perceived,
known by his works."[38]

From his mighty, godlike power, therefore, which transcends
all discourse, it is possible in a way to receive knowledge concerning his ineffable divinity. But God the Word, the Creator of
all, appeared to the world with the flesh; and this not in order to
destroy the existing earth and show us another, new one at present, nor indeed to fashion other heavens after doing away with
the ones that are now, nor to execute something novel and unexpected about the orb of the sun, nor to make something new
about the visible creation. No, it was that he might fashion us
anew unto incorruptibility when we were lying beneath the dev-

32. Cf. Am 5.20.   33. Jn 8.12.
34. Jn 12.46.   35. Jn 10.37–38.
36. Jn 1.18.   37. Ps 19.1.
38. Rom 1.20.

il's feet and were borne down through sin into decay, that he might render us holy and blameless once he had removed us from all defilement according to the commands of his clemency, and that he might set us upon the paths of that life that is faultless.

But[39] since he was a human being as we are, visible according to the economy (for as the prophet says, "He appeared on earth and consorted with human beings"),[40] for this reason, in order to make it clear to us that he is God as well as truly Son of God the Father, he performed his works, showing himself to be connatural and equal in operation to his own Parent, and through the equal and indistinguishable pre-eminence and power he displayed, causing astonishment among those at least who recognized his advent. Senseless Israel, however, was nonetheless stubborn and wholly inclined to disbelief; chattering endlessly up and down the length of the written law and alleging the commandment given through Moses, they resisted the revelations given through Christ, saying, "We are Moses' disciples; as for this man, we do not know where he is from."[41] And they kept insulting him in other ways, nor was there anything ridiculous that they did not say. Giving full rein to their perversity, as it were, and going beyond all limits, they hastened to encompass with death the Author of life, the Redeemer from heaven, the one who justifies the impious by faith and renews unto incorruptibility those caught in death's snares. Kicking against the goad[42] and bringing fire and punishment upon their own heads, they gathered irreligious councils, together with their leaders, to formulate impossible plans. They spoke accordingly as follows, inciting themselves to violence and blazing with a now-unquenchable envy at the very things that ought to have provoked astonishment at the wonder-worker: "What are we to do? For this man works many signs. If we let him go on thus, the Romans will come and destroy both our nation and our country."[43]

And when[44] the one who was foremost in their priesthood

---

39. This sentence does not hang together grammatically, and needs repair at several points. We offer a possible translation, following the Latin.

40. Bar 3.37.   41. Jn 9.28–29.

42. Cf. Acts 26.14.   43. Jn 11.47–48.

44. Reading Ὅτε instead of Ὅτι.

drew as though from the depths of his mind that thought that was lethal to them, and said, "You know nothing, nor does it occur to you that it behooves you that one man die for the people, and that the whole nation not perish,"[45] their counsels ran thence to an unholy end. Those wretches arrested Jesus and delivered him to Pilate, making up some untruths, and urged that he be crucified. And that is what happened, Satan acting as their captain in this and bringing them down into the pit of destruction. But Christ endured it, and willingly submitted even to descending to the death of the flesh for our sake in the economy. For he knew, he knew indeed, the good that was to come from the suffering. For he has not remained among the dead; he came back to life, having bidden farewell to the bonds of death and emptied hell. For "he said to those in bonds, 'Come out!' And to those in darkness, 'Show yourselves!'"[46] And in his own nature he became the way to incorruptibility. For it was renewed in him, and we have sprouted afresh unto life. The blessed Paul confirms this when he says, "Just as in Adam all die, so also in Christ all will be brought to life."[47] Having abolished death's power, accordingly, he ascended to God the Father in heaven. And he will come in due time to render to each according to his deeds.[48]

Since, then, as the all-wise Paul says, "we must all appear before his bench, that each may receive good or evil, according to what he has done in the body,"[49] let us gird up the loins of our minds, let us act courageously in doing good deeds, let us mortify the pleasures of the flesh, and rid ourselves of the stains of all immorality. Let us take pity on orphans, let us support widows,[50] let us assist those in need, let us show compassion toward those in extreme misery, let us visit prisoners;[51] in sum, let us display every kind of virtue. For thus we will fast in purity, beginning holy Lent on the first of Phamenoth, and the week of the salvific Paschal feast on the sixth of Pharmuthi. We break the fast on the eleventh of Pharmuthi, late on the eve of Saturday, according to the gospel precept. We celebrate the feast on the following day,

---

45. Jn 11.50.
46. Is 49.9.
47. 1 Cor 15.22.
48. Cf. Mt 16.27.
49. 2 Cor 5.10.
50. Jas 1.27.
51. Cf. Mt 25.43.

the eve of Sunday, the twelfth of Pharmuthi,[52] adding thereafter the seven weeks of the holy Eastertide for which we so deeply long, so that, by making even this time of relaxation a kind of image of that of the saints in heaven, we may be granted their company, in Christ Jesus Our Lord, through whom and with whom be glory to the Father, with the Holy Spirit, now and for all ages. Amen.

52. April 7, 440.

FESTAL LETTER TWENTY-NINE

A.D. 441

PREFACE

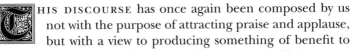 HIS DISCOURSE has once again been composed by us not with the purpose of attracting praise and applause, but with a view to producing something of benefit to the souls of those listening. Do not heap severe criticism upon a failure to achieve the finest eloquence, but listen with an indulgent ear. For the feast that is prepared is not one that comes from the pomp of the orators, but from the vegetables of the Church, as it were.[1]

1. Behold, the time of our holy feast arises once again, filling the souls of those who love virtue with all gladness, removing from our midst the reluctance to engage in good endeavors, and rousing us to undertake all that is held in admiration: those things which accord with the sacred laws, which have results that meet with the approval of God above, and which make for high renown for those who decide to achieve them. As the divinely inspired Psalmist says, therefore, "It is time to act for the Lord,"[2] in making, that is, that holy and all-pure feast which we are accustomed to celebrate for Christ, the Savior of us all. For as the all-wise Paul writes, "Christ our Passover has been sacrificed," "the true Lamb who takes away the sin of the world."[3]

It is, then, always somehow customary for those keeping festival to dress well, to decorate their robes, and to free their cloth-

---

1. Reading οἶον instead of οἷς. Cyril's reference to vegetables here may allude whimsically to Lenten dietary restrictions.
2. Ps 119.126.
3. 1 Cor 5.7. Cf. Jn 1.29.

ing from all soil. Some might well say that it somehow suits this occasion. But I would think that we should by no means concern ourselves with the beautification that comes only from external ornamentation, but rather bend every effort at eliminating the defilements in the soul. For this presents us to Christ pure and well cleansed, distinguished by the grace that comes from him, adorned with him richly as with a garment befitting the saints. For thus writes the all-wise Paul: "Put on the Lord Jesus, and make no provision for the flesh, to gratify its lust."[4] When we are thus prepared, there is nothing unreasonable about wanting to be near the all-good God. For "you will be holy," it says, "because I am holy."[5]

Let us, therefore, keep festival, as the divinely inspired Paul says, "not with the old leaven, nor with the leaven of malice and evil, but with the unleavened bread of sincerity and truth."[6] That means with a faith that is right and exact, added to which, of course, is the splendor of deeds. For if these things are present in you, they will secure a share in the way that leads straight to one's allotted portion, and will raise to the inheritance of the saints those who are the best imitators of their excellence of life.

Come, then, let us reflect on when and how Moses, or rather God acting through him, bade the law concerning the Paschal feast to be observed: it is the first month for the Hebrews, the one upon which the springtime smiles, when the vegetation in copses and gardens is crowned with new foliage that has just appeared, and promises a yield of fruit, the entire plain is green with grass, the arable land is shaggy with crops, the most fragrant flowers are adorned with all sorts of colors, and tender lambs bound around[7] their mothers, bleating sweetly and daintily.

How, then, can it be anything but completely ridiculous to see the whole earth in bloom, while that chosen, godly animal upon earth, man that is, remains spiritually sterile, bearing the unshakeable depression of sin? As sacred Scripture says, then, "let us lay aside every weight, and sin which clings so closely, and let us run with perseverance the race that is set before us,"[8] not dis-

4. Rom 13.14.   5. Lv 11.45.
6. 1 Cor 5.8.
7. Reading περισκαίρουσιν instead of περισκέρουσιν.
8. Heb 12.1.

tressed at the efforts entailed, but eager for the prizes therefrom. For it is not possible, indeed it is not, to attain anything good and admirable while preferring to remain idle. For when one has shackled one's mind with laziness, how can one become worthy of reverence, or be crowned with praise for the achievement of all that is best? Listen to the author of Proverbs: "How long will you lie there, you sluggard? When will you wake from sleep? You sleep a little, you slumber a little, you fold your arms on your chest a little. Then poverty happens upon you as an evil guide."[9] And he has another way of inciting us to the desire for virtue, by taking as an example those tiny animals that are of so little account: "Go to the ant, you sluggard," he says. "Emulate its ways, and become wiser than it. For though it has no[10] husbandry, is not under a master, and has no one to force it, it prepares for itself food in the summer, and lays by abundant store in harvest. Or go to the bee and learn how industrious it is and how respected its work is. It is wholly desired and held in honor."[11]

The labors for the sake of piety are, therefore, worth taking on for those concerned with acting manfully. Laziness, by contrast, is an abomination to be rejected, at least when it comes to those brave deeds that are of the best. For it will always and infallibly befall those accustomed to indolence that they come to lack all that is good. The decision to endure hardship for the sake of virtue, on the other hand, has its reward, and will by no means go without its recompense from on high. That this is true may easily be seen from what happens with us. How can the husbandman, that is, gather an abundant harvest if he folds his hands, refuses to till, and neglects all work with the spade? If such is his disposition, will not the fields be destitute of crops, the garden plants bare of ripened fruit, and the rows of vines idle and without grapes, as though they were paintings in still-life with nothing to them except the bare sight? Or consider merchants: when will they ever find themselves abounding in the profits so dear to them if they persistently shrink from sailing and encountering waves, rather than putting love of gain before all labor and fear? Let me also mention those who bend every effort to win respect

9. Prv 6.9–11.   10. Reading μή instead of μέν.
11. Prv 6.6–8.

in wrestling schools. The divinely inspired Paul mentioned them as well when he said, "They exercise self-control in everything, that they may receive a perishable wreath."[12]

If, then, even with our own affairs, there is none that ever reaches the desired outcome without application and work, how may anyone attain the heights of virtue who does not esteem the necessity of enduring suffering, and is not eager to be borne straight to all that is good as though by the invincible propensities of his mind? Impressing thus the intelligible and lovable beauty of the life of the saints upon our own souls, and portraying it there spiritually, we will make our petitions to God, saying, "Lord, in your will supply strength to my beauty."[13]

Now the counsel and all-effective will of God the Father is the Son. The divinely inspired David sings to him, accordingly, "In your counsel you have guided me."[14] For we have been guided in Christ toward every sort of virtue. And do not be surprised if we say that the Son has been named the counsel of God the Father, since we will find the Father himself honored with such a title. For "counsel" means "wisdom." The prophet Isaiah, then, has written about Christ, the Savior of us all, that "a child has been born to us, and a son has been given to us, whose government is upon his shoulder, and his name is called the messenger of great counsel."[15] For he announced to us what concerned his own Parent, and showed clearly the supernatural beauty of the substance that is above all others,[16] portraying him in his own nature. For he is an image, "reflection and stamp of his being."[17] He said accordingly, "Whoever has seen me has seen the Father."[18] "I and the Father are one."[19]

He is indeed completely one, in the identity, I say, of substance. How is it, then, that he has been called "child?" For, being equal in rank with his begetter, and enjoying identically all of the divine dignities whatsoever, he became a human being, lowering himself in an emptying and submitting to birth[20] from a

---

12. 1 Cor 9.25.
13. Ps 29.8 (LXX).
14. Ps 73.24.
15. Is 9.6.
16. Reading πασῶν instead of παντός.
17. Heb 1.3.
18. Jn 14.9.
19. Jn 10.30.
20. Reading ἀπότεξιν instead of ἀπόταξιν.

woman, like us. The Spirit-bearer,[21] however, says that he "has been given" to us.[22] For it was not for himself that "he emptied himself,"[23] and put on the poverty of our state; it was that we might abound in what is his, and, having washed away sin with its ignominy and profanation, might gain through him purification through faith. For as the Son himself says, "God loved the world so much that he gave his only-begotten Son, that everyone who believes in him might not perish, but might have eternal life."[24]

Faith is, accordingly, something truly salvific. It justifies the impious, and, rendering them free of all guilt, joins them to Christ. It crowns with the splendor of sonship those who cleave to him wholeheartedly, and this through sanctification and justice, the latter not being that which is according to the law, but that which is holy and evangelical. He said to the holy apostles, accordingly, "Amen I say to you, if your justice does not surpass that of the scribes and Pharisees, you will not enter the kingdom of the God of heaven."[25] And the all-wise Paul writes, "Now it is evident that no one is justified before God by the law."[26] And further, "We ourselves, who are Jews by birth and not gentile sinners, yet who know that a human being is not justified by works of the law but through faith in Jesus Christ, even we have believed in Christ, that we might be justified in him."[27]

2. Here you might ask: if the law was of no use at all, and if their abode among the ancient letters was no help at all toward achieving purification for those caught in sin, then why ever was it given in the first place? To this we reply that the law given in writing was ministered by angels, with Moses mediating. It was an image of the truth and a sort of representation of piety leading toward it through figure and shadow.[28] The most holy Paul writes, then, "So that the law was our instructor until Christ came."[29] And this, too, originated from the wisdom above, a

21. Paul.   22. Cf. Rom 5.5.
23. Phil 2.8.   24. Jn 3.16.
25. Mt 5.20.   26. Gal 3.11.
27. Gal 2.15–16.
28. For a discussion of Cyril's exegetical methods, see the introduction in FOTC 118, 9–12.
29. Gal 3.24.

demonstration of skillfulness befitting the divine. For just as those eager to achieve renown in coppersmithery exercise themselves at it thoroughly, and do not work with the material required for it during their first attempts, but practice the art using wax, forming with it the shapes of the vessels; just so, we would say, was Israel educated by the figures of truth so as to proceed little by little toward the fully good. This was the power of the way of life in Christ, the one, I mean, that was proclaimed by the revelations in the Gospels.

There is also another way of responding, not without merit, for those who wish to speak as they should, to the question of why the grace that comes through faith was not given at the outset to those over the whole earth, and why the commandment given through Moses had to precede it and start first. Sin reigned over us, and controlled everyone on earth. For a cruel tyrant pressed us, plunging us into the mire of carnal sensuality, and with easy power conducting the will of each person to every kind of wickedness. And there was no way to be freed from the yoke of his arrogance. What those upon earth needed, what they needed indeed, was then the immeasurably great, incomparable kindness from above, which is from God and which justifies the impious[30] while placing them beyond punishment and penalty. Those whose stain of wickedness had become ineradicably absorbed needed the grace that comes from faith in Christ to shine forth. For it was impossible otherwise to escape both the snares of sin and the cruelty of the devil's tyranny.

In order that the extent of the grace and generosity offered through Christ might be realized,[31] a law was first introduced that in no way justified anyone, but rather convicted the weakness of those[32] at the time. It was, then, a conviction of sin, pronouncing a curse upon those who sinned. For it is written, "Cursed be everyone who does not abide by all the things written in the book of this law, and do them."[33] The most holy Paul will once again confirm that what I say is quite true. He writes,

30. Reading ἀσεβῆ instead of εὐσεβῆ.
31. Reading ἀγνοῆται instead of ἀγνοῆτε.
32. Reading τῶν instead of τόν.
33. Gal 3.10; cf. Dt 27.26.

"The law was established because of transgressions."[34] And further, "Law came in to increase the trespass."[35] With those under the law being weak, and always transgressing, the trespass was excessive. With the law accordingly convicting the weakness of those under it, what those on earth needed was he who justifies in faith, and not from works of the law. This was Christ, about whom it is written, "Yet a little while, yet a little while more and the coming one shall come and shall not tarry. And if he shrinks back, my soul has no pleasure in him.[36] But the just one shall live by my faith.[37] For the God of all has not desired sacrifice and offering. And in burnt offerings and sin offerings he has taken no pleasure,"[38] since, as Christ himself said, "God is spirit, and those who worship him must worship in spirit and truth."[39]

3. This is what he kept teaching in synagogues, adding the miracles to what he said, and those things that befit that nature alone which is above all, he accomplished with the greatest ease, or rather with his all-powerful will. For he had only to decide to do them. But those from Israel despised him in the barren hardness of their minds. They opposed the revelations he offered, giving little if any weight to his miracles, and in their unbridled fury giving vent to the most abusive language. Him who called them to life and who made the knowledge of virtue flash forth upon all, they called a Samaritan,[40] a glutton, a drunkard,[41] a bastard, and a carpenter's son.[42] And for what reason? Because they did not want to have straight paths in life. Bound tightly by the chains of their own passions, accordingly, stained ineradicably by their sensuality, and conquered by unholy dirty money, they did not accept those words which might have led them off in the direction of proper behavior. They are, then, clearly convicted, as Christ, the Savior of us all, says: "Everyone who does evil hates the light, and does not come to the light, lest his deeds should be convicted."[43]

34. Gal 3.19.
35. Rom 5.20.
36. Heb 10.37–38.
37. Cf. Rom 1.17; Hab 2.4.
38. Heb 10.5–6. Cf. Ps 40.6.
39. Jn 4.24.
40. Jn 8.48.
41. Mt 11.19.
42. Mt 13.55.
43. Jn 3.20.

What, then, did they do who did not endure to admit the divine light into their minds? They reviled the one who called them to life, as I said, they stoned the messenger of truth, and finally they crucified him, making up falsehoods and subjecting him who is free of all sin to criticism[44] and accusation. Some of them told Pilate and Caiaphas, "We have seen this man stirring up the crowds, and forbidding tribute to be paid to Caesar."[45] Others said, "He has blasphemed against the divine temple."[46]

But our Lord Jesus Christ has undergone[47] death in the flesh willingly, in order that by treading upon it, and being raised from the dead, he may be recognized[48] as life and life-giver, and as God thereby. For he did not remain among the dead like one of those in our condition; he came back to life, making the new path of resurrection from the dead for human nature. Paul testifies to this when he writes, "For just as in Adam all die, so also in Christ all will be brought to life."[49] Our Lord Jesus Christ has accordingly become for us the root, the way, and the occasion of hope for incorruption. For death reigned from Adam until Moses. But it fell from its tyranny over us, and lost its power in Christ. For we are born no longer for death, as though from corruptible seed, but unto the hope of life, taking Christ as our leader. The divinely inspired Paul writes, then, to those who believed in him, "For you have died, and your life is hidden with Christ in God. When Christ your life appears, then you too will appear with him in glory."[50]

For he will come, he will come in due time in the glory of his Father, and will descend once again from heaven with the holy angels, "that he may judge the earth in justice,"[51] as is written. Since, then, we are to stand before the divine bench, and render an account of our own life,[52] let us conduct ourselves holily, and practice every form of virtuousness, cleansing ourselves of every stain of flesh and spirit,[53] being satisfied with what we have, and

44. Reading μῶμον instead of νόμον.
45. Cf. Lk 23.2.
46. Cf. Mt 26.61; Mk 14.58.
47. Reading ὑπομεμένηκεν instead of ἀπομεμένηκεν.
48. Reading γνωρίζηται instead of γνωρίζεται.
49. 1 Cor 15.22.　　50. Col 3.3–4.
51. Ps 9.9.　　52. Cf. 2 Cor 5.10.
53. Cf. 2 Cor 7.1.

otherwise considering an annoyance whatever is superfluous. Let us share the suffering of those in misery, assist those who labor, remember those in fetters as sharing their bonds,[54] consoling those who are infirm, showing compassion for the tears of the orphan and widow,[55] helping those in poverty as far as possible, and, in a word, practicing every good deed. For then we will celebrate a holy and all-pure feast, beginning holy Lent on the sixteenth of Mechir, and the week of the holy, salvific Paschal feast on the twenty-first of Phamenoth. We break the fast on the twenty-sixth of Phamenoth, late on the eve of Saturday, according to the gospel proclamations. We keep the feast on the next day, the eve of Sunday, the twenty-seventh of Phamenoth,[56] adding thereto the seven weeks of holy Eastertide, so that, by dancing the time of relaxation away with the saints in heaven as they leap and rejoice, we may be granted their company in Christ Jesus our Lord. To him be the glory and the power with the Father and the Holy Spirit, now and always, and for all ages. Amen.

54. Cf. Mt 25.43.   55. Cf. Jas 1.27.
56. March 23, 441.

FESTAL LETTER THIRTY

A.D. 444

HOSE WHOSE sacred ministry is the august and divine proclamation, the one, that is, which comes through Christ, the Savior of us all, are ordered by the Holy Spirit through the Psalmist's lyre to "blow the trumpet at the new moon, on the glorious day of our feast. For it is an ordinance for Israel, and a statute for the God of Jacob."[1] By "new moon" he means[2] in this place the new and, as it were, just-blossomed time of the Advent of our Savior, in which "all that is old has passed away, and all has become new,"[3] as the divinely inspired Paul says, and which is a kind of beginning of a new age. We must therefore blow the trumpet at this time, which means saying to people everywhere in words that resound most clearly and piercingly, "The Lord is God, and he has shone upon us; hold a festival in the coverings unto the horns of the altar."[4] What is meant by the words "hold the festival in the coverings" I will try to explain as best I may.

The tent of old was set up in the desert. But it had a double arrangement; one part was the first, which had the altar for the worship that was according to the law. In it those who still honored God through shadow and figures were bidden to sacrifice cattle and slaughter sheep, with smoke. The second, which adjoined[5] the first and was further within, separated from it by a curtain, was called[6] the Holy of Holies. Here the propitiatory[7] was a figure of Christ, the Cherubim covering it in the posture

---

1. Ps 81.3.   2. Reading φησιν instead of φασιν.
3. 2 Cor 5.17.   4. Ps 117.27 (LXX).
5. Correcting προσευχῆς to προσεχής.
6. Correcting αὐτῷ to αὐτῇ.
7. Reading ἱλαστήριον instead of θυσιαστήριον.

of divine service, their attitude that of those in God's presence. There was located there a golden altar as well, on which the finely compounded ointment was burned, which was so skillfully concocted of such a variety of spices.[8]

But as the all-wise Paul writes, "These preparations having thus been made, the priests go continually into the first tent, performing their ritual service; but into the second only the high priest goes, and he but once a year, and not without blood which he offers for himself and for the errors of the people. By this the Holy Spirit indicates that the way into the sanctuary is not yet opened as long as the first tent is still standing, which is symbolic for the present time, during which gifts and sacrifices are offered which cannot perfect the conscience of the worshiper."[9]

As long, then, as the form of worship in accordance with the law given through Moses held sway, the things that are subject to figures had their position in the first tent. For it was not permitted[10] to those wanting to do so to rush into the holy, innermost tent. Only the one who was chief among the priests went in, once a year, and "not without blood," as is written.

But since, as Paul writes from his expert knowledge of the law and of the sacred writings on which he was nurtured, "Christ, having appeared as a high priest of the good things that are to come, entered once for all, through the greater and more perfect tent not made with hands, that is, not of this creation,[11] into the Holy of Holies, not with the blood of goats and calves but with his own blood, thus securing an eternal redemption,"[12] let us, too, declining to take a position in the first tent, follow Christ, enter into the Holy of Holies, and "hold the festival in the coverings,"[13] where the propitiatory is as a figure of Christ, the Cherubim covering it with their wings. Let us offer God not sacrifices that are bloody, but that fine, composite sacrifice which is the sweet fragrance coming from virtues, the spiritual and unbloody worship.

It seems to me also that I should quote you the words, "Let us

---

8. Cf. Ex 30.34–38.   9. Heb 9.6–9.
10. Reading ἐξῆν instead of ἐξῆς.
11. Reading κτίσεως instead of πίστεως.
12. Heb 9.11–12.   13. Cf. Ps 117.27 (LXX).

cleanse ourselves of every defilement of flesh and spirit. Let us make holiness perfect in the fear of God."[14] For it is not possible for those who do not want to act wickedly, no, it is not, to go into the Holy of Holies with unwashed feet, as it were. That is what the God of all showed us when he said to Moses, the sacred teacher, "Make a bronze laver, and a bronze base for it, for washing, and you will put it between the tent of witness and the altar. And you will pour water into it, and Aaron and his sons will wash their hands and feet with water from it when they go into the tent of witness; they will wash with water and will not die."[15]

2. Now these things are replete with the beauties of truth in figurative form, while it is Christ, who is truth, that frees us from all defilement. How or in what way this is, he will teach us in the words of Isaiah: "Wash yourselves and become clean, remove your iniquities from your souls before my eyes. Cease from your iniquities, learn to do good, seek judgment, rescue those who are wronged, judge the orphan, and do justice for the widow. Come now, let us speak together, says the Lord. Though your sins be like crimson, I will make them white as snow; and though they be like scarlet, I will make them white as wool."[16]

The divinely inspired Psalmist also mentions this so radiant, amiable grace when he says to Christ, the Savior of all, "You will sprinkle me with hyssop, and I will be cleansed; you will wash me, and I will become whiter than snow."[17] [This grace], then, makes [one] white through holy baptism, stopping the mouth of sin and melting away every defilement that is in us in an intelligible and spiritual way. The divinely inspired John speaks as follows, accordingly, when addressing the Jewish…[18] "I baptize you with water for repentance, but after me is coming one mightier than I; he will baptize you with the Holy Spirit and fire."[19] For when the activity and power of the Holy Spirit comes into us and finds a soul rankly overgrown, then indeed it falls upon it like fire and devours what is like useless matter, consuming the pollution of sin.

14. 2 Cor 7.1.   15. Ex 30.18–21.
16. Is 1.16–18.   17. Ps 51.7.
18. The text is corrupt here.
19. Mt 3.11; Mk 1.8; Lk 3.16; Jn 1.26.

Now it is faith in Christ that is found to be the approach to this reality and a sort of road leading to this so splendid and desirable grace. The divinely inspired David, accordingly, all but points with his finger in showing it to us when he says, "This is the Lord's gate, the just will enter through it."[20] For the law given through Moses was revealed to those of the stock of Israel through the ministry of angels. But it was a conviction of sin and demonstration of transgression, quite useless[21] as a means of justifying anyone. The all-wise Paul writes, accordingly, "Now it is evident that no one is justified before God by the law. For the law brings wrath."[22] For it immediately set out the punishments corresponding to each person's lapses.

The law being weak, therefore, and unable to rub away pollution or free anyone from guilt, the God of all gave the grace that comes through faith, and justification in Christ, to those[23] everywhere on earth. The divinely inspired Paul again confirms this when he writes, "For through the law comes knowledge of sin. But now the righteousness of God has been manifested apart from law, although the law and the prophets bear witness to it, the righteousness of God through faith in Jesus Christ for all who believe. For there is no distinction; since all have sinned and fall short of the glory of God, they are justified by his grace as a gift, through the redemption which is in Christ Jesus."[24] It is the special glory, befitting uniquely and particularly the nature that is regarded as beyond all that is generated, to be sinless in everything and, completely unshakeable, to be able in no respect to fail in doing what is right. But we ourselves do not come up to this; we fall short, as Paul in his supreme wisdom says; it is not unusual for us to be caught in the snares of sin and through our tendencies to wickedness to descend to further depravity. As holy Scripture says, however, "For where sin increased, grace abounded all the more."[25] One may indeed observe how thirsty for this grace those people were who did not know the mystery

20. Ps 118.20.
21. Reading ἀνόνητος instead of ἀνόητος.
22. Cf. Gal 3.10; Rom 4.15.
23. Reading δικαίωσιν τοῖς instead of δικαίως ἐστὶ τήν.
24. Rom 3.20–24.
25. Rom 5.20.

of the Incarnation of the Only-Begotten. Paul accordingly writes from his supreme knowledge of the law, "We ourselves, who are Jews by birth and not gentile sinners, yet who know that a human being is not justified by works of the law but through faith in Jesus Christ, even we have believed in Christ Jesus, that we may be justified in him."[26]

3. And do not suppose that God decreed the law of old as sufficing to render some people free of the guilt coming from weakness, and that when he failed of his purpose, it was as though he pondered further and then thought up the way that is through faith in Christ. This was not the way of it, not by far. Realize rather that even before he had so much as fashioned the first human being from earth, knowing as he did what was to be, and the perversity of the devil's cunning, and perceiving in advance the way to render us assistance, the mystery of Christ that is, he established the law through Moses as a conviction of sin and accuser of the weakness that afflicts everyone, and wisely showed the commandment that condemns before the grace that justifies, that the grace might evoke even greater wonder. For it is where there is cause for grief that that which gladdens appears most vividly.

Now we can easily see that the mystery of Christ is something ancient, when sacred Scripture speaks to us again in this way. I mean that blessed Paul speaks again somewhere as follows: "Blessed be the God and Father of our Lord Jesus Christ, who has blessed us in Christ with every spiritual blessing in the heavenly places, even as he chose us in him before the foundation of the world, that we might be holy and blameless before him in love, having destined us to be his adoptive sons through Jesus Christ."[27] You see, then, the ways we have been blessed, even before the foundation of the world, and have been destined to be sons in Christ Jesus. Indeed, salvific baptism itself was prefigured to those of old, and to us after them, through the very ark. For the just man Noah was saved in it through faith, even though the whole earth had been condemned by God's own decree. For he

26. Gal 2.16.
27. Eph 1.3–5.

loosed the flood upon all. It is written of him, accordingly, "By faith Noah, being warned by God before events not yet seen, took heed and constructed an ark for the saving of his household; by this he condemned the world and became an heir of the righteousness which comes by faith."[28]

And that this happened as a figure of holy baptism is confirmed by the divinely inspired Peter when he says concerning Christ, the Savior of us all, "Christ also died for sins once for all, the righteous for the unrighteous, that he might bring us to God, being put to death in the flesh but made alive in the spirit. In which he went and preached to the fathers[29] in prison, who formerly did not obey, when God's patience waited in the days of Noah, during the building of the ark, in which a few, that is, eight souls, were saved through water. Baptism, which corresponds to this, now saves us, not as a removal of fleshly defilement but as a pledge to God of a clear conscience."[30]

Now what does this mean: "a pledge to God from a clear conscience"? It is a confession of faith in Christ, which it is our custom to make in the presence of many witnesses as well, and not just those human ones dignified by the honor of the divine ministry, but also the rational powers who minister to God, zealous to achieve what is for his glory. And those who pronounce the profession of faith unwaveringly must, I claim, avoid being shaken from it in any way. For it is written, "My beloved brothers and sisters, be steadfast, immovable, always abounding in the work[31] of the Lord."[32]

4. For it happens sometimes that men reared in the company of ignorance buffet certain people around, even some of those who have already become believers, giving their neighbor foul perversion to drink, as is written,[33] and as though "from the wicked treasure of their hearts"[34] spewing out their wickedness and belching forth the poison of the devil's perversity. They dispar-

---

28. Heb 11.7.
29. Πατράσι instead of πνεύμασιν as in the received text.
30. 1 Pt 3.18–22.   31. Reading ἔργῳ instead of οἴκῳ.
32. 1 Cor 15.58.   33. Cf. Hab 2.15.
34. Cf. Mt 12.35.

age that substance and glory which are beyond everything, and do all in their power to bring down from his supernal throne the Word engendered from God the Father, numbering among creatures the Creator and Artificer of everything: whom all of his works venerate[35] trembling, gloriously crowned as he is with the dignities of his true[36] and natural divinity. "For every knee bends[37] to him, in heaven, on earth, and under the earth, and every tongue confesses that Jesus Christ is Lord, to the glory of God the Father."[38]

There are, in addition to these, some who divide him who is indivisible, the one Christ, and who pervert the splendid beauty of the truth, even though the divinely inspired Paul has written to us clearly and distinctly, "One Lord, one faith, one baptism."[39] But if there were two lords, then there would certainly have to be two faiths and as many baptisms. Let us give those who think so short shrift as pests and plagues, and, pulling[40] our foot from the snare, let us say in the word of the Psalm, "Blessed be the Lord, who did not give us as prey to their teeth. The snare has been broken, and we have been rescued."[41] For we have been redeemed in the death of Christ, "who gave himself for our sins," according to the Scriptures, "to deliver us from the present evil age, according to the will of God the Father."[42]

For since, as we said, it was impossible to wash away the defilement of wickedness or of sin by means of the form of worship that is according to the law and which has nothing besides figures and shadows, the very Word who is from God the Father, having become a human being on our account and for us, while remaining what he was, God that is, gave his own body to death, that he might ransom us from death and decay by his own blood. He spoke, accordingly, to God the Father in the heavens through the voice of David, saying, "Sacrifice and offering you did not

35. Correcting σείεται to σέβεται.
36. Reading ἀληθοῦς instead of ἀληθείας.
37. Reading κάμπτει instead of συνάπτει.
38. Phil 2.10.
39. Eph 4.5.
40. Reading ἱέντες instead of ἰόντες.
41. Ps 124.6–7.
42. Gal 1.4.

want, in burnt offerings and sin offerings you have taken no pleasure, but a body you have prepared for me. Then I said, 'Behold, I have come. In the roll of the book it is written about me, I have chosen to do your will, O God.'"[43]

Observe, therefore, observe how he says clearly, "A body you have prepared for me." For he was and is incorporeal as God. How is it, then, O Jew, that you have not known the economy that is so ineffable and august? How is it that you have not accepted the incorporeal One who became incarnate for you? the one above all creation who descends in the economy unto the dimensions of humanity? the one who enriches those in heaven and who bears your poverty? the Lord of all who took the form of a slave?

But you may reply: he appeared to be a human being like us. How is it, then, that you have forgotten the writings of Moses? For he spoke somewhere to you about him: "A prophet like me the Lord your God will raise up for you from your brothers, according to all that you asked of the Lord your God in Horeb; him you will hear."[44] The passage indicated that he was to be as a human being and as of the holy prophets. The divinely inspired Isaiah says, accordingly, "Behold, the virgin will conceive in the womb, and will bear a son, and they will call his name Immanuel," which means, "God With Us."[45] And Immanuel's birth was surprising, for he came forth from a Virgin never married. You say, nonetheless, in accordance with the laws of humanity, that he appeared as a human being from a woman, as far at least as his body and appearance went. And yet you saw in addition to this that he had a glory completely befitting the divine, made splendid with the highest honors, fulfilling the Father's works. For the power to bring the dead to life when they are already foul with the stench of putrefaction, to send light into those deprived of eyesight, to render the lame sound of foot, and to free lepers of their disease with a touch and a word of command, dwells solely in that substance which is above all others.

Tell me, then: did you want the Word of God, the Creator and Artificer of the universe, to shine upon those on earth in his un-

43. Ps 40.6–8.   44. Dt 18.15–16.
45. Is 7.14.

clothed divinity? Who, then, could bear a sight so unspeakably frightening? Do you not see that the bodily eye cannot[46] gaze steadily at the glare of the sun's[47] rays? How, then, could it look at that light which is unapproachable[48] and beyond all wonder? He therefore sojourned among us as a human being, making it possible for all to bear his presence, so that, being as one of those who are as we are, and going about together and living with us, he might show us the way to a pious manner of life in order to rescue us from the snares of pagan superstition,[49] and so that he might institute the true and spiritual worship.

But that abominable, malicious, wicked beast, Satan, did not remain quiet; having subjected the whole earth to himself by his deception and greed, and having drowned it in the mires of sin, he saw himself ejected from the domination he had over us, and, unexpectedly expelled from the power he had exercised over those he had seized long ago, he thought that here was just another human being like one of the prophets of old, and nothing else. He had in fact brought about their deaths, having incited the Jews against them in their perversity. He once again, accordingly, injected them with the poison of his perversion. They, for their part, scorning their own salvation, sprang at him boldly, and, in the savagery and murderous hatred that filled them, went so far as to crucify him.

Now did they lay hold of someone who was unwilling, someone who did not know that he would suffer? On the contrary; he saw in advance his suffering, and the audacity of the Jews in their hostility to God, and accordingly he spoke at one time through the holy prophets, "They gave me also gall for my food, and in my thirst they gave me vinegar to drink."[50] And again, "They divided my garments among them, and cast lots for my raiment."[51] And he says through Isaiah, "I gave my back to scourges, and my cheeks to blows, and I did not turn my face away from the shame of spitting."[52]

46. Reading ἔχει instead of ἔχειν.
47. Reading ἡλιακῆς instead of Κυριακῆς.
48. Correcting πρόσβλητον to ἀπρόσβλητον.
49. Reading δεισιδαιμονίας instead of δυσειδαιμονίας.
50. Ps 69.21.   51. Ps 22.18.
52. Is 50.6.

He was not, then, unaware that he would suffer. Able as he was to avoid the snares, therefore, he gave his own body willingly to death for a short time, so that, once raised from the dead, he might destroy the power of death, that he might undo the devil's envy, through which death entered human nature, and that he might refashion us unto incorruptibility and everlasting life. "For just as in Adam all die, so also in Christ all will be brought to life."[53] He was raised on the third day, accordingly, having plundered hell, and after his return to heaven is seated with his own Father. And he will come in due time to judge the living and the dead.

5. Since, then, we are to stand our trial before the judge, let us, once we have cast hesitation aside, hastened away from all sin, and all but bade farewell to the distractions of the present life, practice justice, continence, charity, and love of the poor; let us visit those[54] in prison;[55] let us care for those suffering from bodily illnesses; let us assist orphans; let us commiserate with the tears of widows;[56] and let us love one another fervently. For if we conduct ourselves in this way, we will celebrate the holy and all-pure festival, beginning holy Lent on the sixth of Phamenoth, and the week of the august and salvific Paschal feast on the eleventh of Pharmuthi. We break our fast on the sixteenth of Pharmuthi, late on the eve of Saturday, according to the gospel precept. We celebrate the feast on the following day, the eve of Sunday, the seventeenth of Pharmuthi,[57] adding thereto the seven weeks of holy Eastertide, so that, in considering the time of relaxation[58] to be a sort of image of the repose of the saints in heaven, we may be granted their company in Christ Jesus our Lord. Through him and with him be glory to the Father with the Holy Spirit, now and always, and for endless ages. Amen.

53. 1 Cor 15.22.
54. Reading τούς instead of τοῖς.
55. Mt 25.43.
56. Jas 1.27.
57. April 12, 444.
58. Reading ἀνέσεως instead of ἀναστάσεως.

APPENDIX
INDICES

APPENDIX

The Dates of Easter Announced by
Cyril's *Festal Letters*[1]

Festal Letter	Alexandrian Date	Equivalent	Other Churches
	(19 pharmouthi)	April 14, 412	
	(11 pharmouthi)	April 6, 413	
I (1)	26 phamenoth	March 22, 414	
II (2)	16 pharmouthi	April 11, 415	
IV (3)[2]	7 pharmouthi	April 2, 416	
V (4)	27 pharmouthi	April 22, 417	March 25 in some Western churches
VI (5)	12 pharmouthi	April 7, 418	
VII (6)	4 pharmouthi	March 30, 419	
VIII (7)	23 pharmouthi	April 18, 420	
IX (8)	8 pharmouthi	April 3, 421	April 10 Elsewhere
X (9)	30 phamenoth	March 26, 422	
XI (10)	20 pharmouthi	April 15, 423	
XII (11)	11 pharmouthi	April 6, 424	March 23 in Africa (Roman)

1. The following chart is taken from Évieux, 92–93. It shows the dates of Easter for the whole of Cyril's episcopate and illustrates some of the confusion surrounding the dating of Easter that continued to exist even in the fifth century.

2. Although the twenty-nine letters run in uninterrupted sequence from 414–442, a scribal error has resulted in the omission of a letter three in the manuscript tradition.

Festal Letter	Alexandrian Date	Equivalent	Other Churches
XIII (12)	24 pharmouthi	April 19, 425	March 22 in some Western churches
XIV (13)	16 pharmouthi	April 11, 426	
XV (14)	8 pharmouthi	April 3, 427	
XVI (15)	27 pharmouthi	April 22, 428	
XVII (16)	12 pharmouthi	April 7, 429	
XVIII (17)	4 pharmouthi	March 30, 430	
XIX (18)	24 pharmouthi	April 19, 431	
XX (19)	8 pharmouthi	April 3, 432	
XXI (20)	30 phamenoth	March 26, 433	
XXII (21)	20 pharmouthi	April 15, 434	
XXIII (22)	5 pharmouthi	March 31, 435	
XXIV (23)	24 pharmouthi	April 19, 436	
XXV (24)	16 pharmouthi	April 11, 437	
XXVI (25)	1 pharmouthi	March 27, 438	
XXVII (26)	21 pharmouthi	April 16, 439	
XXVIII (27)	12 pharmouthi	April 7, 440	
XXIX (28)	27 phamenoth	March 23, 441	March 30 in some Western churches
XXX (29)	17 pharmouthi	April 12, 442	
	(9 pharmouthi)	April 4, 443	
	(28 pharmouthi)	April 28, 444	March 26 in some Western churches

GENERAL INDEX

INDEX OF HOLY SCRIPTURE

New Testament